D0779911

After Franklin

BECOMING MODERN:
NEW NINETEENTH-CENTURY STUDIES

Series Editors:

SARAH SHERMAN
Department of English
University of New Hampshire

JAMES KRASNER
Department of English
University of New Hampshire

ROHAN McWILLIAM
Anglia Polytechnic University
Cambridge, England

JANET POLASKY
Department of History
University of New Hampshire

This book series maps the complexity of historical change and assesses the formation of ideas, movements, and institutions crucial to our own time by publishing books that examine the emergence of modernity in North America and Europe. Set primarily but not exclusively in the nineteenth century, the series shifts attention from modernity's twentieth-century forms to its earlier moments of uncertain and often disputed construction. Seeking books of interest to scholars on both sides of the Atlantic, it thereby encourages the expansion of nineteenth-century studies and the exploration of more global patterns of development.

STEPHEN CARL ARCH
After Franklin: The Emergence of Autobiography in Post-Revolutionary America, 1780–1830
(2001)

JUSTIN D. EDWARDS
Exotic Journeys: Exploring the Erotics of U.S. Travel Literature, 1840–1930
(2001)

After Franklin

The Emergence of Autobiography

in Post-Revolutionary America

1780–1830

Stephen Carl Arch

University of New Hampshire

PUBLISHED BY UNIVERSITY PRESS OF NEW ENGLAND

HANOVER AND LONDON

In memory of David Levin

(1924–1998)

teacher, mentor, friend

University of New Hampshire

Published by University Press of New England, Hanover, NH 03755

© 2001 by University of New Hampshire

LIBRARY OF CONGRESS CATALOGING-IN-PUBLICATION DATA

Arch, Stephen Carl.
After Franklin : the emergence of autobiography in post-revolutionary
America, 1780–1830 / Stephen Carl Arch.
p.   cm. — (Becoming modern)
Includes bibliographical references and index.
ISBN 1–58465–114–8 (alk. paper) — ISBN 1–58465–132–6 (pbk. : alk. paper)
1. Autobiography. 2. United States—Biography—History and
criticism. I. Title. II. Series.
CT 25 .A68 2001
808'.06692—dc21   00–012126

CONTENTS

ever, I should note that my method in this study of the emergence of autobiography has led me to exclude many interesting and valuable texts from consideration. Chronologically, my study covers the half century from (approximately) 1780 to 1830. Both dates are relatively arbitrary, but they do encompass a neat half century and they construe the post-Revolutionary period, as Gordon Wood has argued it should be construed, as a broad and sweeping, though fitful, radical transformation of American society. Having chosen those dates, and then insisting that the texts under scrutiny must have been written (though not necessarily published) in those years, I was forced to exclude from consideration such narratives as Elizabeth Ashbridge's *Some Account of the Early Part of the Life of Elizabeth Ashbridge*, which was written before 1755 though not published until 1774, and John Trumbull's *Autobiography*, published in 1841. Trumbull's narrative was excluded from consideration even though he fought in the American Revolution and lived through its tumultuous aftermath, all the while rubbing elbows with many famous revolutionaries.

I focus solely on self-written narratives, and that decision led to the exclusion of another set of texts, a set comprised primarily of African-American narratives. "One should note," William Andrews has written, "that [George] White was the first slave narrator to compose and write down his life on his own" (48). White's *Brief Account of the Life, Experiences, Travels, and Gospel Labours of George White, an African* was first published in 1810, more than halfway through the period under consideration here. Before that date, African-American self-biographical voices were nearly always mediated by white narrators, as in Venture Smith's *Narrative of the Life and Adventures of Venture, a Native of Africa* (1798), which was told to an unnamed white narrator, and John Marrant's *Narrative of the Lord's Wonderful Dealings with John Marrant, a Black* (1785), which was "Taken down from [Marrant's] own Relation, [and then] ARRANGED, CORRECTED, AND PUBLISHED by the Rev. Mr. Aldridge," a white minister (Marrant, 110). Because African-American self-biographers emerge, as narrators who literally control the act of inscribing their written narratives, so late in the period in question, I defer discussion of an African-American self-biographical narrative until the final chapter, where, among other narratives, I discuss William Grimes's underappreciated *Life of William Grimes, the Runaway Slave* (1825).

Chronology and independent authorship generated two criteria by which I judged a narrative relevant to my study of the emergence of American autobiography. So did geography. I chose to analyze narra-

PREFACE

This book is a study of autobiography as it emerges as a literary genre in the years after the American Revolution. It is, first and foremost, an act of recovery. My methods are literary and critical; they are not sociological, philosophical, psychological, anthropological, or even, I am afraid, cultural (studies). I have profited much from studies of the "self" or the "individual" that make use of those various methods, some of which I cite below. And I think my analysis and argument are relevant for scholars in those fields who want to see how the emergent, modern self was shaped in and by narrative in the early United States. But I tend to be skeptical of arguments made by literary critics that ignore the very texts that stand in need of interpretation. I do not ever stray far from an interpretation of a specific text in *After Franklin*. This is a matter both of inclination and of methodological choice.

After Franklin would best be read in conjunction with a handful of key studies that provoked and stimulated my thinking on the subject of autobiography and narrative selfhood: Felicity Nussbaum's feminist study of early autobiography, *The Autobiographical Subject: Gender and Ideology in Eighteenth-Century England* (1989); Stephen Greenblatt's cultural poetics of the Renaissance narrative self, *Renaissance Self-Fashioning from More to Shakespeare* (1980); Charles Taylor's philosophical study of the emergence of modern identity, *Sources of the Self: The Making of Modern Identity* (1989); and Leopold Damrosch's study of philosophical narrative in the late eighteenth century, *Fictions of Reality in the Age of Hume and Johnson* (1989). What these studies have in common is a sensitivity both to the larger contours of literary and historical change and to the specific problems faced by an individual writer as she or he tried to account for the meaning of her or his lived experience. I hope I have learned from them.

I have chosen to discuss particular narratives for reasons that will become clear in the individual chapters themselves; my readings of those texts carry the weight of my argument. On a more practical level, how-

vii

In earlier drafts, this book was titled "Besides Franklin." My initial interest, captured in the pun on "besides," was in what the self-biographers "next to" and "in addition to" the more famous Franklin had to say about their narrative selves in late-eighteenth- and early-nineteenth-century America. I felt then, and I still feel, that Franklin's so-called autobiography obscures the relevance and significance of a number of other worthy personal narratives. As I kept reading the narratives themselves, however, I came more and more to see that Franklin's narrative was at the end of one tradition of self-life-writing, not at its origin. After Franklin, the modern self gradually emerges in Western culture, and—I argue—that self is manifested literarily in the genre of autobiography. It is simply not true that, as Robert Folkenflik has stated, "autobiography existed before the term came into being [in 1786], just as one could catch a disease before it was diagnosed or named" (7). Diseases are not man-made products, and our ability to "read" them is determined by the available technology. I can, indeed, contract malaria without knowing anything about mosquitoes or parasites. But, unlike diseases, genres and the criticism of genres are man-made, and nothing is available to the artist who writes a narrative that is not also available to the critic who reads it. The "technology" of composition and the "technology" of interpretation are one and the same. I cannot write *or* read autobiography "as" autobiography without being cognizant of its generic demands and limitations. It is only "After Franklin" that the genre of autobiography, both in practice and in name, emerges in America.

William Spengemann has for years urged us to see "American" literature in as wide a sense as possible. Indeed, one implication of his argument is the rejection of "American-ness" as a category in the analysis of literary texts; pushed to its logical conclusion, his argument would reconstruct literary history as "literature in English," disregarding geographical and national boundaries (1994[b]). In certain contexts, as when I teach the "long" eighteenth century in my classroom, I agree with him. But arguments, including his, are always made in a context, and I have chosen in this book to contextualize self-biographical writing within an "American" framework, even as I realize that it could just as easily be situated within the larger contexts of Anglo-American self-biographical discourse or modern theories of subjectivity. Studying Franklin beside Edward Gibbon, or studying Stephen Burroughs beside Wordsworth—or studying them all beside Rousseau and Goethe and Alonso Carrió de la Vandera—would be interesting and rewarding proj-

tives that were written and/or published in North America in the period in question and that, as well, describe a subject who spends a significant amount of time in the colonies or states. I was most interested in narratives that reveal a self formed in reaction to events in North America. Doing so excluded narratives like Olaudah Equiano's *Interesting Narrative of the Life of Olaudah Equiano, or Gustavus Vassa, the African,* which was first published in London in 1789 and which describes a person who spent no more than two years in America. Indeed, as Andrews reminds us, "Equiano was a British citizen who addressed his autobiography to the English Parliament as part of a campaign to end the slave trade in the Empire" (56). Or, as Tanya Caldwell has put it, "Equiano's *Interesting Narrative* . . . is wholly a document of the eighteenth-century British empire, and embraces many of empire's fundamental problems. . . . [It] shares the world, the experiences, and the language . . . of Johnson and Burke, Smith and Defoe" (280). Doing so excluded, as well, James Fennell's interesting *Apology for the Life of James Fennell, Written by Himself.* Fennell's *Apology* was published in Baltimore in 1814 and it describes some of Fennell's adventures onstage in Boston, Philadelphia, Annapolis, and elsewhere in the United States from 1793 to 1813; in this sense, one could argue, it is an "American" narrative. But Fennell spends two-thirds of the narrative describing his childhood, education, and entrance onto the stage in London. In that sense, I decided to treat it as an "English" narrative and not devote a chapter to it here. I have no doubt that my criteria of selection can and will be criticized; I would be the first to agree that Equiano or Fennell "belong" in my discussion of the emergence of autobiography. So do many others. But choosing primary materials based on the criteria outlined above did not constrain my argument or force me to analyze unimportant narratives, and hence for the purposes of this study I stand by them.

With those criteria in hand, I read all the first-person narratives written in this half century in the new United States that I could locate. I am certain I have not read all the self-narratives that fit my criteria; nor have I read all the narratives on my final reading list as closely as the ones I discuss in the chapters that follow. Recovery is never wholesale; it is always made in the context of an argument. In that sense, my decision to discuss particular narratives such as Benjamin Rush's *Travels through Life* or Elizabeth Munro Fisher's *Memoirs of Mrs. Elizabeth Fisher* is as much a part of my argument as is my primary assertion that autobiography did not (and could not) exist until after the 1810s.

ects. But they are not the project I have chosen to pursue here. To pursue those broader contexts would merely detract from the act of recovery, both of individual texts and of larger discursive aims, that I want to pursue in the chapters that follow.

That recovery, I want to emphasize, is of two kinds. First, it is a recovery of particular texts that have been for the most part ignored in the scholarship. Of the narratives I discuss at length in *After Franklin*, many will perhaps be unknown even to experts in the field of American literature. Some have simply never been reprinted since their initial appearance and are hard to locate, even on microfilm. Several, like Stephen Burroughs's *Memoirs of Stephen Burroughs* (1798, 1804) and Ethan Allen's *Narrative of the Captivity of Colonel Ethan Allen* (1779), will be recognizable because their authors earned a place in the popular imagination, though not because their narratives have been read and taught and analyzed. There is, I believe, much more spadework to be done on self-biographies and autobiographies in this period, as well as a need for more criticism of the texts we already know.

Second, this recovery is of the discursive practices that formed around the concept of self or personhood or personal identity. I argue, broadly, that in this half century autobiography emerged as a distinctive kind of story with its own generic conventions and expectations out of a whole range of what I call "self-biographical" narratives (memoirs, confessions, histories, narratives, personal relations, conversion narratives, novels, etc.). These "self-biographies" were written by individual authors about themselves, but the self they wrote about was always, in some fashion, depersonalized, unselfed. In self-biography, the self is imagined as a type or a kind or a representative example, not as a unique and original entity. The emergence of autobiography is thus one example of (or site for) the self *as* self, of the individual as a unique and original entity. It is one site, among many, at which Western culture in the nineteenth century was becoming modern. This emergence was not sudden or uniform; it was often subtle, and it was incomplete through the 1820s. I have tried throughout this study to balance my analysis of the emergence of the genre or subgenre of autobiography (which in hindsight seems quite clear to me) with my sense that that emergence was not so clear to those writers who lived through it. It was fitful and haphazard. In doing so, I hope I have been faithful both to their felt experience and to our own blessed rage for order.

S. C. A.

ACKNOWLEDGMENTS

Many of these ideas were formulated in graduate and undergraduate classrooms, particularly a seminar on American autobiography at the University of Nijmegen (the Netherlands) in the spring of 1996 and a remarkable section of ENG 310B at Michigan State University in the spring of 2000. I thank my students in those classes for their questions, insight, and skepticism. I thank the Fulbright Commission for giving me the opportunity to teach in the Netherlands; and Hans Bak, Professor and Director of American Studies at the University of Nijmegen, for his friendship and support. I am glad to count him now among my closest friends.

Thanks to several other friends for their continued support: Tom Prendergast, John Ernest, Ralph Bauer, Richard Wisneski, Patrick O'Donnell, Allan Beretta, Mike Lopez, Diane Wakoski, Jim Hill, Douglas Peterson, Loudell Snow, and Leon Jackson.

Thanks, as always, to my wife, Kristin Peterson; I have been fortunate to be able to dream my dreams with you. Thanks to my children, Eric and Rosalind, for being patient while I went off by myself to read and write. Books are okay, but you are my best offspring.

Versions of several chapters have appeared elsewhere: part of chapter 2 appeared as "The 'Progressive Steps' of the Narrator in Crèvecoeur's *Letters from an American Farmer*" in *Studies in American Fiction* 18 (1990): 145–158; an earlier version of chapter 3, "Writing a Federalist Self: Alexander Graydon's *Memoirs of a Life*," appeared in *The William and Mary Quarterly* 52 (1995): 415–432. I thank the editors and readers of those journals for their input. A version of chapter 5 appeared as the introduction to my edition of Ethan Allen's *Narrative of the Captivity of Colonel Ethan Allen* (2000).

Many thanks to the readers of the manuscript at the University Press of New England. Their criticisms made this a much better book.

Finally, last and first, I thank David Levin, who read part of this book in an earlier draft before his death in 1998. He was a wonderful professor, a tireless reader of my (and other people's) work, a conscientious and scrupulously fair critic, a dear friend. He was true.

PART *One*

Self-Biography

In part one, I clear the ground for my discussion of the emergence of autobiography in early national America in part two. This means, first, in chapter 1, exposing and revising some of the assumptions that have undergirded the study of Revolutionary and post-Revolutionary literature since the early nineteenth century; and, second, in chapter 2, defining some of the cultural and literary frameworks in post-Revolutionary America on which autobiography would be built in the first third of the nineteenth century. The first of these tasks is negative, in that I claim that we have been predisposed to read post-Revolutionary literature (at least until the publication of Emerson's *Nature* in 1836) in condescending and mistaken ways. Criticism in the past twenty years, I am happy to say, has reversed many of those assumptions, though not all of them and not pervasively among the literature's most avid readers. The second task is positive, in that I hope to begin to articulate a set of ideas that might permit us to read the self-biographical and autobiographical texts of the early national period with more sensitivity and insight.

Then, I study three self-biographers who, while espousing what they take to be Revolutionary values, nevertheless describe a self or personal identity that is neither unique nor original. These writers would not have liked one another, I suspect, and they disagree on many things, not the least of which is the meaning of the American Revolution. Still, all three are conservative when it comes to selfhood; each wants to "conserve" a conception of identity that restricts the self and self-formation to known or socially inscribed or natural limits. Alexander Graydon, Benjamin Rush, and Ethan Allen are not yet writing autobiographies. They are, however, grappling imaginatively with some of the problems that would help to generate the emergence of autobiography in the next half century: the sense that other people's motivations are inscrutable and unknowable, the sense that we are most ourselves when accessing an inward or natural psyche or core, the desire to relocate the sources of morality from religion or society to a self-derived emotivism or to one's own "natural" personality, the sense that one's own actions are driven by an internal impulse, and the recognition of the value of ordinary life (though that ordinary life or private domestic space is not presented in the actual narrative). But in the end Graydon, Rush, and Allen cannot embrace the loose and fluid conception of identity that these ideas seem to imply. They cannot accept that we have deep, private, inward selves, and that we access originality or genius when we cultivate that inwardness. Their resistance to this modern conception of personal identity, I want to emphasize, does not lessen the value of their narratives. Like later autobiographers, they struggle with the difficulty of representing a self; that they come down on the side of self-biography—of downplaying the self as an independent, unique, or original agent—does not make their narratives any less interesting or complicated. Indeed, their resistance to or inability to recognize modernity makes them valuable indicators of some of the tensions and strains that all post-Revolutionary writers faced when they set out to write about themselves.

✦ I ✦

The Age of Experiments

THE SECOND HALF OF THE TWENTIETH CENTURY witnessed a remarkable outpouring of criticism on the genre of autobiography. Autobiography has risen from critical obscurity to claim an institutional place in the Modern Language Association (in a Division Executive Committee, "Autobiography, Biography, and Life Writing"), to become the focus of undergraduate and graduate literature courses in many modern language departments in the United States and Europe, to serve as the organizing topic of numerous academic conferences and countless academic discussion panels, and to provide a site for hundreds of textual, cultural, and generic studies in both specialized and general interest journals.[1] In thinking about textual selfhood in post-Revolutionary America, I have been greatly aided by many of the critical works on autobiography written and published since midcentury. At the same time, however, I have been struck by several pervasive tendencies in this scholarship: its desire (and apparent inability) to define the "genre" once and for all,[2] its insistence on the typicality or representativeness or greatness of a handful of narratives (including Augustine's *Confessions*, Cellini's *Autobiography*, Rousseau's *Confessions*, and Franklin's *Autobiography*), and its program to include retroactively in the domain of autobiography pre-romantic works entitled "confessions" or "memoirs" or "true histories" or "narratives." Philippe Lejeune refers to these tendencies as "optical illusions . . . which are in fact variations of one single error," the desire to "*fix* the horizon [of expectations of a literary production], to stabilize it." Many critics of self-life-writing, he notes, wrongly believe either that autobiography has always existed or that it was born at a particular moment. Both errors create a "homogenous milieu," a dehistoricized context in which all self-life-writing takes its place within the "undefined" genre of autobiography (141–147).

3

My purposes in this book are twofold. I want to respond to those tendencies by writing an account of self-life-writing that, though regionally bound, is yet historically sensitive to what I see with Lejeune as the uncertain and haphazard emergence of the genre of autobiography, as distinct from other forms of self-biographical writing. And, I want in the process to recover a handful of literary works whose importance and relevance has been obscured, in part because the tendencies mentioned above have prevented us from seeing them in any vital way. In order to achieve those purposes, I needed early on to address those pervasive tendencies in the criticism and to clarify for this project how I understood them and how I would handle them in the chapters that follow. First and foremost, I had to define the genre of autobiography.[3] Like fictional and historical narratives, autobiographies make reference to external reality and are composed in language that is arbitrary but conventional; unlike fictional and historical narratives, autobiographies are necessarily written by the self about the self. Common sense tells us as much. And many definitions of autobiography stop there, taking any first-person narrative that focuses on the author's life or self or being as an "autobiography." An autobiography, Roy Pascal writes with such a definition in mind, is "the reconstruction of the movement of a life, or part of a life, in the actual circumstances in which it was lived" (9).

However, many critics of the "genre" of self-life-writing (the etymological derivation of the term "autobiography") have tried to define the term in ways that are sensitive to historical and generic change. John N. Morris tentatively suggests that, though the "art [of autobiography] itself was not new [in 1809, soon after the term was first used], . . . the invention of a new name for it and the immediate passage of that name into the standard vocabulary of English suggest that at that moment of invention the art was commanding a new sort of attention" (vii). "Essentially," Morris writes, "'self' is the modern word for 'soul'" (6). Along the same lines, Pascal himself complicates his rudimentary definition by drawing a distinction between eighteenth-century "memoirs," which focus on the public history of well-known figures, and autobiographies, which in his account emerge after 1780 as the narration of a self or person in "a process of development," not "a state of being" (52). The philosopher Charles Taylor goes further than Morris or Pascal: "we have come to think that we 'have' selves as we have heads. But the very idea that we have or are a 'self,' that human agency is essentially defined as 'the self,' is a linguistic reflection of our modern understanding and the radical reflexivity it involves" (177). The historical shift from "soul" to "self," in other words, was not merely a linguistic or generic translation, as Morris suggests; it was a conceptual transformation. It was both an etymological and an epistemological shift in how a writer understood the meaning of his or her lived experience. "Thus by the turn of the eighteenth century," Taylor goes on, "something recognizably like the modern self is in process of constitution, at least among the social and spiritual elites of northwestern Europe and its American offshoots" (185). "Something fundamental changes in the late eighteenth century" (390), Taylor insists. As Jerome Buckley puts it: "By the end of the eighteenth century the personal, fluid, individual self, or rather the many separate selves and 'dead selves' of each man, distinct from all others, had begun to replace the fixed and average public self" (13).[4]

Taylor notes that class factors played a key role in the linguistic and conceptual transformation from "soul" to "self." Feminist critics have in recent years made a similar observation about the emergence of the modern, independent self from the perspective of gender and race. "The fundamental inapplicability of individualistic models of the self to women and minorities is twofold," Susan Stanford Friedman writes. "First, the emphasis on individualism does not take into account the importance of culturally imposed group identity for women and minorities. Second, the emphasis on separateness [of the self] ignores the differences in socialization in the construction of male and female gender identity" (34–35).[5] As Felicity Nussbaum puts it, "first-person texts disseminate a regimen that enables the production of a particular kind of self, assumed to be free and equal. . . . [By] the end of the eighteenth century, a middle class regulates itself through this technology of self, and [that] technology is deployed to maintain gender hierarchies" (xvii). Self-life-writing takes place in the context not just of (changing) philosophical conceptions of reality but of (changing) social and cultural opportunities, needs, demands, and restrictions. Any definition of the genre has to be sensitive to both dimensions.

Lejeune, Morris, Taylor, Friedman, and others demand that the genre of autobiography be viewed historically. William Spengemann likewise insists that "we must view autobiography historically, not as one thing that writers have done again and again, but as the pattern described by the various things they have done in response to changing ideas about the nature of the self, the ways in which the self may be apprehended, and the proper methods of reporting those apprehensions" (1980, xiii).

His statement captures precisely what I hope to do in this book: study the ways in which the self was apprehended, comprehended, and reported in first-person self-narratives in post-Revolutionary America. Since, however, I believe that autobiography simply did not exist, as a genre, prior to the early nineteenth century, I had to begin by defining autobiography in a way that accounted for its gradual appearance in English-speaking America in the first half of the nineteenth century. I did so even while cognizant of Paul Jay's warning that "the temptation in defining autobiography as a genre [will always be] either to create borders that are too exclusively narrow or ones that are so large as to be meaningless" (18). I was, I must admit, warned.

Generically, autobiography emerges haphazardly from the assumptions and conventions of other and earlier genres of self-life-writing—memoir, confession, history, personal relation, conversion narrative, and the novel among them—in response to changing cultural needs and desires in the late eighteenth and early nineteenth centuries. I would define an instance of the genre as it has fully emerged by 1830 as *any narrative written or told by one person in which that person struggles to tell the story of how he or she came over time to be an independent, often original, agent*; and I shall analyze in the chapters that follow some of the textual sites at which that emergence from earlier genres begins to take place and some of the textual sites at which it has fully emerged.

My definition of autobiography excludes some self-life-writing as autobiography more readily and obviously than it does others. "I have not studied in this you read," Anne Bradstreet wrote in her self-biography, "To My Dear Children," in the mid–seventeenth century, before the rise of autobiography, "to show my skill, but to declare the truth, not to set forth myself, but the glory of God" (215). Bradstreet's avowed purpose in talking about herself is not to talk about herself. Similarly, John Woolman begins his 1774 *Journal* with the comment that "I have often felt a motion of love to leave some hints of my experience of the goodness of God" (1): this motion is from God, as Woolman often points out, not from himself. Later, for example, he says, "My tongue was often so dry that I could not speak . . . and as I lay still for a time I at length felt a Divine power prepare my mouth that I could speak. . . . [And I perceived] that the language 'John Woolman is dead,' meant no more than the death of my own will" (215). Bradstreet and Woolman did not imagine or desire to write themselves into being as independent or original agents; each hoped to "mortify" the will and let God's will serve in its place. Did they, in fact, achieve such a selflessness? We have only their texts, and in those texts each narrator imagines and describes a conversion in which the human will becomes an agent of God, not the narrator. In their understanding of themselves, Bradstreet and Woolman are neither independent nor original. They are dependent (on God) and typical (of all converted Christians). David Seed notes that Benjamin Franklin and Jonathan Edwards tried in their self-biographies to harmonize their experiences "with a general pattern of development from doubt to faith, or from poverty to prosperity" (38), not to individualize them. As Ruth Banes writes about eighteenth-century American self-biographers like Woolman (and Benjamin Franklin): they "attempted to efface their autobiographical selves" (237). It is, I believe, more accurate to say that self-biographers like Bradstreet and Woolman attempted to efface *what we have come to recognize* as their autobiographical self or selves. Or as Leo Damrosch puts it in his discussion of eighteenth-century nonfictional prose writers: "The eighteenth-century philosopher is not an isolated hero giving shape to what would otherwise be unintelligible, but a cultural spokesman who explores the ways in which everybody *already does* make sense of the world" (22–23). Woolman's desire to mortify the human will and passively accept the Christic self is merely one attitude, among others, that precludes autobiography of the sort I have defined above from being written by an author. Woolman hopes to make sense of the world in exactly the same way as many others before him have done: as a Christian stripped of the vanity of this world and filled instead with supernatural grace. Franklin, I will argue, makes sense of his world by adopting the postures and models offered by eighteenth-century texts and by upper-class male exemplars: he becomes in his account of his life a practical type stripped of ancient superstition and filled instead with reasonable and socially useful impulses. Soon after Franklin, however, and by 1830 in increasing numbers, authors will make sense of their world by jettisoning other models and taking their own desires or ideas or impulses or body—their own "nature"—as the authorizing source of meaningful experience. They will write autobiographies.

Put more simply, just because an author is talking about her or his own life does not mean that she or he is writing an autobiography, any more than an author who writes a fictional narrative in prose is necessarily writing a novel.[6] I hope to show that many writers in post-Revolutionary America simply did not accept, consciously or unconsciously, the idea that selves should—even could—be independent or original. Later writers as different as Henry David Thoreau, Maxine Hong Kingston, P. T. Barnum, and Richard Wright *did* accept that idea and struggled to comprehend themselves within it, even if because of race, class, or gender some of them were prevented from fully doing so.[7] Hence, I include in my definition the caveat that autobiographers "struggle" to tell such a story: because of social and cultural conditions, not every writer in the West has been able to achieve (a perceived) independence or originality.

Autobiography, in my definition, is a genre constructed in response to a particular historical, philosophical conception of the individual, a conception that emphasizes, according to Taylor, three elements: a sense of "inwardness" or inward "depth," an affirmation of ordinary (rather than extraordinary) life, and "nature" or the "natural" self as an inner moral source. It is constructed, as well, by a particular historical, economic, and social conception of the individual, one that stresses possessive individualism, egalitarianism, middle-class order, the radical social and intellectual autonomy of the self, and, not least, a notion derived from Locke and other sources that the individual grows or changes or comes to know itself and the world more fully over the course of time.[8] It is, in this last sense, a *narrative*, the story of how the author "came over time to be an . . . agent," the active controller of her or his own movements in life. Autobiography (as I have defined it) depends upon the notion that selves can and do change over time and that that change is teleological. Autobiography is the narrative construct of a particular, modern historical formation. It is, of course, in the end, just as "fictional" as the Christic self that Bradstreet and Woolman attempted to write into being.

Second, having hazarded a definition of autobiography, I had in this project, which focuses specifically on American self-life-writing, to decide how to treat Benjamin Franklin's *Autobiography*, a narrative that since the mid–nineteenth century has eclipsed in importance all other narratives written in Revolutionary and post-Revolutionary America. Anyone who comes to the larger subject of Revolutionary and early national writing has to be struck by the preponderant scholarly and critical interest in Franklin's narrative, at the expense not just of Franklin's other work, and not just of other Revolutionary narratives of selfhood, but of the entire body of imaginative writing produced in the United States from 1771 (when he wrote part one) to the mid-1830s.[9] Early in 2000, a search of the Modern Language Association on-line bibliography for articles on Franklin's *Autobiography* turned up more than one hundred entries; a search for articles on Ethan Allen's *Narrative of the Captivity of Colonel Ethan Allen* turned up three, on Stephen Burrough's *Memoirs of Stephen Burroughs* turned up four, on Alexander Graydon's *Memoirs of a Life* (1811) turned up one. Study after study of nineteenth-century American literature begins predictably with Franklin's *Autobiography* only to leap to Brown or Cooper or Hawthorne.[10] One might assume from this that Franklin is simply the best thing going in Revolutionary and post-Revolutionary America. As Larzer Ziff remarked in the preface to his study, *Writing in the New Nation: Prose, Print, and Politics in the Early United States* (1991), "anyone who . . . considered the matter in the abstract could . . . have told me in advance that Benjamin Franklin's *Autobiography* . . . would prove more rewarding than the writings of . . . many others" (xi). Ziff's statement is revealing in its assumption that Franklin's narrative has been and always will be more rewarding than other contemporary narratives and that, in a sense, literary or cultural changes cannot alter that fact. It is revealing because it *makes* the status of Franklin's text a fact, something no longer open to scrutiny but fixed in place as a known element. Given what has happened in the academy since the 1960s, one might be surprised to find any practicing critic maintaining such a blithe attitude toward American literary history. But Ziff is merely stating baldly what generations of critics have been saying implicitly. Literarily, Franklin is pretty much all we have to offer until the emergence of Cooper and Poe and Emerson in the next century. But why, I began to ask as I read memoirists like Elizabeth Fisher and Alexander Graydon and Benjamin Rush, has Franklin's narrative come to seem so powerful, so "rewarding"? What is it that Fisher and Graydon and Rush *lack* that prevents us from thinking or feeling the same way about them? In the end, I came to see that the problem did not lie in the texts themselves but in the criteria by which we make such decisions. The problem is us. My demurral from Ziff's a priori judgment explains my decision to write only a brief part of one chapter focusing directly on Franklin's so-called *Autobiography*. Instead, since he is the one writer whom, I trust, my reader knows, I have made him a touchstone throughout my discussion. But my hope is to shift our focus toward some of the "many others" who have been elided by the literary histories that have shaped our understanding of the past.

This shift will depend, in part, on my re-reading of Franklin's *Autobiography*. Because of the way I read Franklin's narrative, I will insist throughout this study on calling it his *History of My Life*, rather than *The*

Autobiography of Benjamin Franklin. Inside the manuscript itself, Franklin refers to the narrative as "the Account of my Life," "this History," and "this relation."[11] As I will point out elsewhere, Franklin did not have the term "autobiography" available to him in 1771 or 1784 or probably even 1788, when he began each of the three main parts of the manuscript. He did not, indeed could not, think of the narrative as an "autobiography." In a 1788 letter to Benjamin Vaughan, Franklin reported that he was "diligently employed in writing the History of my Life" (1987[b], 1168). It is this reference that provides me with what I take to be a more appropriate title for Franklin's self-biography. In using it, I mean to call attention to the unmodern or not-modern aspects of Franklin's narrative.[12]

At the same time, however, let me say that I believe in criteria that permit us to make aesthetic and cultural judgments about works of art. Some narratives *are* better than other narratives (though of course one must always know what "better" means in order to begin to formulate criteria). I do not want to homogenize all writing in the period under discussion as "just" discourse, all equally significant. It is not all equally significant. Given the focus of my study, I take "better" to include, loosely, these aspects of the narratives I discuss: an awareness of the difficulties inherent in representing personal identity through the written word, an awareness of how the figure of personal identity under construction relates to other known norms or types at that time, the complexity and sophistication of representation (particularly of the figure of the "self"), and the level of interest the author is able to generate in herself or himself as a figure. Taken together, these aspects contribute to the significance of the narrative within the literary terms it has set for itself and the cultural terms within which it was written, a significance that it is up to me to recover in the analyses I present in Chapters 3–9. Following these criteria, Franklin's narrative of his life is indeed better than many contemporaneous narratives, but it is not categorically better than all of them. Stephen Burroughs's *Memoirs* is, I find, as complex, sophisticated, revealing, and interesting as is Franklin's *History of My Life.* I continue to learn from—and be entertained by—both of them, as well as the others I discuss at length in this study.

Third, I had to counter the tendency of scholars to read the term "autobiography," apparently first used in 1786[13] but not in accepted use until the mid–nineteenth century, back onto several key narratives of selfhood written in Revolutionary America, most obviously Franklin's *History of My Life* or *Memoirs* (first published as *The Autobiography of*

Benjamin Franklin in 1868) and Thomas Jefferson's *Memoranda* (published by his grandson as *Memoirs* in 1830 and usually reprinted in the twentieth century as *The Autobiography of Thomas Jefferson*). The retitling of texts like Franklin's and Jefferson's is often offered innocently and without explanation, as if Franklin and Jefferson would have used such a title had they only thought of it. But the fact is that they could not have "thought" of it; the word itself and the concept as I have defined it were not available to Franklin before his death in 1790 and were not readily available to Jefferson before he wrote his narrative in 1821. Such acts of retitling are in reality attempts to make familiar and thus to rehabilitate texts that can never, retrospectively, *be* what modern editors and readers want them to be. Other lesser-known texts such as James Moody's *Lieut. James Moody's Narrative of His Exertions and Sufferings in the Cause of Government* (1783) or K. White's *Narrative of the Life, Occurrences, Vicissitudes, and Personal Situation of K. White* (1809) retain their original titles as they sit unread on the shelves of research libraries or in the stacks of rare-book rooms; they have been left to languish in obscurity as something "less" than or prior to autobiographies. One of my goals here will be to move us back beyond the invention of the term "autobiography" so as to see a group of Revolutionary narratives concerned with personal identity in conjunction and relation to one another. Throughout *After Franklin*, my use of the term "self-biography" to designate preromantic writings in which the author narrates his or her life story is designed to be a reminder that those narratives are not autobiographies in the modern sense.[14]

I am perfectly aware of the difficulty of establishing the "relevance" or importance or value of literary texts in these contentious times. I will say right now that the writers with whom I am dealing in this book are relevant and important and valuable on two counts, at least. They wrote complex, sophisticated narratives that in the context of an American literary history dedicated to diversity in all its many forms deserve more scrutiny; and they, like more well-known writers such as Rousseau and Wordsworth, grappled with the motives and implications of what Paul Johnson calls "the modern." Through the emergent discourse of selfhood, they responded in complex ways to a world undergoing rapid change, deflecting or embracing or simply pondering a new kind of individual whom we now recognize as "us."

This first set of problems I had to identify and come to terms with was historical and generic. A second set was historical and institutional.

Scholars of American Revolutionary and post-Revolutionary literature have since the early nineteenth century been uneasy with their subject matter, primarily because of their suspicions that American Revolutionary literature is possibly not American, probably not literary, and certainly not revolutionary.[15] Their unease has taken many forms. Let me give two examples, both from relatively recent studies and both typical of a more general and long-standing attitude toward the literature. Emory Elliott, in *Revolutionary Writers: Literature and Authority in the New Republic, 1725–1810* (1982), maintains that American Revolutionary writers had a social vision: "This social mission was so burdensome, however, that it weighed down their poetry with meanings and purposes, duties and moral obligations. . . . The artistry drowned in the social and political messages [the writers] included in an effort to achieve the proper didactic effect" (17). Instead of speaking didactically, Elliott blithely asserts, American Revolutionary writers "would have done better to express their frustrations and yearnings for a new unity through a personal symbolic language, as Emerson, Thoreau, Whitman, Melville, and Hawthorne did four decades later" (272). Seeing "no Miltons in America in the late eighteenth century" (18), Elliott asks Revolutionary writers to be romantic writers, speaking to us through the private symbolic imagination in carefully revised and constructed "literary" texts. In this reading, as in countless earlier studies, the literary history of the American Revolution and the early national period is a way station on the road to somewhere else—a better, more interesting somewhere else. Revolutionary and post-Revolutionary writers do not come up to a standard invented by a later age.

Larzer Ziff makes a similar kind of argument, though more subtly, in the already mentioned *Writing in the New Nation*. Though he insists that he values American Revolutionary texts "for the way they reflexively embody their culture and constitute ours rather than measuring them solely in terms of whatever ideological message [he has] detected or decoded" (194), Ziff admits that he is nevertheless unable to "find any good reason to display before the reader . . . many . . . writers [he] studied" (xii). Familiar names—Benjamin Franklin, William Bartram, Charles Brockden Brown—dominate his account, and all are read in ways that emphasize their modernity. Brown, for example, discovers "the power of the subconscious mind" (145), follows "the ideas and images prompted by the subconscious mind" (144), and dramatizes in his novels the romantic connection "between wild nature and the release of the violent self" (178). A few lesser-known authors of the period are resuscitated in Ziff's literary history, but always because they anticipate the romantics: Ethan Allen, for example, creates a "wild man" in his *Narrative of the Captivity of Colonel Ethan Allen* that leads directly to Davy Crockett, Natty Bumppo, and other nineteenth-century "wild figures" (182–189). The American Revolution may have been politically revolutionary, Ziff writes, but American writing had to wait for Cooper, Emerson, Melville, Hawthorne, and Thoreau to achieve its literary "independence" (125). Here, again, the literature of the Revolution and the early national period is devalued because of literary standards erected by modern writers and artists. The literary period becomes, again, a way station on the road to something better.[16]

The refusal to see the early literature of the United States as important in its own right is, in one sense, a peculiarly American problem, a product, R. C. De Prospo says, of our insistent desire to "create a marginal early American literature in the narrow interest of preserving American literary nationalism" (258). Seen from this nationalist perspective, De Prospo argues, colonial Anglo-American literature and American Revolutionary literature *must* be denigrated for the American literature of the nineteenth and twentieth centuries to stand revealed as the highest literary achievement of a unified national people. The story of the emergence of the literary character of the United States demands it.

That nationalist myth complements another historical plot, one whose general outlines I *do* endorse, that is, the story of a paradigm shift in Western consciousness that occurred over the course of the seventeenth and eighteenth centuries. This paradigm shift has been variously characterized in different fields of study as traditional to modern, classic to romantic, patterning discourse to analytico-referential discourse (Reiss), oral to literate (Ong), monarchical-patriarchal social structure to democratic-fraternal social structure (Wood 1992), as well as in other ways. One or more of these shifts is often called upon to explain our modern sense that texts as close to us in time as Joel Barlow's *The Vision of Columbus* (1787) or Timothy Dwight's *Greenfield Hill* (1794) or John Adams's *Defense of the Constitutions* (1788–1789) seem much further away from us in time than, say, Wordsworth's *Prelude* (wr. 1798–1805) or Benjamin Franklin's *History of My Life* (wr. 1771–1789). "English writers of the later eighteenth century were part of a profound shift of sensibility," Fredric Bogel writes, "in the course of which new ways of experiencing the world and themselves came into being" (31). What Bogel says applies to American writers as well. The consciousness of the Anglo-American, if not the Western, mind seems to have been altered profoundly sometime in these years. Of one particular group of Revolutionary American writers, the Connecticut Wits, William Dowling writes: they engaged in "a momentous ideological struggle over the true meaning of classical republicanism, [offering] us [themselves] as the voices of a literary and cultural Augustanism that, for all its earlier importance in bringing about the revolution in the American colonies, would with their own last poems be all but extinguished as a living strain in American thought" (1990, 65). Dowling contends that we can no longer easily read the poetry of the Wits, that we must struggle to overcome the great historical divide between their traditional, classical world and our modern, romantic and post-romantic world. It is that "divide" that has given rise to Elliott's desire to find romanticism in post-Revolutionary writing and Ziff's lament that post-Revolutionary literature is not sufficiently "revolutionary." Many scholars have narrowly attributed to American nationalism impulses that actually derived from this larger cultural shift (of which nationalism itself, American and others, was simply one effect).

Robert Wiebe has perceptively noted that "almost all studies of American history from the 1780s to the 1850s root themselves in either the 18th-century or the 19th-century end of the transformation, and hence remarkably few treat the massive changes in between as much more than an epilogue or a prelude" (xii). In literary history, scholars have nearly always appealed to the second option, to the teleological claim that American Revolutionary writing gave rise to or created the necessary conditions for a truly American, truly literary, truly revolutionary literature: that of the American Renaissance. The pressures of literary nationalism on the one hand and the prejudices of romantic or post-romantic aesthetics on the other seem ineluctably to draw scholars to the view that American Revolutionary literature is somehow inadequate or juvenile or immature or, simply, nonexistent.

This book is one attempt to refute those long-standing claims. One of my contentions is that many other Revolutionary texts besides and after Franklin's can prove vital and rewarding, provided that we can recover the assumptions and problems within which their authors worked. I have chosen to limit myself to one type of writing, but much of what I say could be applied to other kinds of writing in the early republic, in particular what we now distinguish as political and scientific writing. I will argue broadly that American Revolutionary writings, and self-biographies in particular, are for the most part "experimental," though not experimental in our modern sense of the word and not in ways that reflect our notions of reality. In *A Dictionary of the English Language* (1755), Samuel Johnson defined "experiment" as a "Trial of any thing; something done in order to discover an uncertain or unknown effect." He defined the active verb "experiment" as "To try; to search out by trial." Donald H. Meyer writes: "As the terms were used in the eighteenth century, 'experiment' and 'experimental' could refer to the process of testing hypotheses systematically (as in a laboratory 'experiment') or, more generally, to matters pertaining to one's immediate experience—'experimental' knowledge of something being knowledge based on firsthand acquaintance rather than on hearsay or conjecture" (3). These two types of experimentation—systematic and experiential—derive from Francis Bacon and John Locke, respectively. "For the sense by itself is a thing infirm and erring," Bacon wrote in *The New Organon* in 1620; "neither can instruments for enlarging or sharpening the senses do much; but all the truer kind of interpretation of nature is effected by instances and experiments fit and apposite; wherein the sense decides touching the experiment only, and the experiment touching the point in nature and the thing itself" (99). For Bacon, the experiment mediates between sensing/erring man and unerring nature. But experimentation is not simply a passive acceptance of information. The scientist, Bacon insists, does not rely "solely or chiefly on the power of the mind, nor does [he] take the matter which [he] gathers from natural history and mechanical experiments and lay it up in the memory whole as [he] finds it, but lays it up in the understanding altered and digested" (128). This alteration or "digestion" is echoed by many seventeenth- and eighteenth-century self-biographers, who attempt to trace the way their experiences reflect a type or pattern of behavior that exists independently of the individual; experience is given meaning by the understanding's power to refract it through a known model that exists independently of any specific instance of it.

John Locke is also distrustful of the senses, but nevertheless insists throughout *An Essay Concerning Human Understanding* (1690) that "all our knowledge is founded [upon experience], and from that [the mind] ultimately derives itself" (33). "What, then, are we to do for the improvement of our *knowledge in substantial beings*?" Locke asks. "*Experience here must teach me what reason cannot*: and it is by trying alone that I can certainly know. . . . Here, again, for assurance I must apply myself to *experience*; as far as that reaches, I may have certain knowledge, but no further" (351–352, italics in original). Locke often plays upon the close etymological link between "experiment" and "experience"; and by taking a much more constricted view than Bacon did of man's powers—"*the extent of our knowledge* comes not only short of the reality of things," he remarks at one point, "but even of the extent of our own ideas" (279)— he finally collapses one into the other. "Knowledge then seems to be nothing but the perception of the connexion and agreement, or disagreement and repugnancies, of any of our ideas. In this alone it consists" (267). Knowledge, for Locke, is both a constant (and necessarily conscious) experience and a constant (and necessarily conscious) experiment. It is to receive an impression or call up a memory (experience) and, simultaneously, to test that impression or idea against others' impressions or ideas (experiment). It is "the progress of our minds" (79) that Locke sets out to describe, and this becomes in his account a task also similar to some versions of the self-biographical impulse, particularly, I think, those which I will identify later in the book as "autobiographical." For both philosophers, all true knowledge of the world is achieved "experimentally."

"This is the Age of Experiments," Benjamin Franklin wrote near the end of his life (1463). By the "Age," Franklin meant the Enlightenment, the "long" eighteenth century that stretched from the Restoration (1660) and the founding of the Royal Society (1662) to the late eighteenth century and (he assumed) beyond. "The last century," Samuel Miller wrote in *A Brief Retrospect of the Eighteenth Century* (1803), "may also, in a peculiar and distinguishing sense, be called THE AGE OF EXPERIMENT" (II: 415). Franklin and Miller meant Newton's researches into mechanics and optics, Herschel's explorations of stellar astronomy, Lavoisier's discovery of oxygen chemistry and the system of nomenclature based upon it, von Humboldt's travels in Latin America, Lamarck's revision of the Linnaean system, Cuvier's opening of the field of vertebrate paleontology, and Franklin's own discovery that lightning was the same element as electricity. They meant numerous technological innovations, from the steam engine to the hot air balloon, from the lightning rod and Franklin stove to Jefferson's mould-board plow and Herschel's giant reflecting telescope. They meant by the "Age" the belief that mankind was progressively gaining mastery over the natural and physical world by comprehending the laws of nature. They meant what Kant meant when he defined enlightenment as "man's release from his self-incurred tutelage" (1).

We had willingly blindfolded or blinded ourselves. As Charles Thomson wrote in 1768:

> Knowledge is of little Use when confined to mere Speculation; But when speculative Truths are reduced to Practice, when Theories grounded upon Experiments are applied to common purposes of Life; and when, by these, Agriculture is improved, Trade enlarged, and the Arts of Living made more easy and comfortable, and, of course, the Increase and Happiness of Mankind promoted; Knowledge then becomes really useful. (*Pennsylvania Chronicle*, 7 March 1768, quoted in Bridenbaugh, 150–151)

Franklin and Miller—and Kant—meant that, in the eighteenth century, mankind had finally promoted reason over faith, experiments over scripture, experience over tradition, and technological progress over theological debate.

Franklin meant, too, mankind's "experiments" in fields other than what we now call "hard" science or technology. John Locke, Franklin wrote in 1748, was "the *Newton* of the *Microcosm*"; "His book on the *Human Understanding*, shows" that he "*made the whole world his own*" (1249). The essayist Joseph Addison, Franklin remarked in the same volume of *Poor Richard Improved*, "contributed more to the improvement of the minds of the *British* nation . . . [than] any other *English* pen whatever" (1248). In his "Proposals Relating to the Education of Youth in Pensilvania" (1749), Franklin used the works of Milton, Locke, Hutcheson, Rollin, and Turnbull to justify his theory that students should be made to exercise, taught that which is "*most useful* and *most ornamental*," and "inculcated and cultivated" to "serve Mankind" to the utmost of their ability. Such a mode of education would surely result, Franklin argued, in "an Increase of Knowledge" (325–342). In other words, men of letters like David Hume, Lord Kames, Francis Hutcheson, Alexander Pope, and Joseph Priestley were an essential part of Franklin's "Age of Experiments" that we, living in an age when science and the arts have been sundered, have often failed to see with the comprehensive interrelatedness with which contemporaries viewed the period. "The eighteenth century," Dena Goodman writes, "was an age of experimentation—in literature as in politics and science" (4). "This I hope will be the age of experiments in government," Jefferson wrote to John Adams in 1796 (Adams and Jefferson 1988, 260). Newton, Locke, Priestley, Tom Paine, Jefferson, Franklin himself were all "experimenters"—men insistent that ideas be tried "in order to discover an uncertain or unknown effect" (Samuel Johnson)—in various and sundry "fields" of inquiry. The disciplinary lines we have drawn between, for example, bridge building and politics (Paine) or education, government, and human psychology (Locke) or politics, farming, and natural science (Jefferson) were not readily apparent in the eighteenth century. "Eighteenth-century scientists, whether as electrical experimenters, mathematicians, or mechanists, moved with ease between theory and application" (Jacob, 137). Brook Hindle notes in this vein that several of the early steamboat projectors in the 1790s, "conspicuously [John] Fitch, [William] Thornton, [Benjamin Henry] Latrobe, and [Robert] Fulton, achieved notable success in other fields of spatial thinking" (79). Fitch, for example, produced an impressive *Map of the North West* in 1785; he conducted the survey of the land, drew up the map, hammered out a block of copper, polished the resulting sheet, engraved his map upon it, and printed copies from the plate (Hindle, 29). Fitch, surely, was an "experimenter" in Johnson's and Franklin's senses, and not only in "fields of spatial thinking"; he also wrote a tremendously important (though now forgotten) self-biography in the early 1790s (which I discuss in chapter 8). Thornton and Latrobe helped to design the Capitol building, among other architectural projects on which they worked. Fulton was a painter, apprenticing under Benjamin West in London from 1787 to 1791, when he began new endeavors in marble cutting, canal digging, and canal navigation. Experimentation was an attitude, as well as a method, which eighteenth-century philosophers brought to all their endeavors in life. It was, as well, the attitude that many self-biographers brought to the texts in which they attempted to report the significance of their lived experience.

Examples abound of men who "experimented" in various scientific and technological areas in America from 1780 to 1830: Fitch, Fulton, Paine, Priestley, Franklin, Jefferson, David Rittenhouse, Benjamin Rush, Charles Willson Peale, Nathaniel Bowditch, Robert Hare, Alexander Wilson, William Bartram, Benjamin Barton, Samuel Mitchell, Constantine Rafinesque, Oliver Evans, and Eli Whitney are a few of the (comparatively) well-known names. From the perspective of the history of science and technology in the West these names are certainly not as important as those of Newton and Watt. (As in literary studies, a Whig interpretation of early American scientific history obscures the real achievements of many scientific experimenters and deflects our sympathetic understanding into historical generalizations.) But though most of these inventors and innovators felt themselves to be far from the center of scientific inquiry in London or Amsterdam or Paris, none thought that he was excluded from the idealized republic of letters within which experimentation in "scientific," "political," and "literary" discourse was imagined to take place. A story of how American science joined "full partnership" in Western science in the nineteenth century has been told by historians like John C. Greene (128–129), as has a story of how American literature finally became as revolutionary as its politics in the 1840s and 1850s (Ziff). What I have tried to do in *After Franklin* is tell a story about what a few boundary-crossing writers at the end of the "long eighteenth century" in America were doing as they put pen to paper and wrote about their life experiences, and to tell that story without imagining them to be writers who are "lesser" or inferior than the romantic symbolists of the mid–nineteenth century. This story, I hope, escapes the confines of a romantic interpretation of the value of "literature," and focuses instead on the sophisticated ways in which some writers reconsidered the possibilities of selfhood in a Revolutionary, scientific, and increasingly democratic age.

After Franklin makes its argument on behalf of a loose collection of narratives about "factual" selves. Like many recent critics of early American literature, including Cathy Davidson, David Shields, and William Dowling,[17] I will argue that we need to recover particular ways of reading a particular genre, and so I try, at one and the same time, to recover discursive practices and specific "forgotten" texts. *After Franklin* tries to trace the fitful emergence of a new concept—modern, independent selfhood as it was expressed in narrative form. Mine is the story of how a concept and its accompanying genre, autobiography, began to emerge in the late eighteenth century and early nineteenth century in America.

◄§ 2 §►

Forming Selves in Revolutionary America

THERE IS A REMARKABLE MOMENT IN ANNE BRAD-
street's account of her spiritual pilgrimage, "To My Dear Children," written in the mid–seventeenth century, when she admits
to generic uncertainty: "I . . . thought it the best, whilst I was able to
compose some short matters (for what else to call them I know not) and
bequeath [them] to you [i.e., her children], that when I am no more
with you, yet I may be daily in your remembrance (although that is the
least in my aim in what I now do) but that you may gain some spiritual
advantage by my experience" (215). Bradstreet was aware, no doubt, of
Augustine's *Confessions*, yet she did not choose to label her "short matters" a confession, perhaps because, unlike Augustine, her audience was
strictly conceived as her family, not God.[1] She was also no doubt aware
of a tradition of the memoirs and biographies of public men, including
narratives such as Plutarch's *Parallel Lives* and John Norton's *Abel Being
Dead Yet Speaketh: The Life of John Cotton* (1658), but she was a private
woman, reluctant to publish her thoughts[2] and unable to participate directly in the political affairs of the Massachusetts Bay colony. Finally,
she was certainly aware of the Protestant tradition of writing or narrating an account of one's own spiritual pilgrimage, which in the narratives
of John Bunyan, George Fox, and others was coalescing at that very
time, but the seventeenth century simply had no name for that genre.
"To my dear son Thomas Shepard[, Jr.,] with whom I leave these records of God's great kindness to him [i.e., the author]," Thomas Shepard
wrote in 1646 at the beginning of the document we now confidently refer
to as *The Autobiography of Thomas Shepard* (33). This narrative, says the
writer of the "Preface to the Reader" of Mary Rowlandson's *True History*,
is "a *Memorandum* of God's dealings with her" (29, italics in original).[3]

For the genre of autobiography to coalesce in the early nineteenth

20

century out of the strands of novel, confession, memoir, biography, captivity narrative, and conversion narrative, self-biographical authors had
to develop new assumptions and new generic conventions: authors had
to be able to imagine a secular audience beyond locally known friends
and family, a change made possible with the increase in book traffic and
literacy levels in the seventeenth and eighteenth centuries; they had to
be able to imagine themselves as both private and public individuals and
to feel that their experiences in private were worth retelling in public to
people whom they did not know, a change made possible with the
invention of the concept of the public sphere in the early eighteenth
century; they had to see self-biographical writing as something more
than or different from vanity, or at least see vanity (as Franklin has it) as
itself "useful," a change made possible by the depletion of sin as a value
category and by the elevation of personal experience as an indicator of
truth or true "reality"; and they had to invent a sense of a tradition of
self-biographical writing, a tradition that first comes into visibility at
the very end of the eighteenth century. By 1829, when the word "autobiography" was probably first used in the title of an original narrative,
Matthew Carey's *Auto Biographical Sketches*, these conditions had in
large part come to pass.[4] It is not surprising that Thomas Shepard's "records of God's great kindness" were edited and published in 1832 as *The
Autobiography of Thomas Shepard, the Celebrated Minister of Cambridge,
New England.*

The writers with whom I am concerned in part one of this book were
writing at the end of what William Spengemann calls the "historical"
form of autobiography, which was "invented to demonstrate the consonance of an individual life with an absolute, eternal law already in force
and known through some immediate source outside the life that illustrates it"; and they were writing before the rise of what he calls the
"philosophic" form of autobiography, in which the interior, private self
was probed for its originality and genius (1980, 60–63). I disagree with
Spengemann that narrated lives in which the author "knows" him- or
herself "through some . . . source outside [his or her] life" *are* autobiographies; but I agree that what he calls the "philosophic" form of autobiography and what I call autobiography came into existence at the beginning of the nineteenth century.[5] Living in an age in which the notion
of selfhood was under tremendous pressure, when new expectations
were put upon some men and women (by society or by themselves) to
shape and control their own destinies (see Wood 1992), writers of self-

biographies in post-Revolutionary America struggled both to imagine a modern individual free of an "absolute, eternal law" (and, therefore, independent of external forces and models) and to participate in a tradition that had yet to coalesce. As Roy Pascal has written in the context of European autobiography of exactly the same time period as I am studying here:

> This short period, stretching roughly from Rousseau's *Confessions* (1782) to Goethe's *Poetry and Truth* (1832) . . . seems decisive in the history of autobiography. . . . What is common and new is . . . a devoted but detached concern for their intimate selves, a partial yet impartial unravelling of their uniqueness, a kind of wonder and awe with regard to themselves; and at the same time an appreciation that this uniqueness is also the uniqueness of the circumstances in which they lived, hence their attention to the concrete reality of their experiences. (50)

Because the genre fully coalesced in or soon after the period I am analyzing, it has become a critical commonplace to note what G. Thomas Couser refers to as "a special compatibility between American culture and autobiographical discourse" (1989, 13–14). James Cox, for example, argues that the "very idea of autobiography has grown out of the political necessities and discoveries of the American and French Revolutions . . . when the modern self was being liberated as well as defined" (11–12).

Couser refers to a "special compatibility between American culture and autobiographical discourse"; both terms in his equation need more explicit definition. It was a particular ideology and not American "culture" specifically that gave rise to the new genre of "autobiography." That emergent ideology has been variously described as "emotivism" by philosophers (MacIntyre), as "romanticism" by literary critics, as "possessive individualism" (Macpherson) or "democracy" (Wood 1992) or "liberalism" (Hartz) by historians. A number of scholars link its emergence most closely to developing political and social ideas in the United States in the early nineteenth century and beyond. It has, however, been noted by many historians that that emergent ideology never went unchallenged (see Wilentz), and that its triumph was never complete (see, for example, Lasch). (Within literature, it still is not "complete," which is why readers can still buy and read recently published Christian selfbiographies that do not qualify as "autobiographies" under the terms of my definition.) The all-encompassing phrase "American culture" reifies and dehistoricizes a set of ideas still in development at least through the mid–nineteenth century, ideas that most Americans prior to the 1820s simply did not accept, even if they understood or could at least glimpse their meaning and significance. Similarly, "autobiographical discourse," Couser's other phrase, projects autobiography, dependent on modern ideas of authorship, selfhood, and audience, back into time. Revolutionary writers were writing their own lives, surely, but they were not writing autobiographies.

Cox is right to argue, however, that the American and French Revolutions did challenge and eventually alter extant notions of selfhood in the late eighteenth century. One text, albeit a fictional one, in which we can see the pressure brought to bear upon eighteenth-century notions of selfhood during the American Revolution is J. Hector St. John de Crèvecoeur's *Letters from an American Farmer* (1782). It epitomizes what I take to be a central insight, "liberating" for some but frightening for many others, that, explicitly or implicitly, occasions many of the self-biographies and autobiographies I study in this book.

Throughout *Letters from an American Farmer*, the simple, unlettered narrator, James, is fascinated by the concept of progress, especially the "progressive" acculturation of Europeans who have immigrated to America. "All I wish to delineate," he says concerning his short "History of Andrew, the Hebridean," in Letter III, "is the progressive steps of a poor man, advancing from indigence to ease, from oppression to freedom, from obscurity and contumely to some degree of consequence" (90).[6] James's fascination with progress early in the sequence of twelve letters is ironic, since he begins his correspondence with Mr. F. B., his learned European correspondent, as a static personality leading a static existence. Letter II, in which he narrates a brief, tightly focused self-biography, reveals that James's farm was left to him by his father, that he has done nothing to improve it, and that, having once considered selling it, he immediately retreated from such a dramatic change, fearing that in a "world so wide . . . there would be no room for [him]" (52). James ingenuously admits that his life is a direct copy, an imitation, of his father's: "I have but to tread his paths to be happy and a good man like him" (53). In other words, he begins the sequence of letters by drawing upon a conservative notion of imitation as the basis of self-formation. His life will be his father's life, much as Franklin recalls in his real family "the eldest Son being always bred to [the] Business" of blacksmithing (1309). Willingly constrained by the conception that sons should imitate fathers, James initially presents a striking contrast to Andrew the Hebridean in the famous Letter III. Andrew's history is a record of the emigrant's progression from oppressed European to free American. There *is* room for Andrew in the world—and plenty of it, on this side of the Atlantic. Andrew's life will necessarily be different from his father's.

However, James, too, eventually undergoes a "great metamorphosis" in *Letters* and is dislodged from his "narrow circles" (65). His own "progress" is closely linked to the epistolary form and dialogic structure of *Letters*. The text begins with James, his wife, and his minister discussing Mr. F. B.'s request that James become his American correspondent. James is undecided: he is afraid that, with his "limited power of mind" and undeveloped writing skills, he will not make a good correspondent (39–40). His wife is even more reluctant, fearing both that Mr. F. B. is too sophisticated and that James's own local reputation might suffer from his being called a writer. It is the minister who convinces James to write to Mr. F. B. He points out that Mr. F. B., in his first letter to James, asserted "that writing letters is nothing more than talking on paper" and indicated that he wants "nothing of [James] but what lies within the reach of [his] experience and knowledge" (41). The minister agrees with this dialogic understanding of writing: "What we speak out among ourselves we call conversation," he tells James, "and a letter is only conversation put down in black and white" (44). This argument convinces James to go ahead with the project, and the record of this debate becomes Letter I. James closes his initial missive with a final admonition to Mr. F. B. not to forget his limitations: "Remember, you are to give me my subjects, and on no other shall I write, lest you should blame me for an injudicious choice. . . . [And I will record] the spontaneous impressions which each subject may inspire" (49–50).

The first subject provided by Mr. F. B. is American husbandry, a subject on which he has apparently "conversed" at some length in his second letter to James, comparing American farming methods to those practiced in England, Russia, and Hungary. In Letter II James responds to this subject by recounting some of the "spontaneous impressions" he has experienced while working in his fields. True to his insistence that he is "neither a philosopher, politician, divine, or naturalist" (49), James does not overtly discuss politics, science, or other "public" matters at this point in his development. Letter II is a short self-biography revealing that James owns a well-developed farm (inherited from his father), has an excellent wife and healthy children, possesses faithful and industrious Negroes, and is not troubled by unfriendly Indians. James describes an idyllic, if static, existence on his Pennsylvania farm.

Yet the idyllic scenes of Letter II are not quite apolitical. James links them to current political issues at several points. Where, he asks rhetorically, "is that station which can confer a more substantial system of felicity than that of an American farmer possessing freedom of action, freedom of thoughts, ruled by a mode of government which requires but little from us?" (52). His pleasant farm, he remarks, "has established all our [i.e., his family's] rights . . . our rank, our freedom, our power as citizens. . . . This is what may be called the true and the only philosophy of an American farmer" (54). The incursion of such talk into the midst of these "spontaneous impressions" is consistent with the fictional, self-biographical realism established in Letter I; it is consistent with the psychology of a rustic such as James writing in the eighteenth century to someone whom he perceives as his superior. James is quite clearly parroting the minister's arguments, indeed, the minister's vision of America, as the minister expressed them during the debate in Letter I. Here in America, the minister had told James, "'[we] are strangers to those feudal institutions which have enslaved so many. . . . Misguided religion, tyranny, and absurd laws everywhere depress and afflict mankind. Here we have in some measure regained the ancient dignity of our species: our laws are simple and just. . .'" (42–43). James is unlearned and unlettered; in trying to shoot at something beyond his "limited abilities" in Letter II, he falls back on attitudes and ideas he has heard before. He mimics. James's vision of the American dream is as much the minister's as his own. His literal imitation in Letter I (transcribing a conversation) becomes intellectual in Letter II (parroting the minister's ideas).

In Letter III James again responds to a subject provided by Mr. F. B.'s ruminations. James's question, "What, then, is the American, this new man?" (69), suggests that Mr. F. B. has asked him to expand upon his observations in Letter II concerning the "substantial system of felicity" enjoyed by Americans. In response, James first theorizes about the "new man," then narrates the history of one. Theoretically, the American is a man psychologically and morally remade by his exposure to a new and expansive land. Freed from the religious, political, and spatial constraints of the old world, he is "resurrected"; he undergoes a "great metamorphosis . . . [that] extinguishes all his European prejudices [and allows him to forget] that mechanism of subordination, that servility of disposition which poverty had taught him" (83). The American is a "regenerated" human being.

In Letter II James's "spontaneous impressions" led him to recount his personal history; in Letter III James's response to Mr. F. B. leads him beyond "impressions" (and imitative political theorizing) to reflection. His theory of the "new man" in America leads him, for example, to group Americans into three "separate and distinct" classes (71–73). He has gone beyond mere "feelings" and mimicked ideas to assumptions, reasons, and classifications. Just so, his "History of Andrew, the Hebridean," represents another, more extensive act of enlightened reflection: he assumes the historian's task of collecting, digesting, and arranging the events of the past. After first protesting the commonplace nature of his "history," James defines his methodology: "All I wish to delineate is the progressive steps of a poor man, advancing from indigence to ease, from oppression to freedom, from obscurity and contumely to some degree of consequence . . . by the gradual operation of sobriety, honesty, and emigration" (90). James's history of Andrew is rosy: the merchants who deal with Andrew are honest and faithful; the Indians are kind, though slightly mischievous; the neighbors display warmth and friendship; Andrew's lands and possessions prove to be fertile and flourishing. Andrew is a perfect example of the new man in America, his history a perfect "epitome" (86) of the "progressive" transformation that results in that man. For the first time, James rests satisfied with his effort in a letter, concluding that he is more content with his history of Andrew than is the "historiographer of some great prince or general [who has brought] his hero victorious to the end of a successful campaign" (104). Moving from transcription in Letter I to self-biography in Letter II to biography in Letter III, James "discovers" a world outside his own narrow circles, discovers a prospect that is more "entertaining and instructive" (91) than his own in its view of America and the new American man. At this point, his new vision is—this has been often noted—very optimistic.

In the next five letters James, though still responding to Mr. F. B.'s earlier query concerning the precise nature of the "American," takes it upon himself to frame the subject matter of the "conversation." "Sensible how unable I am to lead you through so vast a maze [as America]," he writes, "let us look attentively for some small unnoticed corner" (107), Nantucket Island, which can be analyzed in depth. James has already come a long way from the simple farmer afraid of choosing an "injudicious" subject in Letter I. He begins his narrative of Nantucket Island with a comment on his historiographic method:

> You have, no doubt, read several histories of this continent, yet there are a thousand facts, a thousand explanations, overlooked. Authors will certainly convey to you a geographical knowledge of this country; they will acquaint you with the eras of the several settlements, the foundations of our towns, the spirit of our different characters, etc., yet they do not sufficiently disclose the genius of the people. . . . I want not to record the annals of the island of Nantucket; its inhabitants have no annals, for they are not a race of warriors. My simple wish is to trace them throughout their progressive steps from their arrival here to this present hour; to inquire by what means they have raised themselves from the most humble, the most insignificant beginnings, to the ease and the wealth they now possess. . . . (107–108)

James asserts that he is a historian of America, operating not by the figure of "epitome" (as in Andrew's history) but by the figure of synecdoche. Epitome suggests a simpler, less reflective method of characterizing a whole than does synecdoche. An epitome summarizes or embodies an entire class or type; a synecdoche actively asserts the meaning of the whole through the figure of the part, or vice versa. In James's account, Nantucket becomes merely one typical part of the American whole; "numberless settlements," James says, "each distinguished by some peculiarities, present themselves [to the historian] on every side; all . . . realize the most sanguine wishes that a good man could form for the happiness of his race" (107). Here, too, James conceives history to be the "delineation" of "progressive steps" (108), in this case of the Nantucket Islanders' rise from humble, insignificant beginnings to their present-day wealth and ease. But in this movement from biographer to national historian, James displays a new awareness of his task and, hence, his abilities. He has learned, quite clearly, that history can be written according to any number of methods; he has chosen, in his attempt to "disclose [America's] genius," to examine one small area of the larger whole. This purpose explains why James devotes five consecutive letters to Nantucket Island and Martha's Vineyard, and it reflects the growing role that James's powers of "reasoning" play in his "conversation" with Mr. F. B.

James finds Nantucket a "happy settlement." The islanders enjoy "a system of rational laws founded on perfect freedom" (109); their society is free from "idleness and poverty, the causes of so many crimes" elsewhere (125); many people enjoy great prosperity, all "an easy subsistence" (143); and slavery is not tolerated. Nantucket, it seems, is a restored Eden, a rocky island made into a garden by the "genius" and "industry" of its settlers. Nantucket's settlers emulated their ancestors, creating a more perfect society than the ones the ancestors had founded. Emulation, in this sense, is imitation with the hope of improvement. In *An Essay on Man*, Pope writes: "Envy, to which th'ignoble mind's a slave, / Is emulation in the learned or brave" (II: 191–192). Emulation is a way for those with knowledge or courage to improve upon a known model; it is an upward striving that goes beyond mere imitation. James's extended synecdoche suggests that America is improving. He insists that "what has happened [in Nantucket] has and will happen everywhere else" in America (110). It is, after all, only one singular scene of happiness amid the great "diffusive scene of happiness reaching from the sea-shores to the last settlements on the borders of the wilderness" (154).

James's account of Nantucket Island and its inhabitants is not completely optimistic, however. Darker elements intrude. James admits that the happiness of Americans might not be as unspoiled as he had thought. It is interrupted by individual folly and by "our spirit of litigiousness" (154). He also finds that the history of Nantucket and, since Nantucket functions as synecdoche, of America is tainted by the corruption that European settlers brought to the Indians in the form of smallpox and rum. Even as he writes, James points out, the descendants of those abused Indians are being annihilated. Finally, James's analysis of the history of Nantucket leads to his discovery that some of the islanders had recently moved inland to establish a community in North Carolina named, hopefully, New Garden. But, though it is located in a much more fertile region than Nantucket, New Garden does not create the new, regenerated man of America: "It does not breed men equally hardy [to Nantucket islanders]. . . . It leads too much to idleness and effeminacy" (147). The flip side of emulation and progress is laziness and degeneracy. In his peripheral vision, James can see reasons for refuting the idealized vision of America he expressed so confidently in Letters II and III. He quickly tries to turn away from them.

Essentially, the five Nantucket letters comprise one unit of letters, an integrated history in which, by digging straight down into the history of one region of America (as it were) instead of "cheerfully . . . skipping from bush to bush" along the ground (90), James is made to confront realities gilded by the rhetoric of his and the minister's idealized notions. The entire unit is an extended reply to that famous question of Letter III, "What, then, is an American, this new man?" In Letter IX, then, having glimpsed the darkness beneath, James freely chooses his own topic for reflection for the first time, a sign that he has achieved a certain independence of mind. Charles Town, North Carolina, he writes to Mr. F. B., is one great scene of "joy, festivity and happiness" (168). Now, however, James finds it impossible to ignore the evils that lurk behind that facade of happiness: the climate, which "renders excesses of all kinds very dangerous"; the lawyers, who slowly rob the people of their patrimony; and, crucially, the institution of slavery.

James's subject matter in Letter IX is generated, ironically, by a "spontaneous impression," a phrase that recalls his self-conception in Letter II: on his way to visit a planter, he comes upon a black slave suspended in a cage and left to expire of thirst, of pain, or at the beaks of birds of prey. The slave has killed the overseer of the plantation, James learns, and has been tortured and left to die by what the planter refers to as "the laws of self-preservation" (179), that is, as an example to the other slaves. This scene, James somberly tells Mr. F. B., accounts for my "melancholy reflections and . . . for the gloomy thoughts with which I [fill] this letter" (177). The scene accounts, too, for the tremendous leap James makes from the history of Nantucket in Letters IV–VIII to the "history of the earth" (173) that he begins to analyze in Letter IX. Elaborating upon the intimations of evil he felt upon seeing the slave, James insists that the history of the world, including America, presents nothing "but crimes of the most heinous nature, committed from one end of the world to the other" (173). "What, then, is man?" (170), James asks, echoing his earlier, more famous question. Having moved from simple transcription to self-biography to biography (of Andrew, the Hebridean) to regional and national history (Nantucket and, by synecdoche, America) and now to the history of mankind, James's expanding consciousness arrives at perhaps the most basic and puzzling question the Enlightenment dared to ask. For James, the answer to it is not a sinful being, as Christian philosophers argued, nor a self-loving being constrained by reason, as Pope argued in *An Essay on Man*, nor a reasoning machine, as de la Mettrie and others argued. His tentative answer, following Swift perhaps, is a perverse animal. Human nature itself is perverse (174), and God has abandoned it "to all the errors, the follies, and the miseries, which [man's] most frantic rage and [his] most dangerous vices and passions can produce" (173).

This ninth letter, which James calls a "general review of human nature" (177), moves from his discussion of the institution of slavery to his recognition that man is by nature wretched, his principles "poisoned in their most essential parts" (173–174). James concludes by asking whether he, having realized the true nature of man, should prefer a "primitive" life in the woods to a "civilized" life in society. The question at first seems moot: "Evil preponderates in both" states. But evil, James argues, is "more scarce, more supportable, and less enormous" in the woods than it is in "advanced" society. So, clearly, man should be happier, or less unhappy, in the pastoral state. Yet this "fact" is complicated by man's innate desire and need to people the earth. The dilemma and, more significantly, James's ambivalence are indicative of his state of mind in Letter IX as he approaches the "gloomy" scene at the end. It is as if his realization of the "true" nature of mankind, though the gradual product of his dialogue with Mr. F. B., were still too sudden and too shocking to allow any answers, any firm statements about reality. The ground has shifted beneath him.

It is not by chance, then, that Mr. F. B. initiates the discussion in Letter X, asking James to say something about snakes. Though Mr. F. B.'s choice of subject matter is more than slightly ironic, James certainly *needs* direction. And his recognition of the snake's presence in the new world is a painful but necessary extension of Letter IX. Shocked by his conclusions there, James wishes to turn his face away from the sight of evil: "Why would you prescribe this task?" (180), he asks. James soon finds that the rattlesnake, though "perfectly inoffensive" if not touched and capable even of being tamed, is more likely to kill than not to offend, even after death. He narrates the story of a father and son who were each killed by pulling on the same boot that had two rattlesnake fangs lodged in it. Evil, though not seen, not suspected, preponderates. He shall strike at our heel, indeed, even from the very boots we inherit from our fathers. Once he first notices evil, James finds it everywhere. Retreating to a "simple grove" to watch the hummingbird, "the most beautiful of [birds]," James notes that "sometimes, from what motive I know about, it will tear and lacerate flowers into a hundred pieces, for, strange to tell, they are the most irascible of the feathered tribe. Where do passions find room in so diminutive a body? They often fight with the fury of lions until one of the combatants falls a sacrifice and dies. . . . [The hummingbird] is a miniature work of our Great Parent" (184). Evil "preponderates" in man, in nature, in every work of God, from his most "miniature work" to his most complex.

James's state of mind is figured by an "uncommon and beautiful" battle between a blacksnake and a water snake described at the end of Letter X. He is puzzled by the battle, for the "vindictive rage" expressed by each combatant appears to be unfounded. "Strange was this to behold," he writes. Like the evil he has come to recognize in these later letters versus his own good feelings expressed in the early letters, the blacksnake (the "aggressor") and the water snake struggle, the former solely out of hate, the latter in an attempt to reach "its natural element" (185). The black snake gains control at the end: "The black snake seemed to retain its wonted superiority, for its head was exactly fixed above that of the other, which it incessantly pressed down under the water, until it was stifled and sunk. The victor no sooner perceived its enemy incapable of further resistance than, abandoning it to the current, it returned on shore and disappeared" (186).

The death of the water snake is a metaphor for James's disappearance in Letter XI; he, too, is "stifled and sunk." Letter XI is written by a European traveler named Iw-n Al-z who describes a visit he made to John Bartram, the famous botanist. Iw-n echoes the optimism of James's early letters. Clearly, Letter I and Letter XI are dominated by voices other than James's: the minister and James's wife in Letter I, Iw-n Al-z in Letter XI. And each is followed by a letter in which James's feelings erupt. In Letter II those passionate "feelings" (53) were the result of James's memory of the fear he had experienced when he considered selling his father's farm. Afraid of his own insignificance, James rejected the larger world of experience and remained on his father's farm. Lacking experience, James could at first only retreat in his letters to feelings and impressions, responses conditioned by the thoughts and language of the people he respected: his father, the minister, Mr. F. B. In Letter XII James again retreats to feelings: "Distresses of a Frontier Man." Plagued by the "remembrance of dreadful scenes," not simply the tortured slave, but the battles of the Revolution, James again faces and retreats from his own smallness: "What can an insignificant man do in the midst of these jarring contradictory parties, equally hostile to persons situated as I am?" (205). The ability to reason, which he has discovered in the course of *Letters*, provides no answers, only more questions. "What, then, is life?" he asks, rewriting his most famous question once again. At bottom, he decides, it is "self-preservation" (210). James retreats west, fleeing a world in which he has lost his bearings.

James moves in the course of this fictional self-biography from innocence to experience, from a naive acceptance of the way of life inherited from his father and taught by his minister to a critical awareness of his own need to think, to act, and to create his own future. His progression through the literary genres of simple transcription, self-biography, biography, local history, national history, and human history is an analogue of his intellectual and moral growth. His final step in this progression toward self-knowledge is a painful one, for what he learns to do late in his conversation with Mr. F. B. is to defictionalize his world, to dismantle the many claims colonial and Revolutionary America make on behalf of rational, "objective" truth.

Letters II and III reveal James's unquestioning acceptance of his father's life and of the minister's romantic version of the American dream. By the time he ends Letter IV, James makes note of the fact that the success of the Nantucket islanders is due in part to their simplicity: "I saw neither governors nor any pageantry of state, neither ostentatious magistrates nor any individuals clothed with useless dignity: no artificial phantoms subsist here, either civil or religious" (125). Those who bring their "luxurious" manners to Nantucket, James observes with satisfaction, "could not exist a month; they would be obliged to emigrate" (125). Nantucket Island, in other words, like America itself, has supposedly done away with the "artificial phantoms" that oppressed man in Europe. The "false" has been discarded in favor of the "true," the "real." Of course, this first suspicion of the "artificiality" of religion and government is not all-inclusive. James merely extends the minister's romantic condemnation of the Old World (42–44) to include its manners, government, and religion; he praises Nantucket for reducing class distinctions (125–126), establishing a government "which demands but little for its protection" (109), and practicing a religion "disencumbered . . . from useless ceremonies and trifling forms" (153). One can find a similar sort of rhetoric in many works after 1765 in America. John Adams, for one, argued that, ideally, "government [is] a plain, simple, intelligible thing, founded in nature and reason, and quite comprehensible by common sense." America, Adams went on to say, had thrown off the "arbitrary," artificial tyranny of the Old World's canon and feudal law (1856, 454–455). James, however, soon begins to sense that Nantucket, though it may have simplified life in some ways, has merely replaced one fiction with another. The women of the island, for example, take a dose of opium every morning: "It is hard to conceive how a people always happy and healthy . . . [and] never oppressed with the vapours of idleness, yet should want the fictitious effects of opium to preserve that cheerfulness to which their temperance, their climate, their happy situation, so justly entitle them" (160). Even in this simplified society, mankind willingly chooses fictions, chooses oppressions. In addition, James notices that the law, which he earlier trumpeted as "a bridle and check to prevent the strong and greedy from oppressing the timid and weak" (57), is actually an instrument of oppression. In Nantucket lawyers are an "oppressive burthen under which we groan" (152). The situation is even worse in Charles Town. There, society has become "slaves" to the society of lawyers. James sees that mankind will have its fictions, be its situation ever so simple, free, and happy.

James's first question—"What, then, is the American, this new man?"—is followed by his realization that the American is not so different from the old man. Both are oppressed; both create fictions that complicate an otherwise natural existence. Thus his next question—"What, then, is man?"—collapses the New World/Old World dichotomy. There is no "American," no "European"; there is man.[7] Traditionally, of course, man had been defined as a fallen creature, capable of regeneration only by the saving grace of Christ. Crèvecoeur plays with the notion of regeneration in *Letters*: the black slave in the cage is a Christ-figure, covered as he is by a swarm of insects "eager to feed on his mangled flesh and to drink his blood" (178); the "old man" (the European) is "regenerated" (68) and "resurrected" (82), reborn as a "new man" (the American); the Nantucket islanders found a settlement they name "New Garden." But as James is exposed to the horror and the enormity of evil, he comes to realize that any notion of man's goodness is false. Man is not good. "The history of the earth!" James exclaims. "Doth it present anything but crimes of the most heinous nature, committed from one end of the world to the other?" (193). Men "are always at war" (174); human nature is perverse; existence is but so "many errors . . . crimes . . . diseases, wants, and sufferings" (177). The myths of Eden and of man's regeneration are not true: man could never have been, nor can he be, good.

James's third question—"What, then, is life?"—indicates that his skepticism has been extended to the Enlightenment belief in man's power to remake the world. His immediate answer to the question is pessimistic, almost nihilistic: "Life appears to be a mere accident, and of the worst kind: we are born to be victims of diseases and passions, of mischance and death; better not to be than to be miserable" (210). This is an insight into skepticism that, in the late eighteenth century, James

Boswell will deny with Christianity and Benjamin Rush will deny with an enlightened, universalist faith in progress. But James no longer has faith in his culture's fictions. The "centre is tumbled down" (211), he says in reference to his beliefs and to his society. Unable to believe in "the fictitious society in which [he] lives" (214), James spends most of Letter XII justifying his decision to emigrate to an Indian village somewhere west of Pennsylvania. "Self-preservation," he concludes, "is above all political precepts and rules, and even superior to the dearest opinions of our minds" (210).

The phrasing here—"self-preservation"—is more than slightly ironic: it is the phrase the slave owner used to defend his murder of the slave in Letter IX (179). Language itself has become malleable and fluid in James's world; it does not signify. His world having "tumbled down," James finds it difficult to justify, in language, his intentions. He cannot answer the third question, except in the actual act of his choosing to be left, at the end, where so many later American heroes, also stripped of their illusions, of their naive fictions concerning the world around them, will be left: in a liminal space out of which they promise to project themselves anew in some extranovelistic future.[8] James will light out for the territory.

James's crisis at the end is Crèvecoeur's imaginative projection of the very real crisis experienced by many Americans during the Revolution. Donald Weber has convincingly shown, for example, how Revolutionary ministers, responding to the bewildering events of the 1760s and 1770s, attempted "to arrest [their] metaphysical fall into interpretive contingency, the hermeneutic void of utter disconnectedness," by articulating a sermon rhetoric that was at first fragmented, disjointed, antinarrative. "Language itself," Weber writes, "became unmoored from traditional contexts, referents, and canons of style and form" during the Revolution (152, 154). Myths, of course, are stories a culture invents to confer identity, to achieve and maintain consensus; they are, as Richard Slotkin has shown, stories whose "logic" flows from "the logic of . . . narrative" itself (quoted in Weber, 6). In moments of ideological crisis, such as the American Revolution, those myths are challenged, disrupted, and overturned. They do not adequately explain. "New stories are required when the old no longer resonate with explanatory power" (154). The ministers Weber discusses eventually managed to accommodate "their pulpits to the secular American world of the 1790s" (135), and to invent a rhetoric and accompanying myth that accounted for changed cultural values and their own relation to those values. Their sermons became coherent and dependent on narrative once again.

In his analysis of Crèvecoeur's *Letters*, Grantland Rice makes a point similar to mine and to Weber's:

> Admitting that he has overlooked his "own share" of this evil in his epistemological method of deriving the whole from the part, James confesses his collaboration in mythmaking and asks readers to transform him from his role as author of the text to that of its subject, refiguring in several sentences the entire form of *Letters*. In doing so, he recasts *Letters*, not as an empirical description of America, but as a literary account of the disillusionment of a naïve political philosopher who would eschew the idea of history and historical necessity. (1999, 21)

Recasting himself as the subject of the narrative, James in effect discovers the autobiographical impulse, as I have defined autobiography. His experience has been about himself, not about tradition or America or politics or myth. It has been about his own discovery of himself as a thinking, feeling, changing subject or agent. James becomes an example of Locke's observation that the mind "progresses" by in fact testing or trying personal experience, not against the Christic model or known types, as in earlier self-biography, but against the emergent uniqueness or independence of an agent that formerly did not know itself. James comes to know himself over time through experimentation.

Like the ministers discussed by Weber, James experiences a "metaphysical fall into interpretive contingency." He awakens from his unquestioning acceptance of the world of his fathers into a world in which meanings, values, and language itself are "unmoored from [their] traditional contexts." He is confused both about himself and, in the final letter, Letter XII, about his community, which offers, in the 1770s, only the "extremes" of the Tory and rebel positions (204). "I had never before these calamitous times formed any such ideas" about America, about mankind, about life itself, James mourns; "I lived on, laboured and prospered, without having ever studied on what the security of my life and the foundation of my prosperity were established; I perceived them just as they left me" (201). James's predicament is that, having perceived his society's conceptions as fictions, he has no stable ground or essential concepts with which to replace them; having descended into uncertainty, he cannot find solid ground. He has only fragments that cannot cohere into meaning, fragments from which no consensus can apparently be achieved. They cannot, evidently, even be shored against his ruins.

Read as a fictional self-biography, Crèvecoeur's *Letters from an American Farmer* opens up the terrifying possibility, at least for conservative philosophers in the eighteenth century, that advanced human societies are merely arbitrary fictions. As Leo Damrosch writes concerning British philosophers late in the century: "the unchangeable human nature in which Gibbon, Hume, and Johnson believed was thrown into doubt by the revolution of the 1790s and by a growing consciousness . . . that experience could be unique and change could be irreversible" (128). "There must be something more congenial to our native dispositions than the fictitious society in which we live" (218), Crèvecoeur has James muse. Like an American Candide, James takes to a "garden" in response to that realization; he moves into a wigwam on a plot of land among the western Indians. The Rousseauistic Indians—simple, natural, unlettered, happy (214–217)—represent at the end of James's account a society that is not artificial or fictional, but natural and true. James senses that such a picture is idealized, if not romanticized: "Perhaps my imagination gilds too strongly this distant prospect," he remarks. But, like Rousseau before him, he insists that a society "founded on so few and simple principles" must be less adverse (225) than more complex European and Anglo-American ones. We cannot know for sure if James's brief hesitation about the rosy picture he paints of Indian life is a warning of future disillusionments or is simply leftover skepticism inapplicable to Indian society. He himself, he remarks, "can be nothing until [he] is replaced" into a society of some sort. James, finally, is not a romantic, hoping to locate himself in opposition to or isolation from society, as does Thoreau in the mid-nineteenth century. James's skepticism does not carry him that far; he *needs* society.

The reader of *Letters* is, then, left in ambiguity: we cannot know for sure whether Crèvecoeur intends James to be like Rousseau, rejecting contemporary civilized "fictions" for the truths of a natural existence, or to be like Thomas Paine, rejecting contemporary civilized "fictions" for the eternal truths of trigonometry. But, like Paine, James comes up against the fact that the "mind once enlightened cannot again become dark. There is no possibility, neither is there any term to express the supposition by, of the mind *un*knowing anything it already knows" (Paine 1987, 165, italics in original). The ambiguity is Crèvecoeur's point. He can see the limits of the Enlightenment, but he cannot imagine what lies beyond it.[9] What Crèvecoeur reveals in this fictional self-biography is not so much how people in Revolutionary and post-Revolutionary society would or might choose when they came to see, as Alisdair MacIntyre puts it, "the emergence of the individual freed . . . from the social bonds of those constraining hierarchies which the modern world rejected at its birth" (34), but how they might come to be in the *position* of choosing. Crèvecoeur imagines, I am arguing, the position in which many post-Revolutionary self-biographers actually find themselves, and out of which they are forced or helped or urged to articulate new kinds of selves, and thus help to invent the genre of autobiography. American self-biographers and autobiographers in Revolutionary and post-Revolutionary America are brought by the series of events labeled the American Revolution to recognize the artificiality of a society that, until now, they had either never questioned or never had the opportunity to question. "Our style and manner of thinking have undergone a revolution more extraordinary than the political revolution of the country," Paine wrote. "We see with other eyes; we hear with other ears; and think with other thoughts, than those we formerly used" (1987, 163). This would not be true of everyone, of course, nor even of as many as Paine hoped in 1782. But it did prove to be true for many autobiographers.

To support my reading of Crèvecoeur's fictional *Letters*, let me adduce the example of an actual self-biographer, one who was writing at the very moment that Crèvecoeur's narrative was first published in England. James Moody begins his memoirs, *Lieut. James Moody's Narrative of His Exertions and Sufferings in the Cause of Government* (1783), by stating directly one of the realizations made by Crèvecoeur's fictional narrator: "Choice and plan, it would seem, have seldom much influence in determining either men's characters, or their conditions. These are usually the result of circumstances utterly without our control. Of the truth of this position, the Writer's own recent history affords abundant proofs" (1). Moody's narrative of his experiences uncannily echoes Crèvecoeur's more famous fictional narrative. Like the fabricated James, Moody before the Revolution is "a plain, contented farmer, settled on a large, fertile, pleasant, and well-improved farm of his own, in the best climate and happiest country in the world" (1). Like James, he is incredulous that events should have led to his becoming "a *writer*" (1, italics in original). Like James in Letters I and II, he understands the British constitution to be the "venerable" guarantor of the colonists' "rights" (3). And like James, he desires to remain in georgic privacy in an attempt to avoid the larger world, in Moody's case in an attempt to ignore the "general cry [of] *Join* [the rebel cause] *or die!*" in 1774 and 1775 (5–6). But Moody realizes that what James in Letter XII calls the "extremes" demand a more practical choice than fleeing westward. The extreme passions of rebels and Tories force Moody to make a political choice. Unlike James (who flees west) and unlike Crèvecoeur (who for personal reasons fled east to France), Moody remains loyal to the king and enlists in the British army, where he is employed as a spy.

Moody's *Narrative* is primarily a memoir of his adventures as a British spy. After his early indecision, he never waffles in his loyalty, and he never overtly questions his identity in the face of events. "He . . . has sacrificed his all," he says of himself at the end of the narrative, ". . . [and he] made this sacrifice, because he sincerely believed what he declares and professes" (55). What he "professes," even as late as November 1782, when he sent the narrative to press, is the belief that America has been enslaved by the rebel government. He is, he says, determined to continue the war "rather than outlive the freedom of his country" under British rule in London, where he and many other Tories landed in the early 1780s. Yet for all his professions of loyalty to the crown, Moody reveals the same problem of identity in the wake of social upheaval that Crèvecoeur so eloquently raises through the character of James. Throughout the narrative, he is intensely concerned to establish the authority of his narrative. Early on, he recognizes that "the credit of some parts of [his] Narrative must rest on his own authority," and so he "appeals to sundry certificates and affidavits now in his possession" (4), which he conveniently prints in an appendix to the narrative (59–64). Elsewhere, he appeals to "an eye-witness yet living" to verify an "extraordinary circumstance" (20), and to his own lack of ambition or greed to verify the purity of his motives in writing his story. All narratives, of course, bring with them the problem of authority; histories and self-biographies, in particular, do so, since they claim to point to external, verifiable events and people and places. But Moody's problem is more severe than the problem facing Gibbon in either his *Decline and Fall* or his *Memoirs*, for, in a number of ways, Moody's stance as author and narrator is compromised: he is an American-born loyalist living in London in 1782, when the fatigue and disgust with the war effort led to the preliminary signing of the Treaty of Paris; he is writing the narrative partly as an appeal to the British government to compensate him more fully for his services in the army;[10] and, most important, he is writing as a former spy who spent four years disguising himself, his intentions, and his actions.

Within the context of British and American politics in 1782, the first two problems would have called his motives as author, and hence the truthfulness of his narrative, into question. But it is the third problem on which I want to focus, one that has more general implications for the notion of personal identity in the 1780s and beyond. As Moody tells it, he is quite a successful spy, continually evading detection and bringing important information to the British generals. No rebel jail can hold him; he penetrates picket lines with ease; bullets miraculously miss him. By 1781, the New York countryside is so alarmed by rumors of his presence that the mail is diverted. Moody responds by sending a man who looks like him to a distant part of the country, the man is recognized "as" Moody, the militia from the area is called to apprehend the false Moody, and the real Moody is able to capture the mail. The ease with which he alters his appearance and creates confusion in people's expectations of him suggests that identity was imagined to be an innate or fixed entity in Revolutionary America. But in Moody's *Narrative* it is becoming something to be shaped or molded according to need, much as Charles Brockden Brown imagines Carwin disguising his voice and outward appearance for his own inscrutable motives (in *Wieland*), much as Stephen Burroughs takes on his father's character by simply delivering some of his father's sermons, much as Deborah Sampson actually adopted (or so it is reported) the "character" of a man during the Revolutionary War (Mann, 135). No one suspects Sampson's deceptions, even—for a while —when she is wounded in the groin. She is wooed by another woman, serves honorably in battle, and talks and dresses like any other soldier. Identity was not fixed, unalterable, or even self-evident to writers like Crèvecoeur, Moody, Brown, Burroughs, and Sampson. After 1780, it was becoming malleable, fluid, and self-determined. Character was in one sense a role, not an essential mark of one's individuality or self.[11]

Moody's narrative is one of several Revolutionary narratives in which narrators or characters come to realize that they are not, simply, one essential or typical self. Moody does not develop or thematize the problem as fully as Stephen Burroughs does (see chapter 6, below); Moody relates it only to the problem of narrative authority. How can spies *ever* be faithfully recompensed by the government that employs them? he implicitly asks.[12] By 1782, he thinks he can safely tell the truth. But what records remain, other than the testimony of the spy himself and a few, scattered documents? During the war, Moody learns that (temporary) imitation is easy, so easy that by becoming someone else he apparently loses the authority of the man who can "prove"—Moody claims to be sure of it—that he is singly, essentially one person. James, on the other hand, beginning in the same place, learns that imitation has become pointless in the changed circumstances of the Revolutionary world, because events or the pull of Mr. F. B.'s "enlightened" consciousness (or the combination of the two) conspire to make him a "new man," not regenerate but skeptical. He cannot be or become his own father; but neither is he ready, as John Fitch (and the modern self) will be, to father himself.

As a fictional self-biographer, James represents on a philosophical and narratological level what happened on various other levels—emotional, cultural, intellectual—to other people who lived through the ferment of the 1770s, '80s, and '90s. Charles Taylor defines the modern self in terms of three distinguishing elements, all of which James comes to represent in his self-characterization: an inward depth, an affirmation of ordinary life, and nature or the natural self as an inner moral source. He represents these much more clearly than Moody does, which is why I have chosen to analyze his fictional narrative in much more depth than Moody's. That may have been a matter of talent, as Moody's narrative is clearly less sophisticated than Crèvecoeur's, or it may have been a matter of Moody's real need to ground his story in the "truth." Moody was desperate in 1782, Crèvecoeur less so when he drafted the manuscript of *Letters* in the 1770s. Both authors represent, however, the idea that personal identity was not and could not be a fixed, known thing. The "excess of the passion for liberty, . . ." wrote Benjamin Rush in 1788, "constituted a species of insanity, which I shall take the liberty of distinguishing by the name of *Anarchia*" (1947, 333). In some texts, selfhood in and after the American Revolution indeed becomes "lawless." There no longer seemed to be clear rules for how to think about the self. Writing of themselves in this revolutionary half-century, American self-biographers and autobiographers grappled with the notion of individual identity within a culture that depended less and less on traditional methods to guide the process of self-formation. What happens to James and to Moody as they are moved out of their "narrow circles" of stability and tradition happened to many other people, many of whom pondered their dilemma in written narratives. What I am intent upon showing in the chapters that follow is just how varied those narratives are, and how contested was the ground on which the dominant ideology of personhood in the nineteenth century was finally constructed. After Benjamin Franklin, it turns out, many American writers were thinking about what was and was not, as Benjamin Vaughan puts it in his letter (which prefaces part two of Franklin's *History of My Life*), in "man's private power" (1375).

∂⌐

Post-Revolutionary readers and writers were fascinated by textual self-hood, a fact that can be inferred from the variety of self-narratives written within the first two decades after Yorktown: travel narratives by foreign visitors to North America (such as Rouchefoucault's *Travels through the United States of North America* [1799]), travel narratives by Americans abroad (such as John Quincy Adams's *Letters on Silesia, Written during a Tour through That Country* [1804]), accounts of scientific expeditions (such as William Bartram's *Travels through North and South Carolina, Georgia, East and West Florida* [1792]), memoirs by combatants in the war (such as Nathaniel Fanning's *Narrative of the Adventures of an American Navy Officer* [1806]), memoirs by well-known political figures (such as John Adams's *Autobiography* [wr. 1802–1806]), accounts of captivity among Native Americans (such as John Slover's *Narrative of John Slover* [1783]) and among the British (such as Thomas Dring's *Recollections of a Jersey Prison Ship* [1829]), narratives by former slaves recounting their struggle to be free (such as Venture Smith's *Narrative of the Life and Adventures of Venture, a Native of Africa* [1798]), accounts of spiritual conversion (such as John Marrant's *Narration of the Lord's Wonderful Dealings with John Marrant, a Black* [1785]), accounts of "notorious" figures whose sensational fame created a market for their lives (such as Burroughs's *Memoirs*), and fictional first-person narratives (such as the anonymous *Adventures of Jonathan Corncob, Loyal American Refugee* [1787] or Crèvecoeur's *Letters*). By the 1780s, the market for firsthand accounts of unusual experiences was clearly on the rise.[13] Authors could not yet draw upon the term "autobiography" to describe their narratives, but neither were they as unclear, generically speaking, as Anne Bradstreet had been in the seventeenth century. Within the available categories of self-life-writing, they were hard at work. An audience was available and books could be gotten to them. Many of these authors, particularly the more educated ones writing after 1800, clearly begin to refer to a tradition of self-writing: Benjamin Rush notes in *Travels through Life* (wr. 1800), for example, that Rousseau's *Confessions* taught him to vary his studies to keep his mind from stagnating (91); and Alexander Graydon opens his *Memoirs of a Life* (1811) by contrasting his self-biography to those by Rousseau, Franklin, Marmontel, Cumberland, and Cardinal de Retz (3). Also, many clearly begin to write about themselves with what they sense is a newfound freedom. "It is difficult for a man to speak long of himself without vanity," David Hume wrote in "My Own Life" (1776); "therefore, I shall be short" (962). And Hume's narrative is short, encompassing only a handful of printed pages in which he mainly describes his travels, publications, and public appointments. A self-biography, Edward Gibbon wrote a few years later, in 1789, "will expose me, and perhaps with justice, to the imputation of vanity" (39). More than Hume, Gibbon claims to feel comfortable in "expos[ing] my private feelings . . . without scruple or reserve" (43), yet usually in his oft-begun *Memoirs* he discovers within not the modern self of autobiography but the eighteenth-century type of "man." "The discovery of a sixth sense (i.e., love), the first consciousness of manhood, is a very interesting moment of our lives," Gibbon tells us, for example, "but it less properly belongs to the memoirs of an individual, than to the natural history of the species" (104). In the same vein as Hume and Gibbon, Franklin impishly begins his account of his life in 1771 with a reference to vanity: "I shall a good deal gratify my own *Vanity*" in telling my story (1308, italics in original). In Franklin's comment, we can see that the door to a complete focus on what the eighteenth century called vanity—individuality, singularity, eccentricity—has been cracked open, despite the continued reticence of most self-biographers to talk at length about themselves.

But while these authors had by the turn of the century become more comfortable with the vanity inherent in the act of writing self-biographies, they still struggled with the problem of selfhood. What was the self? How could it be known? How could it be represented? For an earlier writer like Anne Bradstreet, of course, the ideal self was Christic: the point of "To My Dear Children" was precisely to assert that the self known as Anne Bradstreet was inconsequential except as it was subsumed by Christ. Self is vanity, and vanity is sin, and sin must be overcome. Mary Rowlandson wrote with that ideal in mind: "The Lord hath shewed me the vanity of these outward things, that they are *the vanity of vanities, and vexation of spirit*; that they are a shadow, a blast, a bubble, and things of no continuance; that we must rely on God himself, and our whole dependence must be upon him" (65, italics in original). Conversion narratives written during the Revolution make the same assertion, of course; but most self-narratives written during the period were not conversion narratives. They were secular accounts that sometimes retained religious imagery but shifted the significance of individual experience to an entirely earthly plane. During and after the Revolution, authors whose primary interest was secular worked within three related frames of reference about how personal identity comes into existence: the notion that selves are typical and that therefore they are formed through imitation; the notion that selves are ideal and that therefore they are formed through emulation; and the notion that selves are original or singular and that therefore they are formed uniquely. Crèvecoeur's and Moody's insight that the individual self is a constructed entity dependent upon itself and largely unknowable to others was met by Revolutionary self-biographers in one or both or all three of these ways. Let me briefly discuss each.

When discussing the art of virtue in part two of his *History of My Life*, Benjamin Franklin remarks:

> tho' I never arrived at the Perfection I had been so ambitious of obtaining, but fell far short of it, yet I was by the Endeavour made a better and a happier Man than I otherwise should have been, if I had not attempted it; As those who aim at perfect Writing by imitating the engraved Copies, tho' they never reach the wish'd for Excellence of those Copies, their Hand is mended by the Endeavour, and is tolerable while it continues fair and legible. (1391)[14]

Here, Franklin's conception of the process of self-formation is imitative. To imitate, as Samuel Johnson defined it, was "To copy; to endeavour to resemble." Franklin does not identify the "engraved copy" (the tenor of the vehicle in his metaphor) that he tried to imitate in his behavior, though he does list thirteen moral virtues based on his "Reading" and notes that one of those virtues, humility, is based on the precept "Imitate Jesus and Socrates" (1384–1385). This conception of imitation is articulated again in part one of his narrative when Franklin describes his father taking him on walks to see various workmen go about their trades, hoping that he can observe Benjamin's "Inclination and endeavour to fix it on some Trade" (1316). Franklin is not "inclined" to the trades, but he "learnt so much by [observing the men], as to be able to do little Jobs my self in my House, when a Workman could not readily be got; and to construct little Machines for my Experiments while the Intention of making the Experiment was fresh and warm in my mind" (1317). The process is, in great part, mechanical: Franklin suggests that man's moral nature, as well as his skills, can be learned, improved, even potentially perfected through the imitation of others. As David Humphreys wrote in defense of his biography of Israel Putnam: there is an "advantage [in] presenting for imitation a respectable model of private and public virtues" (1968, 243). Imitation is the oldest and most traditional method of self-formation, deriving from the dominant form of instruction available in cultures that do not have wide access to the printed word or that have low levels of literacy. The system of apprenticeship within which Franklin and Fitch and Rush and others were trained depended upon imitation. This, too, is the sense in which Crèvecoeur makes the uncultivated James desire initially to take his father's place.

Franklin's reference to his electrical experiments points us to the section of his memoirs dealing with his "Philosophical Reputation" (1452), and toward the second model for self-formation in Revolutionary America, emulation. In 1746, Franklin sees Archibald Spencer perform "some electrical Experiments" in Boston. "[S]urpriz'd and pleas'd," Franklin imitates the experiments when he returns to Philadelphia, using apparatus that the Library Company received from Peter Collinson. After "much Practice," he becomes expert in the experiments, and even begins to "add . . . a Number of new Ones." These new experiments become the subject of several letters from Franklin to Collinson, letters that Collinson has published in 1751 as *Experiments and Observations on Electricity* and that eventually bring Franklin great fame. Franklin more than imitates in his experiments; he emulates. To emulate, Samuel Johnson tells us, is "To rival; to propose as one to be equalled or excelled" (def. 1); or "To imitate with hope of equality, or superiour excellence" (def. 2). I hope, Humphreys adds in his biography of Putnam, that the narrative will "create an emulation to copy his domestic, manly and heroic virtues" (249).

Brook Hindle has noted how, in the area of technology, Franklin's contemporaries strove to imitate and outdo each other:

> Through competition, one might reach to the ennobled efforts it provoked, to emulation. This word, much more in currency [in the eighteenth century] than today, was frequently applied to achievement in art and the arts. . . . Emulation represented an effort to equal or surpass the work of others; it was more a striving for quality and recognition than a marketplace competition and seems to have emerged from the manner of instruction and improvements in the arts and crafts. (12–13)

Hindle shows how the steamboat was developed through the efforts of a number of craftsmen working from one another's plans, like Oliver Evans refining James Watts's steam engine so as to make it "cheaper [to operate], more compact, and better suited for many uses" (48). By the time Robert Fulton proved the commercial viability of steamboat transportation in 1807, he was at the end of a long line of craftsmen and tinkerers trying to improve on others' plans. Fulton's own "work was creative," Hindle argues, but "not one of [the] components [of his steamboat] was original, as was the work of every predecessor who got a boat running" (54). Fulton was not an inventor; he merely reconfigured the components of other steamboats into one that was commercially viable.

Emulation is what drives Benjamin Rush's career as a doctor: "For many years after I settled in Philadelphia I was regulated in my practice by the System of medicine which I had learned from the lectures and publications of Dr. Cullen. . . . The weight of Dr. Cullen's name depressed me every time I ventured to admit an idea that militated against his System. At length a few rays of light broke in upon my mind upon several diseases." The light, Rush reports, "was like a ferment introduced into my mind. It produced in it a constant endless succession of decompositions and new arrangements of facts and ideas upon medical subjects" (1948, 87). Knowledge in Rush's account is cumulative, and at some point it is reconfigured into a better or more efficient system. Through "time, observations[,] and reflection" (87), he moves from mere imitation (learning Cullen's system from lectures and publications) to emulation (reconfiguring and improving Cullen's system). John Adams, writing to Rush at the beginning of the nineteenth century, defined emulation in just this way: "The human mind is made capable of conceiving something more perfect than any created being that exists. Artists, painters, poets, statesmen, musicians are all capable of conceiving and imagining something in their arts superior to anything they have done or has been done by others. It is a precept in all these arts as well as in ethics to aim at greater perfection than has ever been attained and, perhaps, than ever can be attained" (1966, 65). Again, the desire to emulate operated in all realms, including ethics and human behavior.

Hindle argues that Robert Fulton's work on the steamboat was emulative and "creative," but not "original." His reference to original work suggests a third manner of forming products (including selves) in the eighteenth century, in addition to imitation and emulation: invention. John Fitch tells us that, free of his rheumatism one Sunday morning, he walked to church, only to have the rheumatism "seize me pretty severely in one of my knees [on the way home]. And in the Street Road a Gentleman passed me in a Chair with a Noble Horse. A thought struck me that it would be a noble thing if I could have such a carriage without the expense of keeping a horse.... I soon thought that there might be a force procured by Steam." When a friend later shows Fitch the 1759 edition of *Philosophia Britannica*, which described several steam engine pumps, Fitch remarks: "Till then I did not know that there was such a thing in nature as a Steam Engine" (1976, 113). What Fitch describes in this episode is neither imitation nor emulation. His idea of harnessing the power of steam is a new thought, one that describes something that has never existed "in nature." And even if someone else had already anticipated or experienced his thought, Fitch holds to the originality of his project: "Sir this I can with Truth say that the principle part of the original thoughts of any part of the works proceeded from me . . ." (116). Original, as Johnson defined it, meant "Primitive; pristine; first," and was related in cases like Fitch's to invention, which meant both "Discovery" (def. 2) and the "act of producing something new" (def. 3), as well as "Fiction" (def. 1). The process of invention depends upon the assumption that there *can be* "new" things in nature, of course, an assumption that was simply not available to someone like Bradstreet or Rowlandson or, even, Franklin. "Those RULES of old discovered, not devised," Pope writes in *An Essay on Criticism*, "Are Nature still . . . ; Nature, like liberty, is but restrained, / By the same laws which first herself ordained" (ll. 88–91). Or as Samuel Johnson puts it in his discussion of biographies, "We are all prompted by the same motives, all deceived by the same fallacies, all animated by hope, obstructed by danger, entangled by desire, and seduced by pleasure" (1968, 111).[15] Newton did not "invent" the laws of physics; he discovered them. Yet it is precisely the "art of producing something new" that will undergird the genre of autobiography as it emerges in the nineteenth century. Increasingly, in the wake of the American Revolution, writers will try to articulate the ways in which their lives are unique, unusual, original, or singular.

For those who thought that selfhood *could* be constructed,[16] or that it could emerge naturally or organically, these three models were available in the late eighteenth century to describe its formation: imitation, emulation, and invention. The terms are derived from the eighteenth-century worlds of scientific discovery, technological innovation, and artisanal production, as well as from my reading of the self-biographies themselves, in which the authors describe themselves as they grow, alter, or realize their own workings. Precisely because the worlds of science, technology, and belles lettres were not demarcated in the eighteenth century, the self-biographies written by men like Franklin, Fitch, Rush, and Graydon need to be understood as experiments, attempts to "try" a version of constructed selfhood in a written text. The modern self came into being, in part, through the written words of men like Franklin and Fitch who thought in terms of tools more than "texts." "The intellectual life of early modern Europe did not generally value compartmentalization or even tolerate its most harmless manifestations," Oscar Kenshur has written (4); partly as a result, "individuals lacking a special talent or the traditional aristocratic education [could] claim for themselves the capacity to explain the world by means of their senses, by means of experience and observation" (31). Experimentation, put into use first by gentleman like Bacon and Locke, soon became a method that Franklin and Fitch could put to use anywhere and everywhere, including the technologizing of the self. This has interesting implications for later narratives like Thoreau's, of course, since he grounds his narrative in a world of tools and labor (as well as nature). It suggests more immediately a class distinction: lower- and middle-class white men made the early arguments on behalf of "original" or "invented" selfhood precisely because they were jockeying—and "could" jockey in the changed social environment of the post-Revolutionary period—for social position with upper-class white men. Where those men had "honor" and status to define them, Fitch and Rush had only "character," constructed in actions and, even more, in print.

Ironically, given the decades of analysis of it,[17] Franklin's self-biography—his *History of My Life*—posits a self that is imitative and emulative, but not invented.[18] His narrative, I would insist in opposition to most readings of it, is not an autobiography (as I have defined that genre), nor does it accept or promote the assumptions about selfhood that undergird that soon-emergent genre. Imitation is, of course, an attitude, a method of controlling and managing reality: looking into his ancestry, Franklin discovers that "the Smith's Business . . . had continued in the Family [until his own generation], the eldest Son being always bred to [it]" (1309). Imitation is a conservative gesture, an attempt to stabilize experience, to make the future repeat the past. Throughout the four parts that comprise his narrative, Franklin imitates actual people, as well as models derived from books. Note how, having described the physical

"Constitution" of both of his parents, he describes the "Character" of only his father: "He had a mechanical Genius, too, and on occasion was very handy in the Use of other Tradesmen's Tools. But his great Excellence lay in a sound Understanding, and solid Judgment in prudential Matters, both in private and publick Affairs" (1315). Franklin models himself upon these aspects of his father's character: he learns to use workmen's tools (1317), puts his own mechanical genius to work on problems of woodstoves (1417–1418) and "Glass Tubes" (1453), and attempts to exercise judgment and prudence in both private and public affairs. "He was also much consulted by private Persons about their Affairs when any Difficulty occur'd, & frequently chosen an Arbitrator between contending Parties" (1315), Franklin remarks about his father in a passage that could, just as well, apply to himself as an adult.

Franklin imitates several older men in the course of his narrative, particularly in part one, looking to them as models of correct social and moral behavior. Franklin himself maintains that he is so similar to one of his uncles that, had the uncle died on the day Benjamin was born, "one might have supposed a Transmigration" (1310). A merchant named Mr. Denham adopted the twenty-year-old Franklin, and taught him how to run a business; Denham's unexpected death in 1727 "left me once more to the wide World" (1354). Even characters like Keimer and Keith prove to be "models" for the young Franklin, as they show him how *not* to behave. As he describes it, Franklin constructs himself in accordance with the appropriate male middle-class models he saw around him. This is why he can gain "Character and Credit" (1363) by simply acting industrious: people around him recognize his "Industry" not as something new or original, nor as "ambition"—a word still fraught in 1771 with negative connotations—but as the humble dedication to a particular "calling."[19] Franklin himself takes care to note that he "mention[s] this Industry . . . tho' it seems to be talking in my own Praise, that those of my Posterity who shall read it, may know the Use of that Virtue, when they see its Effects in my Favour" (1363). His *own* narrative is designed to be imitated, by his "posterity" in part one and by Americans more generally in parts two and three, and it is that design which ultimately deflects the criticism that he might merely be talking about himself.

Franklin imitates written models as well. Delighted with "an odd Volume of the Spectator," he thought "the Writing excellent, and wish'd if possible to imitate it" (1319). Reading Daniel Defoe's *Essay upon Projects*

(1697) and Cotton Mather's *Bonifacius* (1710) gave the young Franklin "a Turn of Thinking that had an Influence on some of the principal future Events of [his] Life" (1317). The line in instances like these between imitation and emulation is a thin one. Note how Franklin responds to Melchisedec Thevenot's *Art of Swimming* (1699): "I had from a Child been ever delighted with [swimming], had studied and practis'd all Thevenot's Motions and Positions, added some of my own, aiming at the graceful and easy, as well as the Useful" (1351). Franklin first imitated ("studied and practis'd"), but then emulated ("added some of my own"), elaborating upon Thevenot's system. The line is crossed at various points in Franklin's account of himself: his "Improvements" of street lighting in Philadelphia made use of John Clifton's example "of the Utility of Lamps" ("I did but follow his Example," Franklin remarks) and of the form of globe lamps imported from London, which Franklin redesigned (1426). This is emulation. As Franklin's use of the word "improvements" suggests, emulation is a progressive gesture, an attempt to improve a model or system, to make the future better than the past. "Emulation," wrote Edward Young in 1759, with perhaps more agonism than Franklin usually intended in his self-biography, "is superiority contested, or denied" (1966, 65–66).

In part two of his narrative, Franklin puts imitation and emulation into play in his "bold and arduous Project of arriving at moral Perfection" (1383). The virtues that Franklin isolates for correction are all taken from his "Reading . . . as different Writers included more or fewer Ideas under the same Name" (1384). Having read his Locke, he knows that part of the problem with moral systems is that people use different names to describe similar concepts. By sorting out and simplifying these "names," he improves upon the books that he has read. And as he marks, first on paper and then on erasable ivory tablets, his attempt to purge himself of specific vices and thus provide room for the specific corresponding virtues to sprout, Franklin comes to see that moral perfection is a ridiculous goal, but that "imitating" virtues, like imitating someone's handwriting, can still "mend" the imitator.

Of course, there is a puckish quality to part two. An old man is looking back with fond amusement at his younger, more foolish self. Yet inside his list of thirteen virtues Franklin appears to be quite sincere. Under "chastity," he writes: "Rarely use Venery but for Health or Offspring; Never to Dulness, Weakness, or the Injury of your own or another's Peace or Reputation" (1385). We know from part one that the young man did not follow this advice (1371), but we know also that his advice squared nicely with eighteenth-century medical thought and practical morality, particularly the sort of practical morality that Franklin dispensed publicly throughout his career. His inclusion of the virtue of "humility" at the end of his list, at the suggestion of a Quaker friend who tells him that he was "generally thought Proud," is thus a revelation. To achieve humility, he counsels, "Imitate Jesus and Socrates" (1385). I will discuss in chapter 8 how John Fitch imagines himself to be, potentially, a greater man than Christ. Franklin has no such ambition. Imitate, he asks us, two moral exemplars, one from the pagan tradition and one from the Christian. Neither can be improved upon, either by emulation or by invention.

Aside from their status as moral exemplars, Jesus and Socrates also have in common several key elements: both died at the hands of authorities who did not understand or heed their message, and both died without having ever written a word for posterity. These seem to be unusual models for a man who in 1784 (when part two was written) had survived his confrontation with the empire's authorities and who made his living —constructed his very identity (see Warner)—from the printed word. As with Jefferson's repeated claims that he would prefer to retire to Monticello, Franklin's actions apparently never squared with his own advice. But, in 1784, sensing the end being near, Franklin recognized, I think, that true humility actually renders the self invisible to contemporaries, though visible to posterity. He feared, I would suggest, that his own life, made "as durable as possible, [by] putting it down in Writing" (1307), could never be as substantial or as effective, as a model, as was Christ's or Socrates'. This does not explain why Franklin repeatedly tried to write his life story, but it may help to explain why he never managed to finish it or to publish it.

Part three of the narrative continues to insist upon imitation and emulation as the proper means for self-formation. Franklin picks up his story here at the age of thirty-two, an age when his own character has already been largely determined. As a result, much of part three concerns his efforts to present himself and his behavior as models for others, particularly for civic-minded men who might have "their Country's Interest" at heart (and who wish to have an immediate effect upon society, unlike, perhaps, Jesus and Socrates). He describes the founding of clubs that can direct young men in the "art" of self-formation (1396–1397, 1402–1403), almanacs and newspapers that can convey "Instruction among the common People" (1397–1399), and the scientific experiments and inventions and improvement of institutions that he has made and that others, if they wish, can also hope to make. In defending his experiments on electricity in part three, Franklin remarks: "my Writings contain'd only a Description of Experiments, which any one might repeat and verify" (1454). The same can be said for his understanding of selfhood: it is a found thing, discovered in previous models that one can choose to imitate or emulate.

Nowhere in his self-biography does Franklin imagine himself to be inventive, in the sense of "producing something new," the third method of self-formation that becomes available at the end of the eighteenth century. Franklin always conceives of the self as reactive, either imitative or emulative. The self in his narrative might be compared to Fulton's steamboat as Hindle describes it: creative in its composition, but not original (or unique or independent). Franklin, to quote one of Johnson's definitions of "create," gave "new qualities" to selfhood, and "put [selfhood] in a new state" (def. 5), but in his narrative he never imagines the self he describes as itself original. It is precisely *because* he imagines experience to be bounded by imitation and emulation that he insists on the usefulness of his own narrative. "[My] Posterity may like to know [the circumstances of my life], as they may find some of them suitable to their own Situations, and therefore fit to be imitated" (1307), he remarks in part one. "I hope therefore," he says in part two, "that some of my Descendants may follow the Example [of his project of arriving at moral perfection] and Reap the Benefit" (1391). He reports that his almanacs —and, implicitly, his memoirs—are "a proper Vehicle for conveying Instruction among the common People" (1397). The audience may change in Franklin's several attempts to narrate his story, but his experiences are still a model for others to imitate or emulate.[20]

One might agree, of course, that Franklin thought about himself in terms of imitation and emulation, but then go on to argue that his *narrative* nonetheless, perhaps even in spite of his intentions, was original. This would be to turn the classic-to-romantic dilemma in American literary history on its head, as traditionally the content of Revolutionary writers has been figured as romantic and forward-looking while its form is classic and backward-looking. But the weight of my analysis here and in the chapters that follow refutes that claim, too. For reasons that have been discussed elsewhere (see, for example, Huang), Franklin and his narrative came to claim a prominent place in American literary history:

originality of self and innovative narrative technique were simply not among them.

Most writers prior to 1810 in the United States depended upon imitation and emulation in their conception of themselves in their written narratives. But that does not mean that they did not struggle to articulate particular methods for achieving those goals in their narratives, nor does it mean that they did not see or grasp the implications of new ways of seeing the self. Many of them grappled with individualism and the concept of original selfhood; some of them grappled, too, with the prospect that selfhood was itself a fiction, and with the social consequences of such a view. Hence, I return to the concept of experimentation. If we grant "experiment" its eighteenth-century meaning—"To try; to search out by trial"—we can see that in the testing of the foundations for conceiving selfhood in Revolutionary America many writers were experimental. Crèvecoeur's fictional autobiography, *Letters from an American Farmer*, is an early register of the awareness that events were demanding individuals to respond to the real world in ways that had not been articulated previously elsewhere. In the end, James lacks actual and written models for his behavior. As he turns inward, he discovers, in Roy Pascal's formulation, an intimate self, a sense of uniqueness, and an appreciation for the way that uniqueness is contingent upon circumstances (50). For James, the experience is a terrifying one, reminiscent (I have suggested) of the way in which Calvinist ministers experienced a "metaphysical fall into interpretive contingency" during the Revolution (Weber, 152). In the next three chapters, I discuss how three different writers responded to the changed circumstances in Revolutionary and post-Revolutionary America. Alexander Graydon and Benjamin Rush, in their narratives, make the same discovery as James, and respond to it by reinscribing imitation and emulation in the process of the formation of selfhood. In both conservative (imitation) and progressive (emulation) gestures, they try to control contingency by hooking self-formation to known and accepted models. Ethan Allen, meanwhile, constructs an imitated republican self in his *Narrative*, locating in the natural and universal bonds of sympathy the foundation for correct and just human behavior. Graydon's, Rush's, and Allen's narratives are attempts to relocate a foundation for imitative and emulative self-formation at a time when, for many writers, the model of Christ was being drained of its supernatural, spiritual significance— abandoned to the stark human morality of the "Jefferson Bible"—and classical models seemed increasingly unfit for the times or simply went unread. All three writers are younger than Franklin by at least one generation. In that sense, they come "after" him. But, literarily, they are writing beside him, within the same set of assumptions that deny originality to the self.

In part two of *After Franklin*, I discuss how writers like K. White, Elizabeth Fisher, Stephen Burroughs, and John Fitch begin to revolutionize textual selfhood in Revolutionary America, shifting the grounds of selfhood from imitation and emulation to originality. "Genius," Edward Young wrote in 1759, "is [the] God within" (1966, 31). These American self-biographers begin tentatively to voice in their narratives Young's assertion. Franklin, Graydon, Rush, and Allen mirror and reaffirm the Revolution's foundation in the idea of gradual improvement for self and society; in their insistence on singularity, individuality, and innovation, White, Fisher, Burroughs, and Fitch voice the emerging democratic understanding that the "new order of the ages" is fundamentally the opportunity of all men to pursue, find, and voice his or her individual genius, the inimitable God within.

❧ 3 ❧

Alexander Graydon and the Federalist Self

IN 1811, IN HARRISBURG, PENNSYLVANIA, THE FEDERALIST lawyer and Revolutionary veteran Alexander Graydon anonymously published *Memoirs of a Life, Chiefly Passed in Pennsylvania, within the Last Sixty Years; with Occasional Remarks upon the General Occurrences, Character, and Spirit of That Eventful Period.*[1] Graydon was almost sixty at the time, having been born in Bristol, Pennsylvania, in 1752. He grew up there and in Philadelphia, where his mother ran a boardinghouse, and he studied for the bar in the turbulent years between the Stamp Act and the Declaration of Independence. Commissioned a captain in the Continental Army in January 1776, he raised a company and was taken captive by the British in the assault on Fort Washington on November 16, 1776. In July 1777, he was released on parole and was formally exchanged in April of the next year. After the war, while practicing law, Graydon served as prothonotary of Dauphin County in western Pennsylvania, as a member of Pennsylvania's constitutional ratifying convention in 1787, and as an elector for Washington in the first presidential election. In 1799, he was removed from his post as prothonotary by the newly elected Republican governor, Thomas McKean, thus becoming an early casualty in the "revolution of 1800." He then retired to his farm near Harrisburg, where he wrote anonymously and pseudonymously for newspapers like John Fenno's *Gazette of the United States* and magazines such as Joseph Dennie's *Port Folio.* Graydon died in 1818, apparently leaving behind him no signed traces of his authorship of works intended for the public eye.[2]

Graydon's *Memoirs* falls into three main sections, each occupying about one-third of the narrative: his childhood and education in Pennsylvania in the 1750s and 1760s (1–113); his military experience from 1776 to 1778 (113–262); and his observations on post-Revolutionary politics, especially the political fortunes of Thomas Jefferson and the rise of Jef-

54

fersonian Republicanism (262–378). In the last section especially, but also at points throughout the narrative, Graydon speaks in tones of anger, disgust, irony, or sardonicism about many public figures, including Albert Gallatin, Thomas McKean, and "Mr. Jefferson and his sect" (325). Writing as an unrepentant Federalist after 1800, when the Federalist party was losing direction and public support,[3] Graydon talks about his ideological enemies in ways that his colleagues at the conservative *Port Folio* seven years later still found "bold and unpalatable."[4]

In an issue of that magazine published just prior to Graydon's death, the editors discussed the reasons why Graydon's *Memoirs*, reviewed favorably by them six years earlier, had gone unnoticed by the American public: the "freedom" with which Graydon commented on certain public figures, the obscurity of the Harrisburg press that issued the book, the "mean style" in which Graydon wrote, and the "ambiguous" title he chose (5: 317–318). To that list, I would add the victory of Jeffersonian Republicanism, which, as William Dowling points out (1999), drove some committed Federalists to see themselves as alienated from contemporary society and which eventually ratified (whether Jefferson wanted it to or not) a radically individualistic, capitalistic, and democratic vision of self and society. Like a number of other Federalist publications of the early century, such as the scathing Hudibrastic satires of Thomas Green Fessenden, Graydon's self-biography failed to capture to an audience upon publication[5] and has largely failed to engage readers since. Graydon's *Memoirs* was scarcely remembered in the nineteenth century and has been almost entirely forgotten in our own. Most literary histories pass over it in silence, many critics of American literature seem unaware of it, and no critical essays on it (other than my own) have been published.[6]

Yet Graydon's *Memoirs* is, in the words of the *Port Folio* editors, "one of the most interesting performances which the loom of American authorship has produced" (5: 317). Their defense is that, though *Memoirs* contains "bold and unpalatable" ideas even for die-hard Federalists, "it is a work of unexampled candour and truth; and will conduce more to a veritable history of the times to which it relates, than any other publication now extant [in 1818]" (6: 58). This chapter pursues their idea that Graydon's *Memoirs* can teach us truths about "the times to which it relates" as well as about the time in which it was written. It can, specifically, help us begin to understand the nature and complexity of the discourse on selfhood that fascinated readers in the early republic. By reading Graydon's narrative within the context of other textual constructions of selfhood during the period, we can better understand the ways in which a modern self both came into being in contemporary narratives and was resisted by conservative writers like Graydon. *Memoirs* represents one of the possible narrative choices for individual expression available at the turn of the century, besides Franklin's, and it articulates a deeply held desire to halt or slow the social and philosophical changes being wrought in early nineteenth-century Anglo-America.

Graydon in his *Memoirs of a Life* attempted to refute the prevailing myths of selfhood in 1811, particularly those offered explicitly by Benjamin Franklin and Mason Locke Weems and that offered implicitly (or so Graydon believed) by Jefferson. He offered in their place his own model of impersonal identity through which the corrupted union might yet be saved from liberalism, from democracy, from modernity itself. Constructing himself in print, Graydon intended to counter Jeffersonian Republicanism as a democratic, liberal, capitalist social order in the early republic.[7] In the end, his model proved unacceptable to American readers, but that failure was attributable neither to his presentation (his "mean style") nor to his representation of his self, but to that model's fundamental incompatibility with democratic individualism and the emergent myths that supported it. Graydon's story was doomed to failure because it expressed what had become, by 1811, a residual conception of selfhood.[8]

Our modern understanding of a text like Graydon's *Memoirs* is hampered by the romantic critical tradition that identifies "literary" texts with democratic individualism, the subjective imagination, symbolism, and subversion. When read in that manner, I have argued, Revolutionary and early national texts are easily shown not to meet such aesthetic demands and are elided from the literary histories by which we define our traditions. "Literary critics tend to skip the eighty years from the Great Awakening to the American Renaissance in their haste to associate colonial religious preoccupations with the romantic inwardness of the nineteenth century," Robert Ferguson has remarked (1984, 8). "Historians have a strong sense of the federal era as constituting an ordeal for the new nation," William Hedges adds, but the literary history of the same period "has on the whole been reduced to noting increasing degrees of romanticism or indigenousness and trying to get as rapidly as possible to the promised land called American Renaissance" (1981, 4–5). As romantics and post-romantics themselves, literary critics from Lorenzo Knapp in 1829 to the most cutting-edge post-structuralist have been predisposed to read and recover texts that reaffirm their notion of reality. That reality seldom includes the work of Federalist writers in the early republic. Graydon's *Memoirs* represents a number of texts in the early republic that deserve to be recovered and perpetuated, not because they reaffirm our contemporary notions of reality, but because, to paraphrase Hedges, they reveal the cultural ordeal of the new nation—and of the modernity that defines us. They challenge our conception of a canon of American literature by speaking from within the cultural matrix that first gave form to our modern conceptions of self, community, nationhood, and authorship.[9] If we cannot listen to Graydon, we cannot listen to many writers of the post-Revolutionary generation who did not speak in the emergent idiom of democracy and individualism.

Graydon begins by referring to famous memoirs of the Enlightenment: Rousseau's *Confessions* (1781–1788), Richard Cumberland's *Memoirs* (1807), Marmontel's *Mémoires d'un père* (1804), Cardinal de Retz's *Mémoires* (1717), and Franklin's *History of My Life* (wr. 1771–1789). He is one of the first self-biographers to self-consciously construct an eighteenth-century tradition within which to understand his narrative. It is, however, a negative tradition: unlike those memoirists, Graydon disclaims any "pretensions to fame or distinction in any kind" (4), and he is sensitive to the fact that his readers' interest in his story will have to arise from the narrative itself rather than from their previous knowledge of him (5). In this assertion, ironically, Graydon anticipates the modern autobiography as I have defined it: his motive is in a sense "autobiographical," though his narrative remains firmly embedded in a republican, self-biographical mode.

By 1811, Graydon had been absent from his small role in national politics for twenty years and from his larger role in local politics for more than ten. His few publications had been anonymous or pseudonymous. Former acquaintances like James Wilkinson, a general in the army during and after the Revolution, did not even know whether Graydon was "living . . . or dead" early in the nineteenth century (339). As a man unnoticed by history, Graydon is apologetic about publishing his memoirs, claiming that he does so only because it affords him "a kind of menstruum . . . for the incongruous mass of his materials, serving to harmonize, in some degree, the abrupt transitions and detached details, which, a delineation of the various incidents of 'many coloured life' requires" (4). A "menstruum," as Graydon uses the word, is "a solvent; any liquid agent by which a solid substance may be dissolved" (OED).

Writing about himself, he suggests at the outset, is merely a tool through which to achieve his ends, not an end in itself. His story will not describe the significance of privately lived existence, as the emergent genre of autobiography will tell it; instead, it will be a "solvent" through which something solid can be dissolved and, precipitated out of the reaction, something else revealed.

Franklin was the most important of these memoirists to Graydon.[10] As Graydon's subtitle indicates, his life resembled Franklin's in that it was "Chiefly Passed in Pennsylvania" during an "Eventful Period." Graydon embeds several more allusions to Franklin and to Franklin's self-biography in *Memoirs of a Life*: he shows his familiarity with Franklin's narrative by remarking that Franklin, "as he tells us in his life, . . . had an early and steady abhorrence of tyranny" (303); he quite perceptively understands Franklin's self-biography "as a kind of practical comment on the useful truths, contained in Poor Richard's almanac" (3); and he imitates several of Franklin's actions, both in life and in his writing, "joining a society of young men, instituted for the purpose of disputing on given subjects" (80),[11] for example, and providing the reader with a brief look at his family's not very "illustrious pedigree" (6).[12] More generally, Graydon presents himself as an inveterate reader of books, like Franklin: both men have been formed by the discourse of the eighteenth-century public sphere, which for Graydon embraces such writers as Francois Fénelon, Jean-Jacques Rousseau, Ethan Allen, John Dickinson, Henry Fielding, Laurence Sterne, John Witherspoon, Edmund Burke, Anthony Benezet, and Franklin.[13] Making use of a typical metaphor of Franklin's, Graydon comments about his youthful self: "[Much] profit attended my reading" (17).

Yet Graydon is careful to distance himself from Franklin. He composed *Memoirs* precisely to show how he was *not* like his illustrious predecessor, figuring his own personal failures in an inversion of one of Franklin's organizing tropes, that of "rising": "I have ever found," he remarks early on, "that the morning was the propitious season for the exertion of my mental faculties. But though not materially deficient in attention, [studying] had not the smallest reference to future utility; and something less than 'A wizard might have said / I ne'er should rise by benefice or trade'" (45–46). Early to rise does not make Graydon wealthy or, as he often reminds us, wise. But, though its author is not one of them, *Memoirs* is filled with men on the rise, making their way upward in society and the economy by using their wits, their perseverance, their connections: a coarse, middle-aged Irishman with an "awkward" figure and elocution rises from the "humble post of under-sheriff . . . to his present station at the bar" (92); a friend in the militia (Graydon refuses to name him even in 1811) weaves "a serpentine course" through the "turmoils" of the Revolution by siding with whatever party is in the ascendancy, always "contriv[ing] to be uppermost" (108–109); Major Etherington of the Royal Americans begins his career "in the humblest walks of his profession," marries a wealthy widow, and rises to a colonelcy by 1775 (62–63). Unlike these men, Graydon is not so successful in public life. At the end of *Memoirs*, he deplores "the part [he has] acted in this turbulent" scene of the Revolution and its aftermath: "it certainly makes but a very sorry figure at an era so distinguished for rapid acquisitions of fortune and dignity. To have commanded a company in the continental army at the age of three and twenty, and not to have advanced an inch in the glorious career of personal aggrandizement, makes good . . . my promise of negative instruction" (376). Socially, politically, and financially, he has not "profited" by the Revolution.

Graydon's promise of "negative instruction" is made early in the narrative, and it helps to clarify his relationship to Franklin and Franklin's textual self. Graydon asserts that, though his narrative will not "advance experimentally the sound philosophy of thrift, and [will not] practically mark the routes to private wealth and public greatness, it will yet be found abundantly fruitful, in negative instruction on both points" (5). Franklin's *History of My Life* and other writings on behavior helped to form the early nation's emergent, if not yet dominant, model of rising in the world against which Graydon situates himself.[14] *Memoirs* shows that Graydon possessed talents and advantages that could have made him financially and politically successful in the Revolutionary world: a solid though desultory education, social status (as a lawyer and a politician), connections with the rich and famous, an ability to write. (These were certainly better qualifications than the ones Franklin began with, though in quite different circumstances, of course, in the 1720s.) What he lacked, according to his account, was "the nerve that is necessary [to play the game] to advantage" (376). "A scramble was ever my aversion" (46), he remarks. For Graydon, the figure of the "scramble" defines the "character and spirit of [the] eventful period" from the Stamp Act through Jefferson's presidency, and he detests it. I wish it to be known, he concludes, "that I am not to learn, that this revolution . . . with whatever purity begun, has nearly issued in a scramble, in which all morality and decency being thrown aside, he is the cleverest fellow, that, by trick or violence can emerge the fullest handed" (376–377). It is not that Graydon cannot "learn" this lesson; he clearly articulates its power in the Revolutionary and post-Revolutionary world. He simply refuses to accept it, to live by it. He will not try to rise in a world comprised of men on the make.

So, for example, after Graydon resigns his commission following his formal exchange in April 1778, he considers rejoining the army. But in Pennsylvania a "policy had arisen from the pressure of our affairs, to give every man a commission who was likely to pick up a few recruits." There were too many commissioned officers and not enough noncoms. When Congress began to consider reorganizing the Continental Army in October of that year, officers who had been captured and released became expendable; their "reinstatement in the rank to which they were entitled by the rule of seniority . . . was not to be effected." Only a "very few, who had been willing to engage in the scramble had been retained," and even those were retained with "the chagrin of seeing new men, and numbers who had originally ranked below them, now above them" (294). Graydon refuses to apply for reinstatement. Since the military and Congress cannot or will not recognize true merit, Graydon chooses from "private considerations" (295)—his unwillingness to play "the game" (376)—to stay out of the army.[15]

Having begun by criticizing the idea of rising in the world, then, Graydon suggests that it is only a certain *kind* of rising that irritates him: the ruthless "scramble" for power, position, and wealth. That kind of rising, Graydon claims, dominated American life during the Revolution and has continued to dominate it ever since. There "are so many . . . temptations to a man smitten with a love of public coffers, of influence and power . . . [that] the best, and perhaps only security, for a firm and upright administration, is to be found, in innate dignity of mind" (323). *Memoirs* presents several examples of individuals possessing this "dignity," perhaps even the author himself (as I shall argue below), but the narrative is dominated by men who are tempted by and enslaved to power, money, and influence. "[That] a noble disinterestedness and willingness to sacrifice private interest to public good, should be the general disposition any where, my acquaintance with human nature, neither warrants me in asserting or believing" (286). Though he says nothing about his religious affiliation, Graydon's view of mankind is nevertheless Augustinian, almost Calvinistic. From the friend in the militia who winds a "serpentine course" through the shifting politics of these decades, proving "his fitness for the times in which he has been destined to appear" (109), to Thomas Jefferson himself, whose election in 1800 brings America's "selfish and base" passions into the "ascendancy" (286), the "eventful period" of which Graydon writes is characterized by the "love . . . of influence and power" (323).

Graydon's critique of his era as rewarding a "selfish and base" scramble for power has two purposes, aside from any personal satisfaction he may have felt at venting his spleen. First, he wants to demythologize the American Revolution by showing that the seeds of selfishness and speculation in 1811—the many "unprincipled intriguers" who have put their private interest before the public good—lie in the Revolution itself. "I am chiefly struck," he laments, "with the strong tendency to evaporation, which inheres in a fiery zeal; as well as with the utter insignificance of that dull quality[,] consistency, on the versatile scale of republican virtue" (108). As Graydon describes it, the patriotic zeal evinced by the American public in 1775 and 1776 wore off very quickly: Pennsylvania troops at Fort Washington in November 1776 were "sacrificed to [the] selfish feeling" of the regional loyalty of Generals Israel Putnam (from Connecticut) and Nathanael Greene (from Rhode Island) (171, 189–190); even earlier, by January 1776, "republican spirit" and "sound civism" had become "fashions" that people put on and off with ease (105, 330); and even before *that*, in April 1775, "the canker worm jealousy already tainted the infantile purity of our patriotism" (105). Again and again, Graydon insists that the Revolution was founded more in selfishness and jealousy than in selflessness and public-spiritedness.

This attempt to demythologize the motives of American Revolutionaries is part and parcel of Graydon's more pervasive attempt to demythologize all aspects of the Revolution, to correct the sanitized and simplistic versions of history he sees being written into American culture in the first decade of the nineteenth century. Of course, Graydon does not see his own account of the Revolution and its aftermath as revisionary; having lived through the war, and adhering to strict standards of truth in the composition of the memoirs, even the need "to expose his [own] follies" if need be (87), he can claim that his history is true. But other histories, like Charles Stedman's *History of the Origin, Progress, and Termination of the American War* (1794), John Marshall's *Life of George Washington* (1804–1807), and Mason Locke Weems's *Life of Washington* (1800), are either riddled with mistakes or were written to meet popular demand.[16] For strategic reasons, Graydon's corrections of the history of the Revolution do not begin until his account of his youth gives way to his entrance on the public stage, approximately one-third of the way through *Memoirs*. Graydon seems acutely aware that he has to earn his readers' trust in his narrative voice before criticizing the emergent mythology of the founding.

One of the first corrections has to do with the "spirit of liberty" in Philadelphia in 1776. This "generally diffused" spirit drew in most of the Germans, all the Irish, a few Quakers, the "mechanical interest," and "that numerous portion of the community in republics styled the People." But "notwithstanding this almost unanimous agreement in favor of liberty, neither were all disposed to go the same lengths for it, nor were they perfectly in unison in the idea annexed to it" (107). The truth of this assertion is proved by a number of vignettes. When, for example, the young Captain Graydon scours the countryside for recruits, he is treated with amusement by the locals at a country tavern (118). Later, Graydon hears about a Prussian general who offered his services to the American cause; the general spoke up for "liberty" by claiming that "der koenig von Prusse is a great man for liberdy!" (124).[17] In another instance, on a journey to Albany, Captain Graydon meets so many majors and captains that it becomes clear those titles are merely "very good travelling appellations" (126). "Liberty" had multiple meanings in 1776 and could even be put on as a kind of mask or public persona, regardless of one's actual merit. The unity of the war effort, Graydon shows us, was merely a fiction invented thirty years after the fact by historians like Stedman, Marshall, and Weems.[18]

Graydon makes such corrections with unabated zeal throughout the last two-thirds of the narrative. In 1776, the Declaration of Independence "was not embraced [in the army] with all the enthusiasm that has been ascribed to the event" (140).[19] The "temper of [those] times . . . [shows] that they were not all fire and fury, as certain modern pretenders to the spirit of *seventy-six* have almost persuaded us they were" (284). By 1778, when Graydon was exchanged, Pennsylvania's enthusiasm for the Revolution was "considerably lowered," and hence "Power, to use a language which had already ceased to be orthodox, and could therefore only be whispered, had fallen into low hands" (264). One could think for oneself only "at the peril of tar and feathers" (264; cf. 330), a point, remember, that Crèvecoeur and Moody both confirmed from their vantage points near the end of the fighting. "A revolution in the aggregate," Graydon writes in a footnote to his point that Congress treated Revolutionary soldiers shabbily (213–215), "is a no less glorious thing than a battle, but they both lose many of their charms on an analysis" (215). Graydon's *Memoirs* strips away accumulating layers of "charms" concerning the American Revolution and reveals the sordid reality underneath.[20]

The second purpose of Graydon's critique of his era as "base and selfish" is jeremiadic: he wants to call Americans back to the public-spiritedness that infused the actions of a small group of Revolutionaries in 1776. The "spirit of *seventy-six*," though manipulated for private gain by many people, including some of the founders, did exist at the moment of founding and, for Graydon, can yet be revived in 1811. His instruction in *Memoirs is* "negative" in this sense: he intends his audience to perceive that only by following the example of his own resistance to scrambling and rising—his own example of failure—can the United States in 1811 yet hope to stop sliding "down into the mire of a democracy" (Ames I: 7). "To the sad example of former republics," Graydon says near the end of *Memoirs*, his language echoing a line of commentators stretching back at least to the "country" opposition in England in the 1720s and 1730s, "we are eagerly adding our own, and certifying in colossal characters to the world, the melancholy result of 'this last and fairest experiment,' in favor of free government" (367). His *Memoirs* is designed to halt or at least delay that slide by providing Americans with a selfless, patriotic, and antidemocratic model of behavior. His own life can be a "solvent" that dissolves the widespread belief in democratic scrambling and returns the United States to the republican paths marked out for it by the true patriots of 1776.

༔

Graydon's negative instruction depends upon a basic dichotomy: "To give any chance therefore for the operations of patriotism, we must smother that obtrusive thing called *self*; and by taking away, or rendering power uncertain and fugitive, we must, with pious humility, endeavor to deliver ourselves from temptation" (373, italics in the original). Graydon pits patriotism against selfhood. We can see, perhaps, in his formulation how, by 1811, he was fighting a rearguard action. What has brought "self" into existence in his account is the widespread opportunity for power. As long as people believe that that power is available to them, that belief will call forth what he calls the "self," will call forth a focused and determined drive to accrue power and wealth. Self, here, is presciently imagined as a social construct or effect, but one with real, palpable consequences. The antidote offered by some contemporaries in the Second Great Awakening is alluded to in Graydon's formulation, but it is recast as a communal effort "to deliver [ourselves] from temptation," rather than the Christian's request that God do so. Graydon here is perfectly in keeping with Franklin's insistence in *History of My Life* that the self be constructed by an individual in accordance with externally derived models and that it direct its efforts toward communal or social goals. His quarrel, I think, is not with the Franklin of that narrative but with the Franklin who was (and still is) being read as a "self-made man" or original agent.

With his dichotomy between patriotism and selfhood in mind, we can read Graydon's self-biographical character as he intends for us to read it. In one early scene from his boyhood, he describes being swindled out of a handful of marbles by "a little, skulking rogue" (19) who trades him three times the number of marbles Graydon has because, as the boy argues, Graydon's marbles fit his hand better. The traded marbles turn out to be worthless clay. Graydon comments that it was a puerile episode, but resonant with meaning: "If swindling and oppression beset us in infancy, does experience warrant us in affirming that the state of manhood is exempt from them?" Of course not. The boy's action is a "prototype" of "the more important scene [which] man every day exhibits" (20). And while in one light Graydon is a rube, destined (unlike Franklin) to be forever the butt of jokes and object of swindles, his own dichotomy of behavior makes him a young patriot, trusting and selfless. "I had no cunning," he remarks following the episode, "and consequently, gave no token of those talents which might qualify me, one day, to rise in a commonwealth" (20–21).

Whiling away his later school years in light reading, sports, and carousing, Graydon reports that he never had an interest in "the keener stimulus of profit" that motivated many of his schoolfellows in games and sports. "[Though] I had no dislike to money," he remarks resignedly, "it never impressed me as a primary good. . . . I do not speak of this as a virtue. . . . It is not one of those, at least, which leads to riches and advancement; or which, under the world's law, has a right to look for other than its own reward" (46). It is for this reason that he finds it hard to choose a career, preferring like Rousseau to be mesmerized by the beautiful sound of church bells rather than to be inclined to turn his talents "into pence" (46–47). In contrast, of course, the young Franklin seems almost effortlessly to fall into the trade of printer, and nearly every move in the trade brings him social and financial advancement. Others, writing after Franklin but before Graydon, begin to urge that "advancement" is the key to success in this world. "Beginning with numerous editions of Franklin's *Autobiography* in the 1790s," Gordon Wood writes, "dozens upon dozens of accounts of . . . the individuals' rise to respectability" poured from American presses (1992, 351). Silas Felton, for example, a Massachusetts schoolmaster who was born in 1776, reports reading "Doct. Franklin's life and writings" at about the age of eighteen. "I perceived them attentively," he says in his self-biography, "and found many very valuable precepts, which I endeavoured to treasure up and follow" (129). Graydon resists what he takes to be the terms of such advancement.

As an adult, Graydon is led by his resistance to swindling and even profit making into a number of "failures." He chooses to remain a battlefield captain rather than become an aide-de-camp (a road to preferment for such men as Alexander Hamilton) (139–140). He refuses to rejoin the army after his exchange (294). He refuses to take sides in the acrimonious political contests in Pennsylvania in the 1780s (306–309). On this last matter Graydon summarizes: "But [those who took sides] were rewarded for it: pelf, it appeared, was a better goal than liberty. . . . Those who had fought the battles of the country, at least in the humbler grades, had as yet earned nothing but poverty and contempt; while their wiser fellow citizens who had attended to their interests, were the men of mark and consideration" (308). Such failures, unlike Franklin's "errata," are not correctable. They are, for Graydon, irrevocable decisions that carry with them heavy financial and political penalties. They do not, it should be noted, indicate a simple refusal to become engaged in a struggle; Graydon willingly signed on to the Continental Army in January 1776 and was an early supporter of the Constitution. He would have assented to the Ciceronian ideal that "the whole glory of virtue is in activity" (Ferguson 1984, 74). Instead, his failures indicate that he simply refused to engage in a struggle, any struggle, for personal gain. He expected merit to be self-evident to others, and declined to puff his own merits in order to rise in the new republic. In the eighteenth century, Michael Warner has remarked, "virtue [came] to be defined by the negation of other traits of personhood, in particular as rational and disinterested concern for the public good" (42). Graydon strives to make his virtue impersonal, in keeping with a republican ideal, only to find that his virtue is not recognized.

In all this dichotomizing, Graydon is not unaware of the pleasures of self. As a boy, he prefers games and exercise to studying; as a young man, he attends the old American Company theater and reads Latin classics rather than study law (attending to "the dulce without a particle of the utile" [80], he remarks); as an older man, he sits down to vent his anger through his memoirs. Throughout Graydon's narrative, there is an element of play. But in his representation of himself, he disclaims any desire to put money before morals, social rising before self-worth, private interest before public good. Having at several turns tried to dispel the notion that he was perfect, or even that selflessness came easily to him, Graydon yet insists that he nearly always tried when it mattered to "smother that obtrusive thing called *self*" (373). With Charles Brockden Brown's Jane Talbot, he could say: "Self! That vile debaser whom I detest as my worst enemy, and who assumes a thousand shapes and practices a thousand wiles to entice me from the right path" (1986, 249–250).

Why, then, did an author so committed to the notion of selflessness choose to write a self-biography? Why use the personal facts of one's life to resist the advancement in society of the unrestricted self? On one level, as I have suggested, the act is selfishly, indulgently playful. It is a cathartic cry for Graydon: "I was too high toned and indiscreet even in the opinion of many Federalists; for many there were who saw no wisdom in martyrdom. I am still, however, to speak the truth, a most incorrigible sinner . . . [and] little amended by the chastisement I have received" (369). On another level, however, the act is quite selfless, and the narrative demands to be read in those terms. One of the elements of the narrative that can open up this level is what the *Port Folio* editors called the "ambiguous" title of Graydon's narrative: *Memoirs of a Life, Chiefly Passed in Pennsylvania within the Last Sixty Years.* The term "autobiography" was in use by 1811, of course, though it was still very new, but Graydon chose to employ the eighteenth-century term "memoirs." Rather than an account of himself written by himself, his narrative offers a record of the facts and events connected to two main topics, Pennsylvania in the second half of the eighteenth century and the American Revolution, many of those facts and events already well known. His "own story," he tells us at the beginning, "if he is not misled by self-love," merely serves "to harmonize" the otherwise "abrupt transitions and detached details" of those two topics. Note, too, that the title denies subjectivity in that it refers to "a" life, not to a named life. Unlike, say, Stephen Burroughs in *Memoirs of Stephen Burroughs* (1798, 1804), Graydon has no compulsive need or strategic reason to put his name in front of the reader. Accordingly, *Memoirs* was issued anonymously, and Graydon never once mentions his own name in the narrative itself.[21]

Graydon attempts to elide the self in the narrative as well as in the title. He makes it clear early on that he possessed what "is inaccurately termed diffidence . . . a kind of morbid sensibility [to] ever making self the principal figure in [a] scene" (73). Diffidence *is* inaccurate. Graydon simply does not wish to focus upon his own actions except as they exemplify ideal or typical human behavior. His own ordinary life is insignificant except as it exposes or defines larger contours or patterns of meaning. In the first section, he treats his childhood anonymously, deflecting interest from himself and toward the many visitors at his mother's boardinghouse (54–67) and insisting that in his characterization of himself he "affect[s] not singularity" (76).[22] In the second section, he is forced to speak more directly about himself because he enters the public realm, where his actions resonate with public meaning (such as the loss of Fort Washington, the treatment of American soldiers by Congress, and so on) and can be corroborated by other witnesses. Here, too, however, he resists revealing much of his private self. For example, he leaves his fiancée behind when he joins the army, remarking only that "a disruption of my heart strings, would be a language neither too forcible nor figurative for the occasion" (129). He refrains from any more sentimental language and personal reflection than this, leaving the woman unnamed and referring to his feelings on the matter again only once, more than one hundred pages later when he meets her after his parole: "Were I dealing in fiction," he says then, "a more particular representation might be required, on so auspicious a winding up, of a more than twelve months absence" (261). "Private life is always *real* life," Mason Locke Weems wrote in 1809 in one of the editions of his *Life of Washington*. To our children, Weems insists, Washington's "private character is *every thing*" (2, 4). Graydon could not disagree more. His private domestic life is as "inward" as his identity reaches, and that space is off-limits to prying eyes. *Memoirs* is neither sentimental fiction nor moral melodrama, much less self-revelation. Graydon will say no more.

In the third section, Graydon also tries to elide his self, an especially difficult task since it is here that his diatribe against Jefferson and the Republicans peaks. His personal animosity threatens to engulf the narrative. Upon his parole from the army, however, he begins by remarking: "I shall [now], consequently, be relieved, I hope, from so minute an attention to my own concerns" (262).[23] Graydon tries in several different ways to deflect attention away from himself in this section. In one instance, while recounting the military events of 1777, Graydon calls to mind the name of James Wilkinson, who began his career in the same rank of the Pennsylvania militia as did Graydon but "who is now in the chief command of the American forces." He is tempted to fall into self-pity about his "ill-star'd ambition" but instead retreats to memories of Wilkinson as a student and to an encomium on the pleasures of "early friendship" (277). He resists dwelling on his personal feelings. When he later recalls how he was removed from the office of prothonotary of Dauphin County in 1799 after Chief Justice Thomas McKean, a recent convert to the Republicans, was elected governor, he similarly retreats within himself—"I shall be cold, therefore, upon [this] subject" (363)—and then turns his ouster into a more objective maxim: "A man desirous to know the world ought to place himself in every situation to which the vicissitudes of life, may expose him" (365). His anger, still strong even ten years after the incident, must be overcome. His actions are important for what they exemplify for other Americans, not for what they mean to him.

But as much as he desires to do so, Graydon cannot entirely remove himself from the narrative. The self always returns. This dissonance may help account for the failure of readers to appreciate Graydon's *Memoirs*, both then and in the many years since its publication. He sounds at times like an embittered loser. His narrative does not appear to live up to its own demands. Yet that dissonance is very much an intentional part of Graydon's thesis and method. Intent on demythologizing the Revolutionary past, he could hardly have narrated the story of an aloof, selfless, saintlike martyr to the modern forces of self-interest, speculation, and party politics without substituting one myth for another. Weems's saintlike Washington and Franklin's enlightened Ben were no more true than such a sanctified Graydon would have been. His story of republican selflessness must have some self in it, if only to show that the struggle to be selfless is difficult and ongoing. Like "a revolution in the aggregate" (215), individuals must combat private interests, desires, and temptations at all times. Battles must be lost, though the war itself can be won.

Graydon's negative instruction overtly refers to an attitude and mode of behavior that cannot help readers to advance themselves financially, socially, or politically. It also refers to Graydon's ongoing struggle to live up to his own ideal of republican selflessness. "If the mould in which [my mind] has been formed, is not the most perfect, so neither, do [I] trust, is it absolutely the most worthless. . . . [It] will yet be found abundantly fruitful, in negative instruction" (5). Recounting the American Revolution and its aftermath through the "solvent" of his own experiences, Graydon himself becomes not just the epitome of failure according to the new standards of the republic but also the epitome of the difficult struggle to resist the modern self—rising, untethered, democratic, commercial, self-centered—created or set free by the Revolution.[24] His model of failure, like Franklin's model of the rising self, emerges out of the ruins of a hierarchical society in which personal identity was dictated by social expectations and roles, but it does so as an alternative or complement to the model of the self-made man being read out of Franklin's *History of My Life.* Whereas Crèvecoeur leaves James in the confusion and despair to which events have led him, Graydon experiments with his life in order to locate the values that would bring order out of post-Revolutionary chaos. The model of the rising self led to the very sort of world Graydon saw developing around him in post-Revolutionary America; the model of failure (or, more accurately, what the world around him *deemed* failure) could conceivably lead back to the republic of virtuous disinterestedness that the true Revolutionaries—the selfless ones—had intended to create in 1776.

�𝆺

Larzer Ziff, one of the few critics to have written about Graydon's *Memoirs,* has described Graydon as "a stickler for form" who insisted on being well dressed even "when conducting a revolution." During imprisonment, Ziff claims, Graydon's "claims to gentility" and "exhibition of polished manners . . . gained him treatment as a gentleman from British officers and invitations to the dinner tables of [New York's] leading Tory families." In Ziff's reading of *Memoirs,* Graydon is a pseudo-aristocrat aping British manners. When this Graydon met Ethan Allen in captivity in 1777, Ziff reports, "the magnetism of Allen's elemental energy broke through the stuffiness of Graydon's intense propriety to force an admiration for the savagery blended into his composition and suggest that this [i.e., Allen's savagery] was distinctly American" (185). Allen, the "wild figure" at the center of *The Narrative of the Captivity of Colonel Ethan Allen* (1779), is American; Graydon, by contrast, is British in sentiment, attitude, even (implicitly) literary style. Graydon is the past, Allen the future, of Ziff's version of American literary history. What is at stake in

Ziff's reading of Graydon's *Memoirs* is his argument that the political revolution of the 1770s and 1780s bore little literary or cultural fruit— aside from a few "energetic" and primitive accounts like Allen's—until the mid–nineteenth century. "[N]either the American nor any other political revolution has succeeded in reforming the culture of its society to anywhere near the extent to which, or with anywhere near the speed at which, it has reformed its institutions" (195). Emerson, Thoreau, Whitman, and Melville become the literary embodiment of the political revolution, as do a very few prototypical figures like Allen. Graydon, and his response to post-Revolutionary America, can be safely ignored except as a register of Allen's distinct "Americanness."

To read the two narratives as oppositional is to misread them. As Louis P. Masur has written about a related binary: "when did republicanism give way to liberalism [after the American Revolution]? The answer is that it never did. The two ideologies were as deeply and inextricably intertwined from the beginning as self-denial and self-interest, virtue and vice, reason and passion" (199). Though I defer an extended reading of Allen's *Narrative* until a later chapter, I want to pursue Ziff's bifurcation of the two writers for a moment. I believe that Graydon's own account of Allen reveals the two men's fundamental similarity, not difference. Graydon is first led to discuss Allen when he mentions the inhumane treatment of captured American soldiers by a British provost marshal; Allen mentions the same officer in his *Narrative*, and Graydon quotes Allen's invective against him. Then Graydon apologizes for Allen's "highly wrought" language, excusing it on the grounds "that few have ever more severely felt the hand of arbitrary power than Allen" (222).[25] This in turn leads Graydon to describe Allen as he met him in New York in 1777, to recount hearing Allen tell stories of his imprisonment that "exactly corresponded both in substance and language" to Allen's published *Narrative*, and to observe that Allen's "mode of expression . . . was a singular compound of local barbarisms, scriptural phrases, and oriental wildness . . . unclassic and . . . ungrammatical . . . [but] highly animated and forcible" (223). Though possibly possessing "something of the insubordinate, lawless frontier spirit," Allen appears to Graydon "to be a man of generosity and honor" (223–224). To support his point, Graydon cites a letter in which Washington notes that something in Allen "commanded admiration" (224). Allen then reappears three more times in *Memoirs*, once to verify a fact for Graydon (225), once to assure his fellow captives that they might find "gratification" (as he had) in being shipped to England (239), and once to argue that officers on parole could not on their honor return to their posts. Having given their word to remain out of action, they could not go back on it. Graydon mentions this incident about the integrity of an officer's word "to show, that Allen, however turbulent a citizen under the old *regime*, was not a vulgar ruffian, that the New York royalists represented him" (241).

Though the two men came from different colonies/states, social classes, and educational backgrounds, Graydon recognizes Allen's innate worth and earned merit. Allen opposed tyranny and arbitrary power, remained true to military honor and to his own word when he gave it, and earned respect from his fellow Americans both for opposing arbitrary power and for suffering for two years in captivity under it. Indeed, Graydon accords Allen the status of a gentleman and an officer that Allen, throughout his *Narrative*, demands and fails to receive from many of his British captors.[26]

Graydon's acceptance of and fundamental similarity to Allen is understandable when we recognize that his *Memoirs* does not explicitly or implicitly defend either aristocracy or British tradition, as Ziff's comments about "form" and "propriety" might imply, but instead defends the dual republic of politics and letters. To Federalists in the early national period, one entered the republic of politics by supporting the public order represented by men like Washington, by maintaining a Lockean regard for property, by resisting the temptation to appeal to public passions, by putting the interests of the public ahead of the interests of the self.[27] One entered the republic of letters by engaging in public debate in a rational, objective, impersonal manner, appealing to the authority of reason rather than the authority of church, state, or public opinion. The republic of letters promoted "a discourse in which publicity [was] impersonal by definition. Persons who enter[ed] this discourse [did] so on the condition that the validity of their utterance [bore] a negative relation to their persons" (Warner, 38).[28] For Federalists like Graydon, one danger to both republics was democracy, the pandering appeal to "public opinion" (Buckminster, 96) and public passions, an appeal that Graydon did not find in Allen's *Narrative* (much less in Allen's behavior) and one that, in chapter 5, I also fail to find in Allen's *Narrative*. He could accept Allen's *Narrative* as a legitimate contribution to reasonable discourse and accept its author as his equal precisely because Allen, a gentleman, was willing to sacrifice himself to the cause of liberty on behalf of "rising states of America," indeed on behalf of "the whole world of mankind"

(Allen, 124, 121). To locate a "wild" man in Allen's *Narrative* may be possible for a critic with romantic sensibilities, but it is neither what Allen wanted his readers to find nor what Graydon himself found there.

To read Graydon as an aristocrat or to read his narrative as a completely outmoded form of self-biography is to misread American literature in this period. The boisterous democratic self (which Ziff wrongly associates with Allen) would eventually emerge in American culture in the 1830s and beyond, but in 1811 it could hardly be seen in either fiction or self-biography. Charles Brockden Brown's Edgar Huntly may have eaten raw panther, but he returned to his "senses" (as flawed as they were) and shut down that primitive urge. My point in this discussion of Ziff's reading of Graydon and Allen is this: the debate on selfhood and the representation of selfhood in the early nation was many-stranded, not single-stranded, and Graydon's take on it was still viable for many observers. In hindsight, we can see that new ideas and new forms of discourse would displace the model of "selfless selfhood" that he offered, but to ignore his *Memoirs* is to pretend that the ferment out of which those ideas and discourses would eventually emerge did not exist. It is to flatten out literary history.

Ziff's misreading suggests a final explanation for the disappearance of Graydon's *Memoirs of a Life* from American literary history: we cannot see ourselves and our culture in it. *Memoirs* does not seem American because it cannot be inserted into a line of texts that stretches, say, from Franklin's *Autobiography* to Thoreau's *Walden* or Alger's *Ragged Dick* or Barnum's *Struggles and Triumphs*, and then along one of those (or other) trajectories into the twentieth century. It does not seem to possess literary value, because it resists romantic aesthetic standards that include the use of a personal symbolic language, the perspective of a subversive imagination, the belief in democratic selfhood, and the attitude of a socially alienated self.[29] It does not seem "revolutionary," because Graydon, like a few other recalcitrant Federalists after 1800, believed that the Revolution had been betrayed and that the emergent democracy was a "mire" (Ames, 7). Unlike Ethan Allen, Graydon cannot be (mis)read into our discursive context. Much like John Adams, Alexander Graydon is unable—and unwilling—to help us translate his words into the emergent idiom of democratic selfhood: "In [the nineteenth and twentieth century's] search for a usable past, too much in Adams was simply not usable," Joseph Ellis remarks (1993, 227). Similarly, too much in Graydon, from his anti-Jeffersonian rhetoric to his insistence on man's fallen nature to his mistrust of the self to his adherence to the imagined republics of politics and letters, was not usable.

Reading Graydon's *Memoirs* in the context of self-biographies written during and after the Revolution reveals a conservative discursive strand in the debate on selfhood. Graydon's negative instruction, his particular experimental self, registered the perception on the part of a number of aging Revolutionaries that events had taken a wrong turn, and it figured an exemplary relation of individual to society that could put the nation back on the right path.[30] The "self" for Graydon should not be an agent of its own destiny, as modern autobiography would come to see it, nor could it be original or unique. Individuals should pursue their socially determined roles, subordinating their desires to the public good and rising only on the basis of a merit recognized by others as genuine. Ironically, of course, this is not far from some of Jefferson's own pronouncements, however much his practice and his other ambivalent statements might have deviated from them. Graydon imagined that the self as an active, purposeful agent should be denied, at least in the public sphere (and the private sphere did not deserve to opened to the public), that individuals should passively adhere to known laws of human behavior,[31] and that the collective communitarian goals of the founding fathers (as Graydon understood them) were being undermined by a culture that more and more was coming to accept the individual "self" and its desires as worthy of cultivation. Graydon's notion of personal identity is not modern; it is not really even a "self," and his narrative is not an autobiography. His admonition about the direction that a too intent focus on the value of selfhood would take the nation resonated with the voices of other writers like John Adams, Fisher Ames, Thomas Fessenden, and Joseph Stevens Buckminster, writers whose works have been for the most part ignored by the modernity they were designed to resist, proving in the end the accuracy of Graydon's perception that in a world of rising individuals and myth-making historians he would be a "failure" and his message would go unheard.

❦ 4 ❦

The Revolutions of the Mind:

Benjamin Rush's *Travels through Life*

Here everything is in a plastic state.

—Benjamin Rush, letter, 5 Dec. 1783

IN THE FIRST VOLUME OF HIS *Medical Inquiries and Observations* (1789), Benjamin Rush published "An Account of the Effects of the Late American Revolution upon the Human Body," a short essay in which he argued that the idea of the American Revolution brought about physical effects such as cheerfulness, nostalgia, higher birthrates, melancholy and fever, and even death (the doorkeeper of Congress died from political joy at the news of Cornwallis's surrender).[1] These effects were not the effects of war, Rush insisted; the war and the Revolution were two different things: the "termination of the war by the peace in 1783, did not terminate the American Revolution" (332). "There is nothing more common," Rush wrote in an "Address to the People of the United States" in 1787, "than to confound the terms of American revolution with those of the late American war. The American war is over; but this is far from being the case with the American revolution. On the contrary, nothing but the first act of the great drama is closed" (8).[2] The war itself was fought from 1775 to 1783, but the Revolution began as early as 1774, when the high rate of apoplexy in Philadelphia denoted "a period of uncommon anxiety" (329), and continued until the moment at which Rush wrote in 1788: "The excess of the passion for liberty, inflamed by the successful issue of the war, produced [in the 1780s] . . . opinions and conduct which could not be removed by reason nor

74

restrained by government. . . . [T]hese opinions . . . constituted a species of insanity, which I shall take the liberty of distinguishing by the name of Anarchia" (333). In 1786–1787, of course, the Connecticut Wits had satirized the mid-1780s as the era of "Chaos, Anarch old," whose anti-Constitutional realm is "restor'd" by the "uncreating word" which sinks the "Law" and enthuses the "mobs in myriads" (Humphreys et al. 1967, 6). As Catharine Albanese has written: "[The] men and women who lived through the Revolution seemed to experience it as [a] kind of premonitory chaos and anarchy, [a] dissolution of forms, which would precede the coming of a new and perfect form" (33). Rush fits Albanese's model perfectly. In Rush's mind, however, the ills (or anarchy) of post-Revolutionary America did not need to be treated by politics or social change or even poetry, which, as William Dowling has interpreted the ideology of Revolutionary poetry, saw itself in the 1780s as an "ideological intervention" designed to "clear . . . the ground" for radical reconceptions of society (1990, 26 and 29). They needed to be treated by medical doctors.

Benjamin Rush was the most famous doctor in the early national period. Born in Pennsylvania in 1745, Rush attended boarding school under the watchful eye of the Calvinist minister (and his uncle) Samuel Finley and then attended the College of New Jersey from 1758 to 1760. After agonizing a bit melodramatically over the choice of careers—law or medicine—Rush was apprenticed to Dr. John Redman in Philadelphia, and then completed his medical studies by taking an M.A. at the University of Edinburg in 1768. He practiced medicine in Philadelphia for the next forty-three years, most famously (or infamously, depending on one's point of view) during the yellow fever epidemic of 1793. He held the posts of professor of chemistry in the College of Philadelphia and professor of the Institutes of Medicine and Clinical Medicine in the University of Pennsylvania. He helped found Dickinson College in 1783 and Franklin and Marshall College in 1785. He signed the Declaration of Independence in August 1776 and, along with Alexander Graydon, served as a delegate to the Pennsylvania Convention to ratify the Constitution in 1787. Throughout his life, he was active in schemes and societies to end slavery, reform the prison system, reform educational practices, reduce the use of alcohol and tobacco, and improve sanitation. Benjamin Franklin, not surprisingly, was one of his models.[3]

Rush's belief that ideas, such as the American Revolution, often have physical effects complemented his belief that ideas often have physical causes. In 1786, in *An Enquiry Into the Influence of Physical Causes upon the Moral Faculty*, Rush opines that, "considering how much the shape, texture, and conditions of the human body, influence morals, I submit it to the consideration of the ingenious, whether in our endeavours to imitate moral examples, some advantage may not be derived, from our copying the features and external manners of the originals" (203). Men who look like each other, Rush insists, generally "have the same manners and dispositions." We know this, Rush says, by "experiment" (203–204), by observing in the real world a correlation between people and their physical and intellectual environments. Rush tells us how, as a young man, he stepped into John Wilkes's prison library: "His books consisted chiefly of histories and common place literature from which I formed an indifferent opinion of his taste and judgement. A man's pictures and books are generally pretty correct copies of the intellectual and moral qualities of the mind" (*Travels*, 62). It is for this reason, surely, that Rush throughout his life made a painting of Samuel Finley "a part of the furniture of [his] house" (*Travels*, 32). Virtue, Rush believed, was in great part a "habit," which, though "purely mechanical," was nevertheless as efficacious for society "as if [it] flowed from principle" (196). Climate, diet, music, odors, and even paintings on the wall inculcated habits.

The human body was inextricably linked in Rush's thinking to the intellectual, moral, political, social, and cultural realms. "There is an indissoluble union between moral, political, and physical happiness," he wrote in 1799 (168). This inextricable union of physical and abstract gives us an insight into many of Rush's ideas about disease. His notorious "tranquillizing chair," for example, which he invented in 1810, served "to keep . . . maniacs in the inflammatory stage of their disease in a perpendicular position so as the save the head from the impetus of blood" (*Letters*, 1048). He had noticed that, in a straitjacket, patients were often reduced "to a recumbent posture, which never fail[ed] to increase their disease" (*Letters*, 1058). The "Tranquillizer," as he called it, kept the blood pressure lowered, weakened the pulse, and calmed fears (*Letters*, 1059). The control of the body "acts as a sedative to the tongue and temper as well as to the blood vessels. In 24, 12, 6, and in some cases in 4 hours, the most refractory patients have been composed" (*Letters*, 1052).[4] One's physical state conditioned one's ideas; one's ideas conditioned one's physical state. For just this reason, Rush advocated solitary confinement for criminals because, as he said, "Company, conversation, and even business are the opiates of the Spirit of God in the human heart. . . . [A] bad man should be left for some time without anything to employ his hands in his confinement. Every thought should recoil wholly upon himself" (*Letters*, 512).[5] Rather than continue mimetically to be impressed by bad habits (others' as well as his/her own), the criminal should in solitude be forced to face, as in a mirror, his/her own thoughts, or more hopefully (Rush thought) to face the "Spirit of God" or the image of God in man, which the business of the world had previously occluded.

For the most part, Rush and his ideas like the interdependence of mind and body have been ignored by literary scholars (though they have, in recent years, been probed by social historians like Michael Meranze). Critics like Jay Fliegelman have asserted Rush's centrality to Revolutionary and post-Revolutionary culture, but they have not devoted much attention to his actual writings.[6] Rush "was immensely important in his time," Charles Strozier has asserted, "and yet he has generally fallen between the cracks of scholarship" (415). In this chapter I will make the case that Rush's self-biography, like Graydon's, must be central to our understanding of the variety of choices available to self-biographers in post-Revolutionary America. In his narrative, *Travels through Life*, Rush tests his theory of the interdependence of mind and body against his own experience. Rush imagines the self as a sort of Lockean slate on which ideas are inculcated by fair means or foul. To "inculcate," of course, is to teach or to impress by forceful means or frequent repetition. The metaphor itself links, as does Rush throughout his medical theories, the physical and the intellectual, body and mind. For Rush, learning is abstract, yet impressing is physical. Given Locke's prestige in the eighteenth century, this is not surprising. But to read Rush's self-biography in this way is to see, more clearly, the kinds of problems writers were grappling with in the Revolutionary period, and to situate more clearly the emergence of a different kind of writing and thinking in the early nineteenth century. For at the same time that he sees ideas formed in reaction to the environment, Rush declares that selfishness and ego and ambition are ideas that must be avoided or denied: "I endeavour to have no will of my own," he wrote to his wife in the midst of the yellow fever crisis in Philadelphia in 1793 (*Letters*, 641). This unresolved tension between the passive acceptance of ideas and the active formulation of them preoccupies Rush in his medical thinking and, implicitly, in his self-biography. Like Alexander Graydon, Rush senses the potential for self-invention or self-creation in the modern world; Rush will resist it on both religious and social grounds.

Rush wrote his self-biography in 1800, at a moment when his own life and the nation's life took dramatic turns. Personally, Rush had been freed from the antagonism of William Cobbett. In December 1799, Rush won his suit for libel against Cobbett, who had for three years, with increasing virulence, assaulted Rush in print for Rush's "silly sans-culottish" political ideas and ineffective medical ideas. Throughout the spring of 1800, Cobbett kept up the attack in a broadside called, contemptuously, *The Rush-Light*, but in the face of another libel trial Cobbett sailed for England on June 1.[7] When he began to write his self-biographical account later that summer,[8] then, Rush did so with a sense of relief and a hope that his testament, addressed to his children, would vindicate both his political beliefs and his medical practices.

Nationally, the republic that Rush had helped bring into being was nearing the end of a first Adams administration and was already in the midst of a summer/fall election that would pit Adams against the man who appeared to be his ideological enemy, Thomas Jefferson. Even by early May 1800 it was clear that all the electoral votes in the crucial swing state of New York would go to Jefferson (though the state's actual electoral votes would not be cast until November); in other states, the forces of Republicanism showed their strength early also, as in Pennsylvania, where the "lower house fell under Republican control in 1799" (Elkins and McKitrick, 741). Jefferson's victory would not be assured until February 1801, when the electoral tie with Burr was broken in the House of Representatives, but an observer like Rush was not unaware of the shift in sentiment that was being manifested in what Jefferson came to call the "Revolution of 1800." Writing to Jefferson himself on August 22, 1800, Rush noted that "the issue of the present single and double elective attractions in our parties . . . is difficult to determine. As yet appearances are turbid. Much remains to be precipitated before the public mind can become clear." Nonetheless, he insisted, even though the chemical reaction was not completed, "A spirit of moderation and mutual forebearance begins to revive among our citizens" (*Letters*, 820).

Though a longtime friend to both Adams and Jefferson, Rush embraced the Republican position as it developed in the 1790s. He did so because he feared that the Federalists were determined not to give Jeffersonian Republicanism an opportunity to succeed; the Federalists, he wrote to Aaron Burr in 1792, had sacrificed "public justice and national gratitude to the interested ideas of stockjobbers and brokers, whether in or out of the legislature of the United States" (*Letters*, 623). "We have effected a deliverance from the national injustice of Great Britain," he wrote to Madison in 1790 soon after Hamilton's *Report on Public Credit* was submitted to Congress, "[only] to be subjugated by a mighty act of national injustice by the United States" (*Letters*, 539). Though, characteristically, Adams as president could appoint Rush treasurer of the United States Mint in 1797 (and thereby create many enemies for himself for appointing a "French Democrat" to public office), Rush and Adams exchanged no letters between April 1790 and February 1805, when Adams opened the correspondence.[9] On the other hand, Rush and Jefferson continued their friendship and correspondence uninterruptedly throughout the 1790s and 1800s. Still, Rush in 1800 was, in Cecelia Tichi's phrase, a "worried celebrant of the American Revolution," worried because he could not yet see that the United States had "moderated" enough from the anarchy of the 1780s and the political bickering of the 1790s, but a celebrant nonetheless in his self-biography because he treats the Revolution as a "spring" (*Letters*, 371) that propelled the United States—perhaps even mankind—into a new era. "I consider Federalism and Republicanism as synonymous" (*Letters*, 793), Rush wrote in a remarkable letter to John Dickinson in 1797, anticipating by four years Jefferson's famous comment in his first inaugural that "we are all republicans—we are all federalists." In 1800 both men felt that monarchical and elitist sentiments would, in Rush's metaphor, fully "precipitate" out of the public mind, leaving in their place Jeffersonian Republicanism.

Rush wrote the manuscript self-biography entitled *Travels through Life* in 1800 in ten separate notebooks. Unlike Graydon's *Memoirs*, which was apparently printed under the author's supervision, Rush's manuscript presents several interpretive problems. First, Rush indicates in at least two places that he did not intend the self-biography for publication: "It is my wish," he wrote in the first paragraph, "that [this narrative] may not be read out of the circle of my family, and that it may never be published" (*Travels*, 23).[10] Unlike Graydon, then, who prepared a persona for the impersonal world of print, Rush wrote within the expectations of the privately circulated family memoir, much as Franklin did in part one of *History of My Life*. As a result, Rush's narrative veers into informalities that the world of print would for the most part excise with the emergence of formal autobiography in the course of the nineteenth century. On a technical level, for example, when Rush wants to describe the character of his sister, Rachel Montgomery, he simply appends a newspaper clipping of her obituary to the notebook page on which he is writing. When he wants to describe for his children's "use" his method of commonplacing his reading, he copies decade-old entries from his commonplace books directly into the manuscript. The text reaches outside itself to other, privately held texts, implicitly limiting the reading audience. On the level of narrative, Rush is often moved to provide advice designed (particularly) for his sons, not for a wider audience of readers: "To my sons I bequeath a father's experience, and I entreat them to take no public or active part in the disputes of their country beyond a vote at an election" (*Travels*, 162). We must remind ourselves, in other words, to read Rush's narrative as a manuscript written for his family. "[O]ne does not dress for private Company as for a publick Ball" (1316), Rush's friend Franklin wrote about the first installment of his own self-biography. However, this does not mean that the narrative's relevance lies solely within his family, because in many other ways Rush reveals that he is aware of and writing "for" a larger audience: for example, he provides short biographies of all the signers of the Declaration of Independence; and he consistently analyzes the motives of many of the actors in the American Revolution.

The logic of impersonality that drives Graydon's response to the American Revolution is, as Michael Warner describes it, the logic of "a discourse in which publicity will be impersonal by definition. Persons who enter this discourse [of republican print capitalism] do so on the condition that the validity of their utterance will bear a negative relation to their persons" (38). Graydon elides the self as part of a strategy of public writing, of what Grantland Rice refers to as "a political understanding of authorship" (1997, 11). Rush, too, will elide the self (and hence, in my terms, resist the "autobiographical" impulse); however, he will do so within the logic not of eighteenth-century republican print capitalism but within the more traditional, Christian logic, recast in early psychological terms, of confessional self-biography.[11]

Second, we no longer possess Rush's "entire" self-biographical statement. The tenth notebook, apparently detailing Rush's medical history, was lost in the course of the nineteenth century. We cannot, then, speak of Rush's *Travels through Life* as a "complete" statement about himself. The surviving nine notebooks run continuously from Rush's opening phrase, "My dear children" (*Travels*, 23), through only two chapter headings or fresh starts: "An Account of Political and Military Events and Observations" (approximately halfway through the printed narrative) and "Religious Principles; Domestic Events" (very near the end of the printed narrative). The narrative has a tripartite structure: personal development (the untitled opening section detailing ancestry, education, adult life to the present moment), public events, and private/interiorized aspects. That third section, where Rush provided the history of his spiritual principles, his marriage, and his "body," remains incomplete. His son, Richard Rush, remarked that the tenth notebook made "an interesting addendum to the work, and [will] be looked at with curiousity by others as well as his children" (cited in Corner, 4). Unfortunately, our curiosity there will apparently never be satisfied.

The chapter headings indicate one way in which Rush structured his narrative, and I will return to that structure shortly. He also structured his manuscript self-biography around two moments of sudden and dramatic change. The moments are described in quite similar ways, as I will show, and echo a language that Rush elsewhere employed to discuss both individual and communal psychology. Both moments are presented in the long, untitled, opening section of his self-biography in which Rush narrates his ancestry and education.

In Edinburg in 1766, Rush met a man whose father served under Cromwell in the New Model Army, as did Rush's ancestor, John Rush. The two strangers discovered a "relationship" in this coincidence, and the other man suddenly "opened his mind fully . . . and declared himself to be an advocate for the Republican principles for which our ancestors had fought." Astounded, Rush claims to have listened for the first time to someone call "the authority of Kings . . . in question."[12] "For the first moment in my life I now exercised my reason upon the subject of government . . . [particularly the fact that] no form of government can be rational but that which is derived from the Suffrages of the people who are the subjects of it." That "truth became a ferment in [Rush's] mind." He "now suspected error in everything [he] had been taught, or believed," and determined "to try the foundations of [his] opinions upon many other subjects." Because, however, there was no scope for these republican ideas in Great Britain in 1766, Rush claims that he enjoyed his new ideas for the time being "in theory only" (*Travels*, 46).

The key terms in Rush's account are "ferment" and "try," both of which derive from his devotion to scientific empiricism. The moment is political and intellectual, but Rush describes it in scientific language as a conversion in which the mind experiences a state of tumult or "anarchia," is reconfigured (as it were), and sees the world in a new way. Rush then promises to apply that new vision rigorously to future experience, to "try" it on himself. In the seventeenth century, these three steps might well have been termed "calling," "justification," and "sanctification" (see, for example, Stoever, 123). As Donald D'Elia and John Kloos have each argued, a "religous orientation pervaded the life of Benjamin Rush" (Kloos, 112), and both his deep political commitment from 1774 to 1790 and his devotion to medical investigation and treatment from 1790 to 1812 were informed by the Calvinism he learned from Finley and Samuel Davies in the 1750s.[13] Rush is able to fuse republicanism with the stages of Christian conversion in his narrative precisely because, as he wrote in 1791, "All truths are related, or rather there is but one truth. Republicanism is part of the truth of Christianity" (*Letters*, 584). Writing to Jefferson in 1800, Rush insisted that Christianity is "the strong ground of republicanism. The spirit is opposed . . . to the very forms of monarchy, and many of its precepts have for their objects liberty and equality as well as simplicity, integrity, and economy in government" (*Letters*, 820–821).

Rush's Calvinistic belief in the depravity of man explains why, elsewhere, he calls upon mankind to be converted: "the time . . . will come, when the understanding shall be elevated from its present inferior objects, and the luxated passions be reduced to their original order. — This change in the mind of man, I believe, will be effected only by the influence of the Christian religion" (171). "I am fully persuaded," he effused in 1786, "that from the combined action of causes, which operate at once upon the reason, the moral faculty, the passions, the senses, the brain, the nerves, the blood and the heart, it is possible to produce such a change in [man's] moral character, as shall raise him to a resemblance of angels — nay more, to the likeness of GOD himself" (209). Tranquillizing chairs, gyrators, prisons, and solitary confinement merely complemented Rush's belief that we contract our "habit of virtue" from positive physical causes and exemplary moral types. They worked on the depraved, but other physical causes worked on normal or elevated human beings. "I consider it is possible to convert men into republican machines," Rush theorized in 1798 in "Of the Mode of Education Proper in a Republic" (92). As Michael Meranze has brilliantly shown in his study of reformative incarceration in Philadelphia from 1760 to 1835, Rush's conflation of Christian reform, republicanism, and science was central to the penal reform that liberal society instituted in the late eighteenth century in an attempt to discipline human character (132–138, 168–171).[14]

The second transforming moment also occurs in the long first section of *Travels through Life*. Recounting his career as a physician in Philadelphia, Rush tells us that for "many years" he was "regulated in [his] practice by the System of medicine which [he] had learned from . . . Dr. [William] Cullen" in Scotland. "But time, observations and reflection convinced [him] that it was imperfect and erroneous in many of its parts." This discovery produced "a languor in [Rush's] mind." "The weight of Dr. Cullen's name depressed [him] every time [he] ventured to admit an idea that militated against his system." Finally, in 1789, Rush was appointed Professor of Theory and Practice of Medicine in the College of Philadelphia. In turmoil ("inquietude"), Rush studied "day and night," until he "was gradually led to adopt those [principles]" which would come to characterize his method (*Travels*, 87).

This gradual adoption of principles gives way in the account to a sudden paradigm shift: "The leading principle of my System was obtruded upon me suddenly while I was walking the floor of my study. It was like a ferment introduced into my mind. It produced in it a constant endless succession of decompositions and new arrangements of facts and ideas upon medical subjects" (*Travels*, 87). This "ferment" that rearranges Rush's medical principles is explicitly linked to the earlier "ferment" induced by republican principles: "To the activity induced in my faculties by the evolution of my republican principles by the part I took in the American Revolution, I ascribe in great measure the disorganization of my old principles in medicine. The same republican ferment produced similar commotions and I hope a similar precipitation of the feculencies of error" (*Travels*, 89).

Here, again, is the conflation of republican political ideas, scientific terminology, and Christian conversion. Republican principles, which Rush sees as fundamentally Christian, induce him to reorganize his medical principles. The resulting intellectual "ferment" once again precipitates out error, leaving in its place truth. Rush uses the same metaphor in reference to Jefferson's election in 1800, hoping that it will "precipitate" elements out of the republic and make the people's mind "clear." He imagines in all this that people, including himself, are the products of their learning (the ideas to which they are exposed and the environment that surrounds them) and, then, of their habits. What happens in the moment of transformation is not a Bloomian "mis-reading" in order to clear imaginative space[15] but an Enlightenment appeal to reason's power: "I now exercised my reason upon the power of government" (*Travels*, 46); "The System I adopted was not merely a speculative one" (*Travels*, 88). The converted and enlightened mind "sees" things in new ways and the individual acts in new ways: old learning is transcended and old habits are broken.

The modern editor of Rush's *Travels*, George Corner, has distorted the form of Rush's self-biography by dividing it into nine chapters. (The manuscript, remember, now exists in nine notebooks, but the nine chapters in Corner's edition do not correspond to each of the notebooks.) Rush places both of these accounts of "conversion" in the long, untitled first section of the manuscript. When he comes to the end of this first installment or section, he gestures toward completion: "A few miscellaneous remarks shall close the history of this part of my travels thro' life" (*Travels*, 106). Similarly, when he comes to the end of the part of his travels that he titles "An Account of Political and Military Events and Observations," he gestures toward completion: "I feel pain in a review of my political life, . . ." he concludes. Then, opening his account of "Religious Principles; Domestic Events," he begins: "Having briefly stated the literary, medical and political events of my life, it remains only that I say a few words upon my religious principles" (*Travels*, 162). Structurally, Rush divides his experiences into the categories of personal development, public observations, and interiorized/private thoughts.

It is difficult to generalize about that third section since, as I pointed out earlier, we do not possess it in its entirety. Still, it seems clear that Rush is interested in describing "elemental" ideas in that section: love of God (*Travels*, 163–166), love of his wife (*Travels*, 166) and mother (*Travels*, 166–169), and his own "physical history" (the lost tenth notebook). This seems, if anywhere, a place where Rush might try to open up the interior space of his self, or to reveal the private spaces of heartfelt love and the embodied self, or to affirm the value of ordinary life as he has experienced it. What is "inside" his own mechanically produced sense of self? But this third section is merely tantalizing, both in its brevity and in its reluctance or inability or refusal to adventure into the interior or the private. For instance, Rush describes what most biographers take to be a crucial change in his thinking—his adoption of universalist principles in the 1780s—in much less dramatic terms than he described his "conversions" to republicanism and Rushite medical methods. He laconically notes that he was trained in the Westminster catechism, held the principles of limited atonement "without any affection" for many years, began to read in the controversy concerning salvation, and eventually "embraced" universalism. "From that time I have never doubted upon the subject of the salvation of all men" (*Travels*, 163). Under Joseph Priestley's influence, he has become a necessitarian, but that change is not described as a conversion.

His earlier conversion to Christianity is told just as laconically. He reports that the "early part of [his] life was spent in dissipation, folly, and in the practice of some of the vices to which young men ever are prone." At twenty-one, a "deep and affecting sense of [those errors]" led him to seek God's favor. He received "religious impressions," but they did not lead to "a complete union to God by his Son Jesus Christ." Devotion "was often a mere form, and carelessly and irreverently performed" (*Travels*, 164). Throughout the 1780s and 1790s, Rush reports, he was alternately "drawn" to God and fell away (*Travels*, 165). In the end, however, there is no "ferment" or blinding moment of conversion, as there was in the political and intellectual spheres. "My only hope of salvation is in the infinite transcendent love of God manifested to the world by the death of his Son upon the Cross" (*Travels*, 166). As a universalist, Rush comes to have a firm faith that he (and everyone else) will be "take[n] home." Hence, perhaps, his account does not demand an assured moment of conversion, nor perhaps does it demand an attempt to articulate a sense of that private space. In a sense, of course, for him, it is not private. God's providence belongs to Him, not to us. Rush can rest easy in the rise and fall of "a sense of divine things" (*Travels*, 165).

I take the lack of an account of his conversion to be a significant non-moment in Rush's self-biography, and I need to keep pulling at Rush's narrative to show why. Recounting why his "devotion was often a mere form," he remarks, "I lost a great deal of spiritual sensibility while I was abroad. Travelling is unfavourable to the growth and even to the existence of Religion in the soul. Thousands I believe have lost their all by it" (*Travels*, 164–165). In this context, I think, "abroad" refers to any journey that requires one to be away from home, rather than only journeys to foreign places. Rush, after all, spent only three years "abroad" (1766–1769), in that latter sense, while the passage describes his spiritual life from the 1760s "to the present year 1800" (*Travels*, 164). Also, Rush notes that the "scenes of my political life were likewise unfavourable to the divine life in my soul" (*Travels*, 165). Politics, like "travelling," distracts one from one's relationship with God. These remarks recall his comment, which I cited earlier, that "company, conversation, and even business are the opiates of the Spirit of God in the human heart." In 1790, Rush wrote in his commonplace book: "The powers of the human mind appear to be arranged in a certain order like the strata of the earth. They are thrown out of their order by the fall of man. The moral powers appear to have occupied the highest and first place. They recover it in solitude, and after sleep, hence the advantage of solitary punishments . . ." (*Travels*, 185). This passage begins in Brockden Brownian fashion—the mind as a subject with layered depth—only to retreat to a Renaissance notion of faculty psychology. Rush sees in people a Miltonic fall, not Freudian neuroses. Solitude and sleep are conceived in the passage as static conditions in which the mind recuperates its natural, divinely ordained order. They are opposed to society, business, and traveling, all of which distract the mind from this natural order.

But this conception as Rush develops it in the third part of *Travels* is at odds with his conception of solitude in the first part. There, amidst his narration of his intellectual development, Rush remarks that he does "not recollect ever acquiring a single new idea by sitting still and doing nothing in [his] study" (*Travels*, 91). Instead, he says, new ideas came to him "when riding, walking, . . . writing," lecturing, reading, and conversing with others (*Travels*, 91–92). This conception accords with a set of lecture notes prepared in 1809 in which Rush points to "observing, reading, thinking, recording, conversing, and composing" as "the Best Means of Acquiring Knowledge" (*Travels*, 347). There is, in other words, a tension in the self-biography between intellectual knowledge and spirituality: intellectual knowledge comes about through stimulation, spirituality through sensual privation. (This suggests, again, why solitary confinement played such an important role in Rush's understanding of penal reform. The soul would necessarily, mechanically, reform itself in isolation.) The tension recalls Pope's formulation in *The Essay on Man*:

> Two principles in human nature reign;
> Self-love, to urge, and reason, to restrain;
> Nor this a good, nor that a bad we call,
> Each works its end, to move or govern all:
> And to their proper operation still,
> Ascribe all good; to their improper, ill.
> (II: 53–58)

For Pope, self-love is the motive force and reason the stabilizing or balancing force. Both principles are inherent and necessary in his system. Similarly, Rush posits intellectual knowledge as a motive force and spirituality as a static, stabilizing force. But in his self-biography, Rush writes only about the first (motive, intellectual) force; the second (passive, spiritual) force remains outside the bounds of discussion.

In a sense, the tension merely suggests the depth of Rush's early Calvinism: solitude may be a way of recovering our Adamic senses, but God has nevertheless enjoined us to "delight in Society" (*Travels*, 46). We must live in the world, while striving to be above it. Protestants destroyed the monasteries in the sixteenth century for a similar reason. Even more, however, the tension suggests the extent to which Rush is willing to see the "soul" as an aspect of the self that need not be addressed at length or in depth. Rush devotes three pages to his soul's conversion and eighty (in the first part of the self-biography) to his intellect's; and he conflates the stages of Christian reform with the language of empiricism and science in order to render that intellectual conversion in dramatic terms. The mind is Rush's focus in *Travels*, as it is in his later medical treatises,[16] not the soul. Metaphorically, the title *Travels through Life* picks up on the tension, since it suggests that Rush is traveling not toward salvation (though he does think that he will be saved, indeed that we all will be) but toward higher intellectual truths. He apparently feels, as a universalist, that that first journey—interior, private, spiritual—is simply beside the point as he reviews his life. "They misrepresent the Christian religion, who suppose it to be wholly an internal revelation, and addressed only to the moral faculties of the mind" (211), Rush once wrote. He chooses in his self-biography, however, to focus *only* on the ways that his moral faculties emerged in his life, and emerged through the particular events that happened to him. Christian religion is "wholly an [*external*] revelation" in his account of his own life.

Rush's interests, throughout his life, can best be described as outwardly directed. From his dilemma as a young man about choosing medicine over the law—the ministry apparently was never a serious option for him—to his 1812 treatise *The Diseases of the Mind*, Rush aimed, as he expressed it in 1761 at the age of sixteen, "to spend and be spent for the Good of Mankind" (*Letters*, 3). His medical practice, his political involvement, and his public writings were all designed to improve human life, to minister to "this earthly frame, a minute fabric, a center of wonders" (*Letters*, 3). Rush consciously believed in the ideal of self-effacement in order to serve a larger good. No wonder, then, that he could work so closely with men who themselves were so very different: Thomas Paine and John Adams, for example. Paine could see in Rush's republicanism a revolutionary social reformism that resembled his; Adams could see a radical Christian reformism that struck a chord with him. Rush's "thought," William Hedges once wrote perceptively, "is a startling amalgam of the daring and the reactionary" (1973, 300). His contemporaries could find many congenial ideas in Rush because Rush himself accommodated a variety of ideas from religion, medicine and science, politics, and law.

Paine, Adams, Jefferson, Graydon, and many others shared with Rush the ideal of self-effacement.[17] Adams, in his own grumpy way, felt that many people "advertised" their disinterestedness and so forfeited the principle itself (Adams and Rush, 92–95), but he, like the others, believed ideally in the principle. Or, to phrase this more clearly, they believed that certain people ideally effaced themselves, notably white men with education, influence, power, and/or wealth. They believed, in other words, that some men *had* a self, a distinct, perhaps original or independent, agency; that that agency both gave them their power and was a sign of their social status; and that they had a responsibility to deny or downplay that agency. The "spur of fame" was not available to everyone. Most people inhabited a world, so Adams and Jefferson and others felt, in which they simply could not or should not aspire to agency. Republican disinterestedness, after all, was by definition a stance that denied agency and power to all people except propertied men. Rush in the second section of *Travels* makes the necessary gestures in this direction: "I derive pleasure from the recollection of the integrity of my public pursuits. I sought not honors. . . . I was animated constantly by a belief that I was acting for the benefit of the whole world, and of future ages, by assisting in the formation of new means of political order and general happiness" (*Travels*, 161). Much of this section of the self-biography is taken up with sorting out who was and who was not "animated" by heartfelt republican principles (self-effacement among them): the categorization of motives for different kinds of Tories and Whigs (*Travels*, 117–119), the narrative of his battle with Shippen during the war (*Travels*, 131–138), the "characters" of all the members of Congress who signed the Declaration of Independence (*Travels*, 138–154) and of some patriots who did not (*Travels*, 154–158). Benedict Arnold, for example, is revealed not as a traitor to the republic—those actions were recorded in "printed histories" already—but as a man whose "language was ungrammatical," whose "character . . . was never respectable," and whose "person was low" (*Travels*, 158). He was a climber, Rush suggests, who clawed his way toward the top from selfish motives: shades of Graydon's critique, but offered from what is more clearly a republican perspective. Rush tries to look behind the public facade, the "advertisement" of the self, so to speak, to find true motives. We should have anticipated Arnold's behavior, he suggests, from his ungrammatical speech; the outside necessarily and mechanically reveals the inside. John Hancock, in contrast to Arnold, "was a disinterested patriot" who sacrificed personal wealth to aid the country. If his conversation was "desultory" and his temper "peevish," he could be excused since the gout caused him serious infirmity. Behind Hancock's advertisement of irritability, in other words, was real self-effacement. Grammar you can help; the gout you cannot. It is easy to ridicule Rush's logic in all this: he is defending those he likes and attacking those he does not. But the issues go deeper, and touch the heart of eighteenth-century concerns that "character" might, in the end, be just "characterization." Rush hopes not for a core at which "character" rests, which is how autobiographers will later imagine the self, but for a perceivable convergence between inner and outer, motive and action, cause and effect. We are and must be our "characterization," our habits that experience has inculcated upon our minds.

Rush's defensiveness about his own motives in this section, like Graydon's in his *Memoirs*, is in part self-serving. His own errors, when he makes them, are made out of "indiscreet zeal" (*Travels*, 137) rather than bad or mistaken motives, while on the other hand he is persecuted by many people whose own motives are, he says, sullied by ignorance, greed, and ambition. Rush intends, I think, for the first section of the self-biography to bear upon the narration of events in the second (and upon his spiritual and domestic life in the third): his motives in section two (in the Revolution) are grounded in his intellectual revolution, laced with religiosity and interpreted "psychologically," which he described in section one. To speak of himself and other patriots being "animated" (*Travels*, 161), after all, is to return to a conception of behavior as determined by causes, both intellectual (Arnold's ungrammatical language, for example, or Rush's own intellectual revolution) and physical (Hancock's gout). The entire three-part structure of his self-biography depends, in Rush's understanding of human behavior, on his political and intellectual conversions in the first part. He is, it appears, "animated" by the principle of republicanism that he discovered there, and will be animated in just that way until (if) another "revolution" reorients him or until he dies. It is mechanical. His ideas have real, ongoing, physical and behavioral effects.

In placing that sort of determining power on his intellectual conversion, Rush exposes the contradiction that Jay Fliegelman has brilliantly examined in Jefferson and other American Revolutionaries: "the Whig . . . insistence on historical agency and self-determination was . . . in flight from a fear of [mechanical] instrumentality and determinism. Yet paradoxically the discourse of mechanical determinism (recast as a determinism of psychological and natural motives) was essential to shield and exculpate individuals from the ultimate and uncomfortable responsibility of their newly heightened historical agency" (1993, 142–143). When Rush anxiously asks at the end of the second section if the Revolution might have been a deception, and his own and others's "hopes [simply] visionary," he falls back on the notion that he had been "acting for the benefit of the whole world, and of future ages" (*Travels*, 161). As Fliegelman notes, acting means both theatricality and historical agency (1993, 89–94). Rush intends the latter; he intends his sons to see that he "acted," not from a script and not out of self-interest, but from a principle. He is not responsible, at some level, for what happened in the Revolution. He, and others, appropriated agency, but that agency was undermined by the fact that it was animated by a principle. The principle truly believed will assuredly "cause" patriotic behavior. The principle "animates." Failing in the middle of the election year of 1800 to see that principle actuating absolutely every American, Rush finds a natural metaphor that explains the drama he witnessed: "the seeds of all the great changes for the better in the condition of mankind . . . have been sowed years and centuries before they came to pass" (*Travels*, 161). The principle that drove the American Revolution will, in time, triumph and convert others, even if it has not done so yet, but until that time it will be resisted by men who are themselves driven by other, inferior principles. The American Revolution in that sense is just like universalist Christianity; in the end, we will all necessarily be converted.

"I consider it is possible to convert men into republican machines" (92), Rush wrote in 1792. By controlling the environment, people could be "disciplined" (as Foucault has it) into republican behavior, much as Rush's behavior in the 1770s and after was "disciplined" by his conversion to republican principles. But would such citizens be republicans by choice, or would they merely be the determined product of physical and intellectual causes? On one level, it does not matter: "purely mechanical" habits are as efficacious for society "as if [they] flowed from principle" (196), Rush wrote. But on another, more important level it does matter, for the principle to which Rush ascribes truth, republicanism, is a reasonable one: "no form of government can be rational but that which is derived from the Suffrages of the people who are the subjects of it" (*Travels*, 46). To determine a person's habits, however, is to determine their "suffrage"; it is to posit a power or being who can determine the environment and, then, at second remove, determine ideas.[18] For Rush, of course, that power is and remains the Christian God, who subsumes reason and republicanism within his Being. "Republicanism is a part of the truth of Christianity" (*Letters*, 584). "True Whigs like true Christians always love one another" (*Letters*, 189). "It seems to be reserved to Christianity alone to produce universal, moral, political, and physical happiness" (*Letters*, 799). Not surprisingly, Rush gradually moves toward a millennialism in which mankind is eventually brought within the discipline of Christian rationalism: "There is a great deal of preparatory work to be done before [the millennium] can take place. . . . Civilization, human knowledge, and liberty must first pervade the globe. They are the heralds of religion. They do not confer happiness, but prepare the minds of mankind for it" (*Letters*, 834). When it is all over, we will *all* be republican machines! And, we will be in heaven, or in a heaven on earth. Rush's universalism is not only religious, it is social, intellectual, and political. In the end, *everyone* will be self-effacing, republican Christians. Rush is simply already there.

Rush's self-biography is, then, a sort of confessional self-biography, despite its scientific inflections. It tells the story not of his soul's conversion but of his mind's, that locus of knowledge and liberty which for Rush is the herald of religion. In *Travels through Life* Rush tests his intellectual conversion against his lived experience and against his era's experience, finding in the process that he has, indeed, acted according to the dictates of "civilization, human knowledge, and liberty." His interests in social reform, revolution, and medicine (the "reform" of disease, both theoretical and practical) all reflect his millenarian sense that the world needs to be prepared for universal salvation. "The majority of mankind are madmen at large," Rush wrote in 1811. "They differ in their degrees of insanity, but I have sometimes thought the most prominent in this general mental disease are those men who by writing and reasoning attempt to cure them" (*Letters*, 1090).[19] We can see in this how close Rush was to Freudian psychology, just as his insistence on the physical causes of mental disease put him close to modern psychiatry[20]—close, that is, if one ignores the fact that the fundamentally spiritual/religious dimension of his thought was still based on faculty psychology. For his actions were always grounded in a belief that salvation was man's universal, destined end, and that the dialectic of physical and ideal—body and mind, material and spiritual—would, step by faltering step, lead mankind to it.

For Graydon, the self must be resisted because it leads to democracy, capitalism, and romantic self-infatuation; accordingly, Graydon wrote a "selfless" self-biography. For Rush, the self is structured according to the model of faculty psychology, with mind and soul at the top of the list of the powers of man; but only the mind is susceptible to full-scale reformation (though apparently the soul follows). Accordingly, he wrote in *Travels through Life* a history of his mind's development, but one in which the mind is in great part determined by the environment. His own intellectual revolutions move him upward to higher truths, but they prove to have been themselves conditioned by previous events and ideas. In effect, Rush does not open any space between mind and environment for agency to manifest itself; indeed, he is not able to theorize clearly, at all, how ideas or environment (each animated by the other) can move forward in the dialectical manner he imagines, except as a transcendent God can manipulate the process. Everything, as Rush says, is indeed in a plastic state, at the mercy of other forces or ideas, constantly changing, which condition them. Like Graydon, then, Rush could not yet put his faith in a mind that was a powerful agent of its own destiny or that was, in any sense, original or unique or interiorized. Mind merely followed matter. And until mind or the "self" could be theorized more clearly as an agent of its own imaginings and action, original or unique, autobiography could not fully emerge in the United States.

❧ 5 ❧

Ethan Allen and the Republican Self

I REMARKED EARLIER THAT THE PAUCITY OF CRITICISM on Revolutionary self-biographers is a surprising, but revealing and significant, fact of American literary history. It is most surprising, perhaps, in the case of Ethan Allen, whose *Narrative of the Captivity of Colonel Ethan Allen* was first published in 1779 and then republished at least eighteen times before the Civil War (Jellison, 219). Allen's *Narrative* has been readily available in the archive,[1] and it also made its way into fiction and poetry (like Melville's *Israel Potter*) read by critics with other interests. It would seem to have provided all sorts of readers with possible critical openings: Progressives with a critique of the founding; New Critics with a tight, carefully controlled narrative; New Historicists with a node in a web of Revolutionary discourse on class and status; historicists with a complement to Franklin's master narrative; Bercovitchean neo-Marxists with yet another instance of auto-Americanbiography; post-structuralists with a persona who invents himself in language; and so on. Yet only one critic, Daniel Williams, has really grappled with the language and implications of Allen's *Narrative*.

Williams astutely reads Allen's *Narrative* as a "captivity narrative [that] reflected the conventions of earlier Indian captivity narratives" (1989, 331). Redemption or freedom for Allen comes to mean liberty, not conversion to a truer or renewed or more heartfelt Christianity as it did in many of the early captivity narratives. Through his trials and torments, Williams argues, Allen teaches his readers "that submission to tyranny resulted in a death of one sort or another, that happiness depended on liberty, and that liberty demanded total commitment" (1989, 340). Allen's lesson, Williams concludes, is a self-conscious representation—an "artistic process of self-creation" (1989, 341)—in which Allen remakes himself into the person he wants to be: an honorable gentleman

93

whose motives are pure and disinterested and self-evident. Allen's "artistic process" can, I think, be analyzed more closely, not with a view of refuting Williams but of expressing more clearly even yet Allen's achievement, and, particularly, of articulating his conception of personal identity. Though he seems at times to anticipate the hero of a tale of the Old Southwest, and thus to speak in an individualistic, autobiographical voice, Allen actually embeds the figure of himself that he creates in his *Narrative* within several conventional late-eighteenth-century conceptions of identity, including sentimentalism, (republican) liberty, and gentlemanliness. These rhetorical moves are "revolutionary" in that Allen, of all people, should assume them, but they are not revolutionary or innovative or original in their actual uses. Allen appropriates, as best he can, the language of revolutionary sentiment and feeling, and he does so in order to pull himself upward socially and pull Vermont "upward" politically. But he operates, in the end, as an agent of larger forces—sentiment and liberty—not as an agent of his own personal desires. His *Narrative* remains in this sense firmly ensconced within eighteenth-century self-biographical norms.

Ethan Allen was taken captive in September 1775 as he tried in an ill-conceived attack to take Montreal from the British. He had no commission from the Continental Congress or from a colonial government ("though," he says, the officers commissioned by Congress "engaged . . . that I should be considered as an officer the same as tho' I had a commission" [10]), which created problems both for the British who captured him and for Allen himself in captivity. He was finally exchanged for a British colonel in May 1778. Throughout his narrative of these two-plus years, Allen takes great care to describe the cruel treatment he and others received at the hands of his British captors. Writing in late 1778 and early 1779, of course, Allen, like Philip Freneau in his 1781 poem *The British Prison-Ship*, was trying both to exercise literary revenge and to reinvigorate the Revolutionary cause, flagging as the war dragged on.[2]

So, for example, onboard the *Mercury* en route to Halifax in 1776, Allen found himself under a cruel captain named Montague, who "was loaded with prejudices against every body; and every thing that was not stamped with royalty" (34). Montague "seemed to think," Allen says, "that heaven and earth were made merely to gratify the king and his creatures" (35), and as a result he denied his American prisoners food and medical assistance. The entire British prison system, Allen remarks bitterly near the end of the narrative, may "with propriety [be] called the British inquisition" (62), directed by "an abandoned British council" and "perpetrated" in America by "monster[s]" like William Howe, Joshua Loring, and John Burgoyne (63). Allen describes in detail wretched conditions on prison ships and in the makeshift New York prisons, lingering in exquisite detail on brutal punishments, rotten food, unsanitary floors and bedding, the lack of medical attention, and epidemics. Captivity in his account is truly and sensibly horrifying. He clearly wants his contemporary readers to *feel* the realities of captivity, a point I shall return to later in this chapter.

Williams has rightly argued that the Indian captivity narrative was a shaping influence on Allen's account of his captivity. Traditionally, the Indian captivity narrative represented a binary opposition between "us and them," between darkness and light, savagism and civilization, demons and saints (Pearce). We might expect, given Allen's characterization of the British prison system as an "inquisition," that the binary system at work in his narrative will be American versus British. Yet Allen often meets with a "generous enemy" (16). "One of the officers [on one of the prison ships], by the name of Bradley, was very generous to me; he would often send me victuals from his own table" (17). "My personal treatment by lieut[enant] Hamilton, who commanded [Pendennis] castle, was very generous" (25). "The guard which was set over us [in Halifax], was . . . touched with the feelings of compassion" (37). The British as Allen presents them are not entirely demonic or monstrous.

Nor are the Americans entirely sanctified in liberty. One guard over Allen in New York "was composed of tories from Connecticut. . . . They were very full of their invectives against the country, swaggered of their loyalty to their king, and exclaimed bitterly against the 'cowardly yankees'" (46). The American Tories watch with "delight and triumph" (47) as prisoners from the Continental Army die in crowded churches in New York. "I have observed the British soldiers to be full of their blackguard jokes," Allen writes, "and vaunting on those occasions, but they appeared to me less malignant than tories" (48). The American Tories figure as do Howe and Burgoyne, as "monsters" perverted in their designs.

Allen does figure the conflict in his *Narrative* in binary terms, then, even if those terms are not "American" and "British." Daniel Williams and John McWilliams both note how Allen divides the men he encounters into those who recognize him as a gentleman and those who do not (see also Ziff, 183–184). "Early in his life," Williams tells us, "Allen had claimed for himself gentleman-status, and now, during his captivity, his greatest struggle was to maintain this status in the most abject circumstances" (1989, 334; see McWilliams, 269–270). I am not sure that a reading of either the biographies of Allen or of Allen's *Narrative* itself warrants an assertion that Allen claimed "early in his life" the status of a gentleman, but he does claim it in the *Narrative* when he is fighting for the rebel cause. This desire to be seen as a gentleman is, in fact, where Williams finds Allen "remaking" himself. Born in 1738 on the frontier in western Connecticut, lacking any sort of formal education, and isolated by the rigors of frontier existence (see Pell and Jellison), Allen proclaims himself a gentleman in his *Narrative*, demonstrating in the process "his power of self-creation" (Williams 1989, 341).

In one incident, for example, Allen says he was paraded in front of "numbers of gentlemen and ladies" while held at Pendennis Castle. He asked one "gentleman for a bowl of punch, and [the gentleman] ordered his servant to bring it, which he did, and offered it me, but I refused to take it from the hand of his servant; he then gave it to me with his own hand," and Allen drank it down (27). A gentleman himself, Allen will accept the drink only from the hand of another gentleman, not a servant. Elsewhere, Allen is often treated as a private soldier, housed with the other privates, denied the luxuries normally afforded to commissioned officers, and told explicitly that he is not a "gentleman." Many of the British commanders, Allen sighs, "knew not how to behave towards a gentleman of the military establishment" (23). But, in defense of the British military, Allen had no commission from a colonial government or from the Continental Congress—not that the British recognized such commissions in the early years of the war—nor did he "appear" to be a gentleman. He swears grievously (18), dresses barbarously (23), acts (by his own admission) like "the madman" (47), and "swagger[s] over those who abused" him (18). In England, two clergymen come to see him and are "surprized" that Allen "should understand a syllogism or regular mode of argumentation. . . . To see a gentleman in England [argue thus], regularly dressed and well behaved, would be no sight at all; but such a rebel, as they were pleased to call me, it is probable was never before seen in England" (27–28). Allen looks and acts like a rough frontiersman, not a member of the gentry.

Many people do, however, recognize Allen as a "gentleman" and treat him accordingly. Sailing from Halifax to New York, Captain Smith of the *Lark* met Allen on the quarterdeck and "assured me that I should be treated as a gentleman." Allen tells Smith that he can probably never repay such generosity: "Capt. Smith replied, that he had no reward in view, but only treated me as a gentleman ought to be treated" (42). At Pendennis Castle, Lieutenant Hamilton sends Allen a few marks of gentlemanly status: "fine breakfast and dinner from his own table, and a bottle of good wine" (25). Held on a prison ship in Cork, Allen is given food, clothes, and money by some "gentleman of Cork determined to make my sea-stores equal to the Captain [of the ship]." From a "large acquaintance with gentleman of [Ireland]," Allen says, he can tell the nation abounds in "liberality and bravery" (30). Some people are able intuitively to penetrate Allen's frontiersman's clothes and his rough behavior, and see behind them his internal gentlemanly merit.

Allen's definition of a gentleman can be derived from the incidents of his *Narrative*. It involves, first, a sense of honor and a concomitant self-consciousness that that honor has a public dimension—in other words, reputation. Both terms are weighted with a sense of class, aristocratic privileges in which certain members of society "inhabit" a set of behavioral expectations that must be deferred to by others. Musing on the possiblity that he might die in prison, Allen reasons that the "cause I was engaged in" was a "worthy" one, worth dying for if need be, and that if he should die he would "be as well treated as other gentleman of my merit" in the world of spirits (26). He resolves not to show fear in the face of death, so that while living he "might exhibit a good example of American fortitude" (26) and so that his "last act [will not be] despicable to my enemies, and [hence will not] eclipse the other actions of my life" (26). Here and elsewhere, Allen is intensely aware of the way his actions will be perceived by others. He is a "sight," as the two clergymen imply, someone whose behavior is assessed not simply for what it says about himself (that is Williams's argument), but for what it says about other things: liberty, gentlemanliness, America, American identity. Later, for example, when some prisoners approach Allen to help them overthrow Captain Smith of the *Lark*, Allen tells "them that they might depend on it, upon my honor, that I would faithfully guard Captain Smith's life" (43), thereby indeed repaying Smith's initial gentlemanly generosity. The enemy is not the British: it is anyone who fails to understand that society should be directed by certain men with internal merit, merit revealed not by traditional means of dress, manners, language, and style, but by the passionate adherence to an ideal. The Revolution itself, Allen reminds his reader at the outset of his *Narrative*, was caused by the "systematical" attempt of Great Britain "to enslave America" (5), that is, to deprive American subjects of their innate equality to British subjects (see Bailyn 1967, 232–234). British soldiers are not the enemy because they are British; they are the enemy because they (some of them, at least) seek to subjugate their fellow countrymen, their political and social equals in the eyes of Allen. Allen wants to be regarded as a gentleman, and even though in the end he will not argue that everyone is a gentleman or that everyone should have an opportunity to become a gentleman, this desire marks his *Narrative* as a "revolutionary" social document in 1779.

For the British, of course, honor is class-based; many British officers cannot see Allen as honorable, because he is not of noble birth or superior social position (see Mason). Allen knows this: in his introduction he asks his audience "to excuse any inaccuracies . . . as the author has unfortunately missed a liberal education" (4), one of the signs of gentle breeding for men in the eighteenth century. But his bid in the *Narrative* is to shift the definition of honor from heredity and training to individual, innate merit. In this, his bid is similar to Jefferson's repeated attempts (beginning in 1779) in Virginia and the United States to make education available to all "those persons . . . whom nature hath endowed with genius and virtue . . . without regard to wealth, birth or other accidental condition or circumstance" (365). At one point, Allen writes about two American brothers held in New York by the British. After one brother dies, the other approaches Allen and asks him whether he should "deceive the British by enlisting, and [then] deserting the first opportunity" (50). Allen, not afraid of disguises and "strategem[s]" (24) himself, tells the young man he should. Allen then reflects on the incident:

> it seems that [the two brothers] could not be stimulated to such exertions of heroism from ambition, as they were but obscure soldiers; strong indeed must the internal principle of virtue be, which supported them to brave death, and one of them went through the operation, as did many hundred others. (50–51)

He refers to this sort of behavior as "public virtue" (51), and portrays himself as one of its greatest exemplars, along with Washington (53–55), John Fell (61), and numerous others whose brief stories Allen embeds in his own. In this sense, Allen, like Alexander Graydon thirty years later, intends his written life to counteract selfishness and ambition, teaching instead the "virtue" and honor of liberty, sociability, openness, and equality. Though it may seem like self-aggrandizement to us, Allen's behavior demands to be read in the context of his own narrative as the selfless expression of American liberty.

Allen's notion that virtue is disinterested creates tension in the narrative, a tension that can allow Williams to read his actions as "self-creation" and, at the same time, me to read his actions as "self-less." When, for example, a year into captivity, Allen continues to insist that his "rank" entitles him to preferential treatment, he juxtaposes a British class-based notion with an American republican one. "I now found myself on parole," he writes at one point, "... where I soon projected means to live in some measure agreeable to my rank, though I was destitute of cash" (46–47). What merit or virtue or honor entitles him to more than the two brothers whose "internal principle of virtue" stimulated them to heroism? For that matter, why is Allen entitled to have ambition, while the two brothers' obscurity suggests that they are somehow below it? That, after all, is exactly how many of the British aristocrats in the *Narrative* understand Allen. Ideally, the proprieties of class should, in Allen's republican vision, be unrelated to true virtue. But they never are; Allen desires "rank" and its accoutrements even as he suggests that they are vestiges of an outmoded hierarchical system. Allen himself never consciously recognizes this tension, though elsewhere he quite clearly states the republican ideal:

> I shared the same fate with the [other prisoners], and though they offered me more than an even share, I refused to accept it, as it was a time of substantial distress, which in my opinion I ought to partake equally with the rest, and set an example of virtue and fortitude to our little commonwealth. (36)

Here, equality of merit, combined with dehumanizing conditions, equalizes men, creating a commonwealth that mirrors the larger commonwealth that their suffering is intended to help bring into being.

Virtue and reputation, seen through a specifically republican lens, are thus central to Allen's notion of gentlemanly behavior. The other trait that defines gentlemanliness for him is sentimentality. Allen's *Narrative* returns again and again to feelings: "This I could not reconcile to my own feelings as a man, much less as an officer" (12); "The guard which was set over us, was by this time touched with the feelings of compassion" (37); "I ... am sure that I express the sentiments and feelings of all the friends to the present revolution" (71). When Captain Smith first offers to treat Allen as a gentleman, Allen responds as would Henry Mackenzie's Man of Feeling and Laurence Sterne's Mr. Yorick: "This was so unexpected and sudden a transition, that it drew tears from my eyes, (which all the ill usage I had before met with, was not able to produce) nor could I at first hardly speak" (42). This is one of the genuine signs offered by Allen in the course of the narrative—genuine because spontaneous, physical, and uncontrollable—and it contrasts to other blustering actions that readers have taken for the "real" Allen, like his cursing, his legendary exploits, or his rustic frontier clothing. Not only does Allen often tell us that those other actions are disguises, as when he says that it was "political to act in some measure the madman" (47), but they are always characterized by Allen's forethought and control, unlike his weeping. Indeed, this is the rock on which Ziff's reading of Allen's *Narrative* founders: Ziff takes Allen's "strategem[s]" for Allen himself, not as poses designed to speak within specific, local, and temporary contexts. I shall have more to say about this in a moment.

The "sensible feelings of humanity" that Allen and others like him wore on their sleeves were very much in vogue in the 1770s and 1780s.[3] No matter how one understands the origins of the vogue—French *sensibilité*, Scottish Common Sense philosophy, New Light sensationalism, Shaftesburyean *Sensus Communis*—Allen's use of sentimental language places him squarely within a group of fictional characters who dominated the Anglo-American literary scene well into the 1780s: Harley (*The Man of Feeling*, 1771), Mr. Yorick (*A Sentimental Journey*, 1768), Sir George Ellison (*The Man of Real Sensibility*, 1766), Werther (*The Sorrows of Young Werther*, 1774), and Dr. Primrose (*The Vicar of Wakefield*, 1766). These novels were both imported from abroad and reprinted in the colonies. Sterne's *Sentimental Journey*, for example, was reprinted three times in the American colonies prior to 1778, when Allen began to write his *Narrative*. All five works cited above went through three or more American editions alone by the end of the century, in addition to being imported in English editions (Winans). It is unclear to me yet, I must admit, where exactly Allen picked up the language of sentimentality and sensibility.[4] Charles Jellison, his most reliable biographer, reports that Allen read no more than "a half-dozen" books in his entire life (14). But the narrator of Allen's *Narrative* is, nevertheless, a sentimentalist, a man of feeling.

That sentimentality is a trait shared by gentlemen is pointed out at numerous times in the narrative. A captain named (ironically) Royal told Allen that "his express orders were to treat [Allen] with . . . severity, which was disagreeable to his own feelings"; Royal could never bring himself to "insult" Allen, even though "many others who came on board did" (17). Before Captain Smith ever comes to Allen's aid, his commanding officer upbraids him for sympathizing with a "severe" letter in which Allen, demanding "gentleman-like usage," gave "the British . . . their true character." Do "you take the part of a rebel against me?" the commanding officer asks Smith. Smith responds: "he rather spoke his sentiments" (41). The "true character" of some of the British officers is that they cannot feel. In one instance, Allen tried to gain the aid of a purser on a ship. After his request for stores was denied, Allen tried "to reason the matter with [the purser]." Unsuccessful, Allen then "held [the purser's] honor up to view . . . but found his honor impenetrable." Allen next "endeavored to touch his humanity, but found he had none" (35). Reason, "honor," and "humanity" are different aspects of the mind or soul, representing various eighteenth-century schools of thought about the nature of man. Allen probed them all, unsuccessfully in the purser's case. Other officers, however, and Allen himself, "terrifyingly conscious" of and vulnerable "before the formative influences of uncontrollable impressions, distractions, and random events" (Fliegelman 1982, 63), reach out to others with honor and humanity, figured by Allen as generosity, charity, benevolence, sentiment, and sympathetic friendship. One captain (Allen cannot remember his name) tells Allen: "there is a greatness of soul for personal friendship to subsist between you and me" (45). These two men have opened their innermost recesses to each other, and come disease, imprisonment, poverty, and destitution that personal connection persists. Allen remakes the world in his *Narrative* so that true community is grounded in sensibility, not reason; feeling, not intellect.

Allen's *Narrative* is like no other document from the war years so much as it is like Thomas Jefferson's draft of the Declaration of Independence. Garry Wills has, of course, studied Jefferson's Declaration as a "sentimental paper" (1978, 257–319), focusing quite rightly on Jefferson's use of such language as "agonizing affection," "unfeeling brethren," and "bands which have connected" people. Wills locates the origins of Jefferson's thinking in Scottish Common Sense philosophy and, perhaps more surprisingly, given Jefferson's mistrust of the novel, in Laurence Sterne's writings. His insight has been developed by other scholars, such as Andrew Burstein, who in his portrait of the "inner Jefferson" (1996) analyzes Jefferson's sensibility, in part as it was developed through an extensive, indeed lifelong, reading and re-reading of Sterne's works.

In his draft of the Declaration, Jefferson presents evidence of insensitive, unnatural behavior, particularly of the king's desire to create an "absolute tyranny" over the American states, heretofore his dutiful children. "To prove this let facts be submitted to a candid world" (19–20), Jefferson writes. Allen grounds his *Narrative* in the same rhetorical move. "I took [care]," he says at one point, "to inform myself . . . of the very designs and aims of Gen. Howe and his council; the latter of which I predicated on the former, and submit it to the candid public" (56). Allen's descriptions of physical punishment, of deprivation, "of the assuming tyranny, and haughty, malevolent, and insolent behaviour of the enemy [from 1776 to 1778]" (68) rise in crescendo in the course of the narrative. Like Jefferson, he wants to appeal to his audience by virtue of the sheer number of instances of depraved and unfeeling behavior, and also through the rhetoric of wounded sensibility, which gives those facts their true meaning. Jefferson, accordingly, has the king of England "plundering" seas and "ravaging" coasts, waging "cruel war against human nature itself" and "prostituting" his negative (21–22); he makes the people of Great Britain "deaf to the voice of justice & of consanguinity" and, like unfeeling brothers, willing to ignore a sibling's "agonizing affection" (23); and he imagines the American audience as moved, as injured, as wounded by the ungenerous, unnatural, unfeeling behavior of the British king and people. Allen's focus is on the unnatural and unfeeling British commanders and soldiers; by 1779, of course, the king had been effectively "killed" (Jordan 1973), and what was needed was a vilification of the enemy to encourage enlistments and continued sacrifice. Allen's ideal audience is a sympathetic, sensitive American people who, once informed of the truth of the facts—for which Allen, like Jefferson and other eighteenth-century gentlemen, "stake[s] my honour" (4; see Jefferson, 20)—will respond with emotions and, then, with action.

In his 1825 letter to Henry Lee, Jefferson claimed that the "object" of the Declaration of Indepedence was

> Not to find out new principles, or new arguments, never before thought of, not merely to say things which had never been said before; but to place before mankind the common sense of the subject, in terms so plain and firm as to command their assent, and to justify ourselves in the independ-

ent stand we [were] compelled to take. Neither aiming at originality of principle or sentiment, not yet copied from any particular or previous writing, it was intended to be an expression of the American mind. (1501)

Though recalled romantically at the distance of fifty years, Jefferson's object as he remembered it was quite similar to Allen's in 1779. Allen was not writing an original self into narrative being, nor did he see himself within a tradition of previous self-biographical selves. He attempted to frame the Revolution as a conflict between head and heart, between inhuman/inhumane men and — *novus ordo seculorum* — the feeling, generous, sentimental revolutionaries. "If our country," Jefferson wrote in his famous letter to Maria Cosway in 1786, "when pressed with wrongs at the point of the bayonet, had been governed by it's heads instead of it's hearts, where should we have been now? Hanging on a gallows as high as Haman's" (875). Hanging and dismemberment were the punishment for treason in Great Britain in the eighteenth century. Allen knows that: his first inhumane British persecutor tells him he "shall grace a halter at Tyburn" (16). That he does not hang is, indeed, attributable in his own account of his captivity to his willingness to listen to the dictates and impulses of the human heart.

The self-biographical Ethan Allen is, then, virtuous, gentlemanly, and sentimental. Like Royall Tyler's later stage creation, Colonel Manly in *The Contrast* (1787), Allen is "manly" in the eighteenth century's sense of that word. Within the plot of the narrative, during the thirty-four months of his captivity, Allen asserts that this identity is constant: removed from jail to a general's quarters near the time of his release, he remarks "that I was the same man still" (71). Captive or free, jailed or paroled, he is "the same man still." The process by which he became this fixed identity is occluded in the narrative; Allen, in a sense, leaps fully formed onto the first page of the *Narrative*. We can, however, infer the development of this self from two key moments in the narrative, one at the beginning and one at the end. The moments frame Allen's *Narrative* and are, quite clearly, ways for him to "enter" and "exit" the story.

"Ever since I arrived to a state of manhood," Allen begins, "and acquainted myself with the general history of mankind, I have felt a sincere passion for liberty." Reading the "history of nations doomed to perpetual slavery" because their people yielded "their natural born liberties" to "tyrants," Allen reacts with what he terms a "philosophical horror" (5). We have no way of knowing what histories Allen has in mind here: he himself, remember, admittedly "missed a liberal education" (4), his biographers report that he read very little, and the *Narrative* itself yields very few (if any) classical or contemporaneous historical references. Bernard Bailyn reminds us that, though the writers of the Revolutionary generation drew citations from a whole range of classical authors, most colonists had "detailed knowledge and engaged interest" in "only one era and one small group of writers. . . . [that is,] the political history of Rome" from the early first century B.C. to the end of the second century A.D. (1967, 25). As for eighteenth-century influences, Trenchard and Gordon's *Cato's Letters* (1721) was well known, as were works by Molesworth, Molyneux, Macauley, Bolingbroke, and others (Colbourn, 3–20). Allen does not offer us anything more precise than his comment on nations "doomed to perpetual slavery" by giving up their liberties to tyrants, but we can, I think, safely read his reference as a republican one.

Note what Allen says next. The clash at Lexington in 1775 was "the first systematical and bloody attempt . . . to enslave America." He echoes the paranoia of Jefferson in the Declaration of Independence and Adams in "A Dissertation on the Canon and Feudal Law," a paranoia that Gordon Wood has quite rightly noted is endemic in the writings of the Revolutionaries (1982). Allen says that that event, in light of his reading in (apparently) the Whig, republican tradition, "thoroughly electrified my mind, and fully determined me to take part with my country" (5). This figure of electrification is not repeated or alluded to elsewhere in the *Narrative*, so it is difficult to ascertain how much to make of it. On one level, of course, Allen means that he was shocked or startled or thrilled by his perception that events in 1775 could be made comprehensible by his previous reading. At the same time, however, the figure invokes Benjamin Franklin, of whom, famously, Turgot wrote in 1778 on a bust of Franklin: "Eripuit coelo fulmen sceptrumque tyrannis" (He snatched the lightning from the sky and the scepter from tyrants). Simon Schama has noted how "the link between the fall of tyrants and celestial fire" in Turgot's inscription suggested "that liberty was a natural and hence ultimately irresistible force, and contributed further to a growing polarity between things natural . . . and things artificial" (46). Schama was writing about pre-Revolutionary France, but his insight is relevant here. Allen's "electrification" at the very beginning of his narrative overtly links three distinct elements: manhood, reading (in a Whig, republican tradition), and the American Revolution. Manhood, in this context, is natural, something to which Allen "arrived"; it is a natural state that requires only time to achieve. When Kant defines enlightenment, he does so in terms that suggest as well the importance and the inevitability of reaching adulthood: "Enlightenment is man's release from his self-incurred tutelage. Tutelage is man's inability to make use of his understanding without direction from another. . . . 'Have courage to use your own reason'—that is the motto of the enlightenment" (1). Allen's narrator is indeed "enlightened"—something else, not surprisingly, that electricity can do—at the moment his narrative begins.[5] Reading history from a Whig perspective is also presented as something of a natural process: Allen "acquainted [him]self with the general history of mankind," and unproblematically read therein the pattern of nations yielding liberty to tyrants. To "take part with my country," then—or, seen from the other side, to rebel against the king of England—follows naturally from these conditions; the conditions, we might say, naturally "electrise" Allen:

> To electrise plus or minus, no more needs to be known than this, that the parts of the tube or sphere that are rubbed, do, in the instant of the friction, attract the electrical fire, and therefore take it from the thing rubbing: the same parts immediately, as the friction upon them ceases, are disposed to give up the first they have received, to any body that has less. (Franklin 1908, II: 185)

Liberty, to switch metaphors, is contagious among Whig men, crossing—like sympathy or electricity itself—from person to person without regard to rank, national origin, or religion. Franklin, Kant once remarked, was a new Prometheus who had stolen fire from the heavens. It was a fire that could reach through books and events to convert or transform farm boys into exemplars of liberty.

Near the end of his narrative, Allen is converted again. Curiously, he inserts General John Burgoyne's 1777 Proclamation to the inhabitants of America "as a specimen of [England's] arrogance" (66–67). Burgoyne claims that the rebels are arbitrary, tyrannical, and unnatural, and he calls upon Americans to welcome and aid his troops in their tireless efforts to "re-establish . . . the blessings of a legal government" (67). In the narrative itself, his Proclamation comes on the heels of Allen's extended description of the many "murders and cruelties" (63) committed by the king's commanders and troops in America (46–63), and so is meant to reveal, ironically, the hypocrisy of England. Not only is England's spirit "opulent, puissant and haughty" (68), but in its "vanity" (70) it has no qualms about hypocritically adopting the language of senti-mental republicanism to achieve its enslavement of America. In using such language to describe the Tories, Burgoyne's Proclamation exposes the hypocrisy of phrases like "affecting interest" (66) and "friends to lib-erty" (67), both because Allen's extended description of Tory behavior belies their meaning and because Burgoyne himself ends the Proclama-tion by attempting to frighten Americans with his suggestion that he has "but to give stretch to the Indian forces under [his] direction (67) to overtake America. The "affecting interest" of friends, any sentimentalist could have told Burgoyne, cannot be moved by threats or intimidation.

The Proclamation initiates a three-page meditation by Allen, which he ends by declaring his true "feelings" for England: "as a nation I hate and despise you," he writes, despite the presence in the nation of some Englishmen "who still retain their virtue" (70). "Virtue, wisdom and policy," Allen points out, always, "in the nature of things," direct na-tional power, and when they are departed, as in England's case, then that nation's "glory is departed" (68). Severing the ties to England, as Jeffer-son and Paine had done in 1776, Allen then commits himself to a new affectional relationship: "My affections are frenchified" (70). The verb indicates, as did "electrified" earlier, a conversion from one state of being to another. Then, it was the mind that was altered; it was a way of look-ing at the world and at the affairs of men that changed. Now, it is the emotions, the affections, the heart. The feelings have changed.

Allen intends that this conversion be an analogue to the foreign pol-icy of the United States in 1778, that is, that he be understood as saying that his affections will be directed toward any state "courteous" enough to accept his feelings and sentiments. He is not saying that he has be-come French, or that he wishes to become French (although, indeed, he claims to be studying the French language). "Mankind are naturally too national," he asserts, and it is a function of commerce—on February 6, 1778, American commissioners in Paris signed two treaties with France, one political and one commercial—to permit countries "reciprocally [to] exchange . . . customs and manners," as well as "commodities" (71). Commerce, he says, echoing an English argument that goes back at least to *The Spectator*,[6] erases "the superstition of the mind" formed by local, regional, and national interests, and ties humankind more closely to-gether. Affections, like electricity and like trade, reach across space to re-form communities according to the dictates of the heart.[7]

It is at this moment, precisely, that Allen remarks "that I was the same man still." He was "still," in other words, a republican and a sentimentalist. These aspects of the self are essential to the persona depicted in the *Narrative*. They are the center or the core that Allen protected, when threatened, by adopting "stratagem[s]" or ruses. So, for example, in captivity Allen occasionally acted as if he was "delirious"; "my extreme circumstances at certain times, rendered it political to act in some measure the madman" (47). By doing so, he received better treatment from his captors, allowing his "blood" and "nerves" and "strength" to recruit themselves.[8] Because of his behavior, the British "gave out that [he] was crazy, and wholly unmanned," but Allen insists that his "vitals held sound" (47). Within his sentimental system, of course, it is they who have been "unmanned" by ambition, greed, and power.

His stratagems included lying, cursing extravagantly, acting insane, and dressing in rustic clothing. This behavior is linked, through the word "stratagem," to General Washington, whose "sagacity" at Princeton in early 1777 "suggested a stratagem to effect that which by force to him was at that time impracticable" (53), namely leaving his campfires burning and marching his men to the British rear where they attacked successfully. Like Washington's, Allen's stratagems were usually performed selflessly: when he felt extreme anxiety about his fate, for example, he concealed it from his fellow prisoners and from the enemy, hoping to "exhibit a good sample of American fortitude" in his "daring soldier-like manner" (26). In another instance, he wrote an affecting letter to Congress that he pretended to think would actually be sent; in the letter he described his ill treatment in captivity but urged Congress to retaliate "not according to the smallness of my character in America, but in proportion to the importance of the cause for which I suffered" (25). The letter, a British officer exultingly told him, was sent to Lord North instead of Congress. "I had come yankee over him," Allen smugly remarks, for the letter was supposed to go to North, where it might "intimidate the haughty English government" by showing the resolve of men like Allen, and where it might, as well, save Allen from hanging.

Allen extends the conception of his narrator as selfless through a series of biblical allusions, the only text that is specifically alluded to in the course of the *Narrative*. The allusions are rarely as dramatic as his demand at Fort Ticonderoga that the British commander surrender "In the name of the great Jehovah, and the Continental Congress" (7), but they serve the same purpose of elevating the action of the story to a grand, providential level. Hence, Allen's attack on Montreal was "a day of trouble" (13),[9] he and his men endured despicable conditions "About forty days" before their arrival at Falmouth (23), and General Howe's offer of a large tract of land on the New Hampshire grants resembled Satan's "offer of land to . . . Jesus Christ" (57). These allusions increase in frequency late in the narrative (see, for example, 58, 59, and 68), culminating in Allen's resurrection from the dead at the very end of the *Narrative*: arriving in Bennington on May 31, 1778, "I was to [the Green Mountain Boys] as one rose from the dead" (72).

Ethan Allen's metaphoric resurrection was (locally) into the arms of his feeling comrades—"now both their joy and mine was complete," he writes—and (nationally) into the "rural felicity" of "the rising states of America" (72). Allen rises, and so do the united states. Like Lazarus in the Gospel of John, Allen rises both as a type and as an exhibit. As a type, he stands in for the not-yet-completed Revolution in 1779: he shadows forth the triumphant union/reunion that will belong to Americans and, in a way, to all sentimental republicans throughout the world when the Revolution finally succeeds. As an exhibit—Lazarus is visual proof of Christ's mediating power for the doubting disciples and friends (John 11.7–44)—Allen stands as a character of or figure for the cluster of ideas his narrative tries to imprint, across space, on the reader's heart: liberty, sentiment, manliness, perseverance.

Exhibition, after all, is a figure that weaves itself in and out of Allen's *Narrative*.[10] Let me return to an incident I cited earlier. The two ministers who discussed "moral philosophy and christianity" with Allen before Pendennis Castle in 1775 led Allen to note that "such a rebel" as himself "was never before seen in England." He was indeed a "sight" (28). I hoped, he says in another instance, to "exhibit [in my behavior in captivity] a good sample of American fortitude" (26). Allen puts himself and others on display in *The Narrative of the Captivity of Colonel Ethan Allen*. From the "monsters" who seem "to wear a phiz of humanity" but are in reality "devils" (63), to the many officers and noncoms who display a true "magnanimity of soul" (60) in their physiognomy, Allen paints visual pictures meant to touch his readers' hearts. A letter he wrote on behalf of John Fell, a member of Congress imprisoned by the British, describes his intentions in the *Narrative* itself:

> I therefore wrote a letter to Gen. Robertson, (who commanded in [New York]) and being touched with the most sensible feelings of humanity, which dictated my pen to paint dying distress in such lively colours that

it wrought conviction even on the obduracy of a British General, and produced his order to remove the now honourable John Fell, Esqr. out of gaol. . . . (61)

Dictated by "sensible feelings," the pictures Allen paints in his *Narrative* are meant to be affecting, reaching through prejudice and indifference and lassitude to reshape conviction in the hearts of a people that, by 1779, have lost much of their enthusiasm for war.

As a self-biography, Allen's *Narrative* puts the "self" on exhibit in ways that Graydon's *Memoirs* does not. But, like Graydon, Allen is not interested in himself as original or unique: what makes him a sentimental patriot is precisely an emotional attitude that privileges community over isolation, society over solitude, passion over intellect. Allen is most human when he transcends his own conditions to locate a more powerful connection to other sentimental beings. What readers of his *Narrative* are meant to discover is not Allen but themselves, or, more accurately, the social, sentimental dimension of themselves as human beings. As I suggested earlier in my discussion of Graydon's *Memoirs*, Graydon's and Allen's conceptions of the self, though I have labeled them "Federalist" and "republican," are fundamentally compatible. Both writers resist the self as it will come to be figured by later writers, discovering ultimate meaning not inside the individual but elsewhere. They are, in this, like Jefferson and Adams, whose self-biographies similarly resist the self: "I am already tired of talking about myself," Jefferson sighs midway through his memoirs (43). That, beside Franklin, Graydon and Allen locate meaning elsewhere than in the individual suggests the variety of options open to self-biographers in the early national period, most of whom were wary of according the "self" the power to shape its own destiny.

PART *Two*

The Emergence of Autobiography

In part two, I focus on a handful of self-biographies that begin to adopt the assumptions and conventions of autobiography as I have defined that genre. Stephen Burroughs imagines people as being able to adopt masks or take on characters, though he insists—how seriously depends on one's reading of the text—that behind those masks lies a core or central self. He anticipates autobiography's focus on inwardness. K. White and Elizabeth Fisher imagine personal identity as oppositional, eccentric, and self-directed, anticipating autobiography's focus on an independent self. Like White and Fisher, John Fitch imagines personal identity as oppositional and eccentric, and to justify or explain that eccentricity he pushes hard on the concept of his own natural originality or singularity, anticipating autobiography's fascination with the self as its own moral source. All four writers reveal the emergence of individualized personality, rather than the social roles or typed personhood characteristic of earlier self-biography. Unlike Franklin in his *History of My Life*, these writers probe a self defined inwardly, not outwardly by social expectations, books, class status, or family roles. Finally, in chapter 9, I survey the decade of the 1820s, tracing the fitful emergence of those ideas in several key antebellum autobiographies, examples of what is by the end of the first third of the century the fully emerged genre of autobiography.

❧ 6 ❧

The Enigmatic Character

of Stephen Burroughs

IN THE LAST CHAPTER OF *Memoirs of Stephen Burroughs*, the author arrives in 1794 in the southernmost state of the union, Georgia. He was, he tells us, complying with the solicitations of an old college friend, a lawyer, in hopes of "realizing . . . a sufficiency of money" to support his (Burroughs's) wife and three children. He does not tell us what occupation or enterprise his friend had in mind for him, although previously Burroughs had performed "the office of a physician on board [a] ship" (37), taught school in at least four different communities in the north, posed as a minister, and served more than three years in prison for counterfeiting (on one occasion) and "open lewdness" (on another). Burroughs was only twenty-nine years old. The friend, it turns out, had left Georgia and was dying or already dead in South Carolina. Burroughs, having begged, borrowed, and speculated his way from Long Island to Georgia, "now fancied the end of [his] trying pilgrimage had arrived, and that I should here find a resting place from further trouble" (340). He has bottomed out, geographically, socially, and financially.

But, as so often happens in Burroughs's narrative, an apparent ending generates a new beginning. Down and out, Burroughs hears that an "academy" in the nearby village of Washington is in need of a rector. He offers—in language that I shall return to later in this chapter—"to act in the capacity of Rector of the academy." The trustee to whom he makes this offer asks Burroughs for his credentials. "I . . . observed," Burroughs laconically responds, "that my credentials were in my head" (341). His assertion is, of course, revolutionary. In eighteenth-century Anglo-America, "credentials" came in many forms: family connections, which signified social status and influence; dress and speech, which signified social class and occupation and (perhaps) economic self-sufficiency; reputation, which signified the conception one's neighbors or colleagues or peers developed of a person over time; and so forth.[1] An inherent, inward sense of self-worth was not, generally, a credential. It was, in fact, as I have argued, a sign of ambition that upper-class white men like Adams and Jefferson tried to resist in order to mold themselves to a republican or classical or Christian ideal,[2] and that most lower-class white men, most women, and most African-Americans stifled in order to perform their determined roles in a classist, sexist, and racist culture.

Burroughs landed the job. From his position as schoolmaster, he then moved on to become a land surveyor in Indian territory for Robert Morris. "This circumstance opened a new field for my enterprise," Burroughs remarks with some understatement. Given what we know of Burroughs at this point in the narrative, it comes as no surprise that he should find his way into the Yazoo land fraud. When it is exposed and Morris is "embarrassed" (348), Burroughs returns to his family home in New Hampshire only to fade, in the editor's account of Burroughs's present-day (in 1804) whereabouts, into rumor and mythology: "it is hazardous to state anything with certainty relative to this extraordinary man" (367).

Stephen Burroughs pushes at the limits of his culture's conception of identity. Where Crèvecoeur, Graydon, Rush, Allen, and Franklin attempt, in their different ways, to ground the self in an external, credible, stable conception of identity, Burroughs welcomes the self as a theatrical production, a rough-hewn subjectivity that is always in the process of formation. Caught posing as a minister, Burroughs revealingly remarks: "I . . . violated that principle of veracity which we implicitly pledge ourselves to maintain towards each other . . . as a general thing in society" (67). Society, Burroughs recognizes, functions smoothly only because we agree to "maintain" consistent stories about ourselves. On a Sunday morning, when we see a man in the pulpit delivering a sermon to a church congregation, we trust that the man is a minister: the church hired him; he cites the Bible; he claims, in effect, to be a minister. Never mind, in the case of Burroughs, that his clothing is "gay," even gaudy. He has other "credentials" for the position. When the congregation learns that he is posing as a minister—that he lacks the proper credentials—Burroughs is chased across the countryside. His parishioners feel cheated. Burroughs has told them he is something that he is not. That episode functions as a synecdoche for Burroughs's conception of selfhood in *Memoirs*: Burroughs must always tell us that he is something—a minister, a dutiful son, a loving husband, a sensitive friend—even though the "external" credentials for those selves or aspects of the self go missing. What he says he is and what he "says" he is (through description, dress, style, etc.) are always two different things. Burroughs accepts that fact; he rests content in the knowledge that, while (he claims) what he says he is is stable, what he appears to be constantly shifts. There is no sure ground on which the self can anchor itself. Self-consciously, with what seems to be a bemused sense of his narrative project, Burroughs fabricates himself in language, anticipating the performative gesture of narrative self-creation of Thoreau much more than he repeats or mimics the description of the social creation of identity in Franklin. His imprisonment in the 1780s, ironically similar to Thoreau's later retreat to Walden, is a metaphor for where and how the self can begin to find its own "credentials."

ॐ

Memoirs of Stephen Burroughs exists in at least three distinct published forms. The first volume of the narrative, which recounts Burroughs's youth, education, posturing as a minister, involvement with counterfeiters, three-year imprisonment for passing counterfeit notes, and release from prison, was published in 1798 in Hanover, Hew Hampshire. The second volume, which recounts Burroughs's tribulations as a teacher, his trial on a charge of rape, and his involvement in the Yazoo land fraud, was published in Boston in 1804. Subsequently, beginning in 1811, the two volumes were usually published together as one complete text. Volume one, it could be argued, is a separate and complete text, removed from the second volume in time, place of publication, and even theme. It is structured around Burroughs's attempts to escape both literal punishment and readers' scorn, and moves eloquently, if only proleptically, toward a proposed "journey to the westward" (219) that had already begun to take on mythic dimensions in American literature by 1798.

Volume one also was published in an abbreviated form in Hudson, New York, in 1809 (and many times thereafter) under the title *Sketch of the Life of Stephen Burroughs*. The *Sketch* recounts Burroughs's life only through his imprisonment for passing counterfeit money and his subsequent rumination on the psychological effects of imprisonment. To speak of Burroughs's "story," then, is to disregard the three versions in which that story became available in the years between 1798 and 1811: the shortened *Sketch*, which ends with Burroughs being flogged for his attempted escape from Castle Island; the longer volume one of *Memoirs of Stephen Burroughs*, which ends with Burroughs's meditations on identity, penal reform, and self-reform; and the combined two-volume *Memoirs of Stephen Burroughs*, which ends with Burroughs's own "embarrassment" in connection with the Yazoo land fraud and his disappearance, recounted in the editor's appendix, into ambiguity and rumor.

I am most interested in this last text. In this chapter, as elsewhere in this book, I am less interested in questions about actual reception—where the different textual versions of Burroughs's story would be crucial—than in questions about rhetorical strategy and authors' constructions of "ideal" readers (Iser). The fullest version of Burroughs's life provides the fullest evidence we have for Burroughs's conception of himself.

Burroughs's *Memoirs* is constructed as a series of letters, recalling Crèvecoeur's fictional *Letters*. Like that narrative, *Memoirs* is technically a one-way correspondence: the author writes only to the unnamed correspondent who may or may not be the editor/publisher of the narrative, but who in any case never formally responds with letters of his own.[3] Volume one is, in fact, a single enclosure within a July 25, 1794, letter that Burroughs wrote to his "Friend, who had requested a Narrative of his Life." Burroughs claims to have written the long narrative in lieu of relating it verbally: "it being more convenient to peruse it at your leisure, than to listen to the dull tale of egotisms which I must make use of in a verbal relation" (1). Note that a written relation is neither better nor worse than a verbal one; it is simply more "convenient." A written text is useful because it gives the reader control over the pace of the narrative.[4] The relation is needed, Burroughs tells us, because the friend has claimed that Burroughs's "character . . . is an enigma" (1). Burroughs claims, in other words, to construct his story in response to the notion that his character is a riddle, an obscure speech or writing. A "puzzling, ambiguous [and] inexplicable" (*American Heritage Dictionary*) character is to be explained through the (hopefully) straightforward and clear narrative that follows.

Volume two picks up the rhetorical strategy seamlessly, but, whereas volume one ends with Burroughs's (printed) signature, volume two ends with the complete withdrawal of the author from the text. In a postscript—the rhetoric of letter writing continued—"the proprietor of the manuscript" informs us that Burroughs has abandoned the text and is now living, happily, in lower Canada. A subsequent appendix, written by the publisher or editor or "proprietor" (it is not clear which), informs us that Burroughs might or might not have taken to counterfeiting in Canada and that he might well have continued and be continuing "in his mad career" (367).[5] No one knows. The story or explanation of his enigmatic character is left entirely in the readers' hands, as author and editor/publisher/proprietor absolve themselves of the responsibility of explaining to what end Burroughs's actions have tended.

Internally, *Memoirs* also makes extensive use of letters. Nearly fifty letters are scattered throughout the text, many of them from Burroughs himself attesting to his "character" both as an author and as a person. Others attest to Burroughs's motives or behavior from the sentimental or sympathetic perspective of family members and friends. Modern-day readers would tend to read the letters not written by Burroughs himself as weak evidence to support his explanation of his enigmatical self. Burroughs, however, operates very much within the sentimental discourse that shaped and defined Allen's narrative, and hence the letters by (prejudiced) family members and friends speak—he hopes—naturally and artlessly to his character.

Burroughs's method is, then, epistolary and sentimental. The sentimentality is pervasive: Burroughs repeatedly appeals to his readers in terms of vibrations (144), sensibility (42), "the language of nature" (226), "the language of the heart" (162), "the weakness of a woman" (11), "propensities, feelings, and sentiments" (59), the "harmony of friendship" (77), "the shock of electricity" (180), "inward sensations" and "shower[s] of tears" (332). He uses, in short, the full panoply of terms available to the late-eighteenth-century sentimentalist. Several times, he reaches emotional pitches at which language utterly fails him:

> This intelligence was like heaven's artillery, charged with tenfold vim. The wheels of nature ran backward! The blood curdled in my veins, and I fell almost senseless into a chair! ... God of nature! what greater scenes of distress are reserved in store? What sharper arrows yet remain in thy quiver? .... May I hide myself with a mantle of darkness, and retire from the stage of action, into eternal obscurity. (46)

The second (long) ellipsis is Burroughs's, and it draws upon the stock, sentimental moment when language proves inadequate to the emotions of a woman or man of feeling. "There is a language of the heart which we cannot express, it so far exceeds the descriptive power of speech" (101).

For Burroughs, this sentimentality is the key to understanding his character. He remarks near the end of volume one that scientific objectivity, feeling "indifferent towards an object" of investigation, prevents a person from gaining a "true estimate" of that object. "We must feel interested in an object," he says, "in order to call forth our attention towards it, sufficiently to examine its merits. When we feel indifferent towards an object, we pay no attention to it, and of course remain ignorant respecting it; therefore, are incapable of forming a just estimate concerning it" (216). Most commentators on Burroughs's *Memoirs* sense that he is playing a confidence game, of sorts; Jay Fliegelman writes that *Memoirs* "reads, in its shamelessly self-interested way, as a plea to the new nation to embrace the new age of deception and invention" (1982, 245).[6] Fliegelman's own, later meditation in *Declaring Independence* on the tension in Revolutionary America between sincerity and deception, naturalness and acting, stable selves and self-invention, focuses on the problem that Burroughs foregrounds: are we to read him objectively in terms of his external actions, or are we to read him sympathetically in terms of his motivations, desires, ideas? Burroughs himself insists upon the latter, and in doing so will articulate a vision of selfhood that, like John Fitch's, radically democratizes the self. Burroughs's self is not radically autonomous, as (I will argue in the next chapter) Fitch's theoretically is, but it has been freed from imitation and emulation, as well as from the institutional authorities on which imitation and emulation were based. "His autobiography actually implied a sweeping rejection of traditional dogmas and hierarchies in favor of an egalitarian social order based on natural reason and fraternal benevolence," Daniel Cohen perceptively remarks (160). The two elements of his method that I have discussed thus far, the epistolary and the sentimental, depend upon each other, then. Burroughs is both literally and metaphorically writing to a "friend" in his *Memoirs*: his correspondent is one friend who is in need of a clearer picture of Burroughs's "character," and the sentimental reader is another. Of course, this latter reader, in order to be a "friend," must be sentimental; reading objectively, he or she will see Burroughs's character only from the outside, as a counterfeiter, a rapist, a con man. The problem, as Fliegelman understands so well, is that the line between "character" as an expression of inner selfhood (revealed by behavior, by emotions, even by handwriting[7]) and "character" as a persona or actor (a character in a novel or drama) is very much a concern for late-eighteenth-century orators and writers. Indeed, as Felicity Nussbaum has written about eighteenth-century England, "the crisis of 'character' . . . surfaces in part as a struggle to debate the meanings of the word and its public manifestations" (107).

ॐ

If Burroughs's method centers on letters and sentimentality, the story that he constructs to explain his enigmatic behavior centers on education. Burroughs notes that he begins his narration with apparently "insipid anecdotes of [his] childish years" because "the greatest events depend on circumstances so minute, that they often pass unobserved" (4).[8] His attention to the details of his childhood reveals three main errors in his education: he was educated with a Presbyterian "rigor" by his father, a method that ill suited his "volatile, impatient temper of mind" and forced his spirits to seek release in practical jokes, hijinks, and extravagance; he read too many novels, which led his "mind from the plain simple path of nature, into the airy regions of fancy" (5);[9] and he formed his early character in imitation of schoolmates who, like him, were rebellious and unmotivated. All three errors suggest, implicitly, some form of educational reform, and can be seen as part and parcel of the project of educational reform that many of Burroughs's contemporaries, like Franklin, Jefferson, Noah Webster, and Judith Sargent Murray, advanced in the 1780s and 1790s. His father's mistake of trying to squelch Burroughs's natural "temper of mind" suggests that educators (and parents) should be nurturing, rather than tyrannical (see Fliegelman 1982, 9–35); his own immersion in novels, and his subsequent confusion between imagination and reality, suggests that students need to be led carefully through a broad course of reading;[10] and his imitation of his schoolmates suggests that teachers must "inform [the] judgment" rather than impose "dictatorial dogmas" or "lessons of reason" (6).

Waxing eloquent on his own miseducation in chapter 1 of *Memoirs*, Burroughs tells the story of how he, as a schoolteacher, once solved the problem of an unruly student. The student, named Dodge—metaphorical, perhaps, of the eccentric tendencies of the youth—"had been expelled from all the schools in the country." Rather than taking a hard line with him, Burroughs places him in front of the class, insisting to him that he really does "esteem" his "merit." Astonished, Dodge responds with two weeks of exemplary behavior, only to fall into dissipation by "scandalously insult[ing] some young women." Burroughs pretends not to believe the charges against his pupil; Dodge almost faints when he sees that Burroughs's trust in him is unshaken. After that, Dodge remains an exemplary student.

It is this sort of story, exactly, that makes readers suspicious of Burroughs's motives as a writer. The story, after all, is told proleptically. Before Burroughs (supposedly) reclaims a wayward youth accused of scandalous behavior, he himself becomes a wayward youth accused of scandalous behavior. Implicitly, he suggests that his own behavior could have been modified or curtailed by the influence of a sensitive monitor of the sort that he himself (supposedly) eventually became. To suggest this is to deflect, in advance, some of the responsibility for his "lewd" behavior onto others: parents, educators, and neighbors who did not understand him. Like Elizabeth Fisher, Burroughs is a victim. Second, the story suggests that education is based upon deception: Burroughs disbelieves a report that is apparently true, in the interest of shaping or molding Dodge to his own specifications. The model here is no doubt Rousseau, who insists not only that no punishment should be inflicted upon children but that a student's natural propensity to goodness be encouraged even by deception.[11] The instructor in this model acts as a "hidden hand," molding the student's "natural" self through unseen motions. Such a sympathetic, gentle pedagogy contrasts, of course, with Burroughs's own education, during the course of which he was beaten, bullied, and controlled. Burroughs suggests that his miseducation made him what he was, an unnatural member of society, while Dodge's fortunate education under his shaping hands permitted Dodge to return with dignity to his true self.

Although Burroughs impersonates a doctor and a minister early in his career, he considers schoolteaching his true calling. In the course of *Memoirs*, he teaches in no less than five different towns. This interest in education is, in and of itself, not remarkable: many of the self-biographies written in the late eighteenth century focus on education, particularly its role in shaping the developing self. Graydon, Rush, and Franklin are typical, as (on the English side) is Gibbon. However, what is new in Burroughs's account is the insistence that, following Rousseau, the natural self is warped or deformed by the pressure of traditional pedagogical methods, whether those methods are religious (his father's "presbyterian rigor") or formal and classical (he leaves Dartmouth because his tutors persecute him). This does not mean that Burroughs, any more than Rousseau, gives up on education; instead, it drives him to contemplate educational reform. As teachers, he remarks near the end of chapter 1, "our commands . . . ought to be reasonable, humane, and parental, calculated to promote, not only the good of the subject of our government [i.e., the pupil], but likewise embracing for their object, the benefit of the whole community" (8). The teacher, as well as the parent, Burroughs suggests, must be affective, humane, sociable, and noncoercive. As Jay Fliegelman puts it, "For [his] authority to be effective—in the broadest sense of establishing normative values—it must be grounded on filial 'esteem,' perhaps the most crucial word in the Lockean lexicon" (1982, 13).

Fliegelman has traced the revolution in the late eighteenth century from a patriarchal model of the family and education—Burroughs's father's "rigor" might be seen as typical of that older model—to an affectional one (1982). On a figurative level, Fliegelman argues, that revolution can be detected as a shift from the image of the Prodigal Son, owing delayed obedience to the father, to the image of the questing pilgrim, owing obedience to God or nature or (in its final romantic formation) the potential inner self. Throughout *Memoirs*, Burroughs's parents deploy the image of the Prodigal Son both to explain what has happened in their family and to urge Stephen to return to them and to their values. In 1787, while the states are beginning to ratify the Constitution and while their son is nearing the end of his three-year confinement on Castle Island, Burroughs's parents write a pathetic letter to him in which they cast themselves as the Prodigal's parents:

[we] consider you as being lost to God, to your parents, and to your generation. . . . But we fully believe, that our times and changes are in God's hands. . . . It would be acceptable to us, to have a line from you, specifying the state of your mind, and what your purposes are, in relation to your future pursuits. In the meantime, take this as a testimony of love intermingled with the most heartfelt grief and anguish, from your afflicted and sorrowful parents. (174)

Burroughs is ambivalent in that role. On the one hand, as he writes in response to that letter, his "most sincere desire" in life is to see his parents happy. Volume two even ends with Burroughs's assertion in 1797 that he has "tumbled at last into the bosom of [his] family. I now behold around my fireside, my wife and children, parents and sisters, with plea-sure pictured on every countenance" (363). In one ending, the romance of a family united apparently caps the diffusive, eccentric journeying of this prodigal son. But, on the other hand, Burroughs continues to wan-der from 1787 to 1797, living with a sympathetic uncle rather than with his parents (and marrying that uncle's daughter), leaving his wife and son to journey to Long Island, Georgia, and the West, and writing home only to extenuate his conduct. In the appendix, the editor/publisher/ proprietor informs us that the idyllic family romance of 1797 soon came to an end: "About a year [later], a sense of propriety and duty obliged the disappointed and dejected father to notify [a] friend, that he had lost all confidence in his son" (367). In this other ending, the "mad career" of a kind of modern pilgrim, restless and cut loose from family, religion, and society, continues on its eccentric course.

Burroughs's attitude that education must be affective, humane, so-ciable, and noncoercive can be seen more clearly in the long episode in volume two in which he attempts to begin a subscription library. I have implied at several points that books and libraries served both a real and a metaphoric function for many eighteenth-century self-biographers. For Franklin, books are a food that metaphorically nourishes the mind. At one point, he even makes the metaphor literal, describing how he saved money by not eating meat and then used those savings to purchase more books (1320). For others, like Rush, they are a form of sociability that sustains the self when alone. For many, including Burroughs, they are also a sign of the spread of Enlightenment values, of the light of knowledge itself. "By 1765," Michael Warner writes, contemplating John Adams's *Dissertation on the Canon and Feudal Law* (1765), "print had come to be seen as indispensable to political life, and could appear to men such as Adams to be the primary agent of world emancipation" (32). In 1771, Franklin wrote that the subscription libraries he helped to form in the 1730s "have improv'd the general Conversation of the Amer-icans, made the common Tradesmen and Farmers as intelligent as most Gentlemen from other Countries, and perhaps have contributed in some degree to the Stand so generally made throughout the Colonies in Defence of their Privileges" (1372).

One of Burroughs's teaching positions, as he says in volume two, was in a school in Bridgehampton on Long Island. Burroughs sets the "scene" for us by describing the "leading characters" (267) in town, including Aaron Woolworth, the minister, and Elia Halsey, a reasonable though sometimes passionate friend. The character of the townspeople themselves is "uniform, contracted, and uninformed. . . . This people are at the lowest ebb in their improvements, either in agriculture, manufacture, or domestic economy. They are," Burroughs concludes, "the genuine picture of ancient time, when their land was first settled by its white inhabitants. These effects are produced, in great degree, by their insular situation" (271–272). His school thriving and he friends with the minister and other local figures, Burroughs hatches a scheme to raise money to buy books for the children of the district. Insularity, Burroughs knows, can be overcome by reading, as well as (the eighteenth century argued) by travel and commerce. Halsey encourages him to proceed, pointing out, however, that Woolworth has already tried to establish a local library. Woolworth failed, Halsey says, because he set the subscription rate too high and because the townspeople feared that he would buy only "books in divinity" (280). When approached by Burroughs, Woolworth indicates that Burroughs should pursue his scheme, and that he, too, will subscribe if it becomes successful.

Burroughs raises forty pounds, promising subscribers a library dominated by "histories, and books of information on secular subjects" (283), and a committee is formed to purchase such books. Woolworth and Burroughs are both placed on the committee. Woolworth "immediately" produces a catalogue of books—mainly theological—to which all the members of the committee except Burroughs silently submit. They know their places. However, Burroughs protests that the list is inappropriate for the townspeople, who need their narrow views enlarged. Woolworth responds that "his people" do not know what they want; as their "spokesman," he understands "what books would suit them" (284). A long, complex series of negotiations ensues, with Woolworth taking a patriarchal view of his relation to the "people" and Burroughs arguing that the subscribers have a right "to purchase such books with [their] money as [they wish]. . . . This [is] a right which we inherited from nature, and which we [do] not intend to give up" (291). What is at stake in this episode, of course, is the question of who shall lead the new republic: traditional authority figures—ministers and aristocrats—or the "people" themselves. For Burroughs, as for H. H. Brackenridge and Jefferson and Adams and Brown, this question is central to the new republic's definition of itself.

It is a local battle that Burroughs cannot win. Woolworth turns against him "with contempt," and the townspeople do not have the courage to go against their minister. Burroughs's list of titles, which included Hume's *History of England* (1778), Plutarch's *Lives*, and Henry Brooke's collected works (4 vols., 1778), is ignored by Woolworth, and Jonathan Edwards's *History of the Work of Redemption* and tracts on baptism lead the list of titles to be purchased. Ironically, Burroughs discovers a few months later that Edward Bancroft's *History of Charles Wentworth* has snuck into the collection, and he gleefully points out that its morality runs counter to Woolworth's professed principles. The authorities—religious and civil—turn their focus on Burroughs then, threatening him with civil action for slander and eventually trumping up charges of rape against him. At trial, the jury finds him innocent of rape but guilty of the lesser charge of "assault." He pays the fine and leaves Bridge-hampton for good.

ॐ

Education is the central theme of Burroughs's *Memoirs*. Burroughs writes from the point of view of an eccentric outsider who comes to see how the nation really and truly operates. Because he does, it seems to me persuasive to read the narrative within a constellation of ideas that mark the narrative as typical of the anxious waning years of the century: representation, authenticity, deception, counterfeiting, causation, contingency, liberty, and freedom. Burroughs, it seems clear to me, both engaged these issues at the level of individual behavior and critiqued them as social virtues/vices. He lived them (he claims), and he wrote critically of them in his *Memoirs*.

Representation was, of course, central to the polity of the new nation. To adduce this, one could point to numerous late-eighteenth-century sites: the Constitution, the debates surrounding it in 1787–1788,[12] the anxiety over linguistic representation (Gustafson, 19–36; Kramer; David Simpson), the concern for accurate geographic representations of the United States and its adjoining territories, and so on. The question of the "relationship between aesthetic or semiotic representation (things that 'stand for' other things) and political representation (persons who 'act for' other persons)" is obviously not a simple one (Mitchell, 11). But I think I can depend here on a substantial body of criticism[13] to assert that the anxiety was pervasive. Indeed, my argument in this book is that selfhood itself was a site that post-Revolutionary culture attempted to represent in a variety of ways, some of which were aligned with romantic representations that would become dominant in the nineteenth century, some of which looked back to more traditional representations.

For Burroughs, representation is an issue at several points. I have already described his battle with Aaron Woolworth, in which Burroughs argues that the "people" themselves should directly enunciate their rights, without representation, and Woolworth argues that appropriate representatives should speak for them. Burroughs has in mind something like Paine's argument in *The Rights of Man, Part Two* (1792):

> Representation was a thing unknown in the ancient democracies. In those the mass of people met and enacted laws (grammatically speaking) in the first person. . . . It was the want of some method to consolidate the parts of society, after it became too populous, and too extensive for the democratical form . . . that afforded opportunities to . . . unnatural modes of government to begin. (1995, 564–565)

If America should ever need representatives, Burroughs suggests, they should not be ministerial or aristocratic or hereditary, but elected. Ideally, the people should simply speak for themselves.

More often, however, Burroughs treats representation as a social construct, not a political one. When he decides to impersonate a minister, early in his career, he considers carefully how, lacking qualifications, he should represent himself: change his name, move to a town where his family is not known, appropriate ten sermons written by his father, and "fortif[y his] countenance with all [his] resolution" (50). What he cannot change is his "curious dress" of a gray coat, green vest, and red velvet breeches; being broke, he decides that he "must make the best of it" (48). In the Massachusetts community that hires him, Pelham, elders and townspeople notice his dress—the representation of a dandy—but the force of Burroughs's characterization, which comes to include his mouthing of the proper religious "orthodoxy" (51) in interviews and in the pulpit, obviates the visual evidence that he is not a minister.[14]

The townspeople first become suspicious of this interloper when they notice that he always has a sermon ready on short notice. Given that Burroughs is only nineteen at the time, they find this remarkable. He has apparently overplayed his role. When a church elder catches a glimpse of his sermon notes, written in his father's "character," Burroughs is forced to admit that, occasionally, he has read someone else's sermon from the pulpit. The elders set him the task on the following

Sunday of lecturing on a prescribed biblical passage, Joshua 9.5: "And old shoes and clouted upon their feet, and old garments upon them." The passage is an ironic one, though we cannot tell as readers if the elders are being ironic or if Burroughs (as the author of *Memoirs*) is being ironic. In Joshua 9, Joshua is deceived by the Gibeonites, who, seeing what Israel has done to their neighbors in Jericho and Ai, dress themselves in old clothes and shoes and load their donkeys with moldy bread. When they appear thus in Joshua's camp, they claim that they have come from afar and extort a pledge from him and the other princes that they will watch over them. When Joshua finds out that he has been tricked by the Gibeonites' disguise, he insists that he must abide by the pledge and the oath that sealed it, but he curses the Gibeonites and enslaves them as "bondmen, and hewers of wood and drawers of water for the house of my God" (9.23).

In the pulpit, Burroughs explores the passage as a statement about deception: the Gibeonites were jealous of the Israelites, they hid that "odious and hateful" attitude under a disguise, and thus their deception epitomizes mankind's effort to cover over or disguise the "doleful monster" inside all of us. Put off your disguises, he urges the congregation, and put on the gospel of peace. This seems to satisfy the congregation, but it cannot satisfy us, since we cannot discern the appropriate target of irony. Did the elders intend Burroughs to be the target, marking him as a Gibeonite (disguised; apparently from afar, but in reality a neighbor; etc.) who becomes their "servant" in his ministerial guise? Or did Burroughs invent or adapt the incident to his own ironic purposes, playfully turning the congregation into Gibeonites who are deceptive in their hearts while he, a Joshua, passes judgment on them from above? We cannot tell. Having passed the literal test, Burroughs performs a final makeover into a minister by purchasing new clothes and continues to minister to the people.

His deception is fully revealed only when an old friend calls him by his real name. He goes into hiding to escape suspicion, but this only inflames the townspeople, who now recollect that Burroughs "ever had a very deceitful look" on his face (66). After a brief chase, he is cornered in a barn (the site of his published "Haymow Sermon"), only to make a final escape from a tavern where, as a truce, Burroughs was to buy a round of drinks. Burroughs embeds a two-sided commentary on this entire episode in the scene at the barn. The townspeople hold that Burroughs deceived them: he is not an authentic minister, they claim, and like the Gibeonites he practiced a deception on them. On the other hand, a "bystander" holds that Burroughs was engaged to preach, he preached and was paid, and so both parties should be happy (70–72). The townspeople's concern is an old one: Cotton Mather writes in *Magnalia Christi Americana* (1702) of several cases of "wolves in sheep's clothing" (VII: 30), including that of Samuel May, who "enchanted" the citizens of Boston in 1699 with his stolen sermons; and Franklin in his *History* recounts the controversy in Philadelphia over a young Irish preacher, Hemphill, whom Franklin supports (he gives "practical" sermons, which Franklin likes, but which the "old clergy" perceive as heterodox) even after it is discovered that he, too, has been delivering stolen sermons. Mather, of course, sees only sin and deception in Samuel May's behavior: he represented himself as something he was not. Franklin sees only usefulness and economy in Hemphill's behavior: "I rather approv'd of his giving us good Sermons compos'd by others, than bad ones of his own Manufacture" (1400). This shift or transformation from imposture as sin to imposture as role playing is a feature of the long eighteenth century, and Burroughs dramatizes a late instance of it superbly. Is virtue an internal feature, he asks, or is it located in external behavior? The Pelhamites (and Cotton Mather) argue that it is internal: your self is equivalent to the roles to which God (or society or birth) has called you. To pretend otherwise, like the Gibeonites, is to sin. Franklin believes that virtue is located in behavior—he is a made, a "constructed," man—but that that behavior is socially constructed: "In order to secure my Credit and Character as a Tradesman, I took care not only to be in Reality Industrious & frugal, but to avoid all Appearance to the Contrary" (1369). Franklin's self requires a society to call itself into being. Burroughs's position is similar to Franklin's in that he understands that selfhood is located in behavior and that behavior can be modified to enact a desired self; but Burroughs goes beyond Franklin in claiming that one's motivation to enact a desired self is not social but private: "I have aimed at nothing but a bare supply of the necessaries of life" (67), he says about his motivation; this deception was designed "to answer the present calls of nature" (47).

Burroughs is aware that the private internal self and the public external self are separable, and that the public self can be constructed or manipulated. He often uses the language of theatrical role playing to describe his behavior: "Here I had a new situation before me, and another part to act" (23); my father "let me loose upon the broad theater of the world, to act my part according to my abilities" (30); in a court proceeding he notes "the perfect propriety with which every character had played his part" (336).[15] He probes the problem of why the two selves do not coincide: "We cannot discern the operation of the human heart in man, until we are in such a situation, as to prevent his wearing a disguise. This situation must be very abject, and then we become of so little consequence in society, that the notice of man is removed from us, and he acts in our presence without disguise" (129).[16] Disguises, Burroughs suggests, are forced on us by society; with others' eyes upon us, a person must of necessity "act" a role, one that does not coincide with her or his "heart," our true inward self. It is no wonder that Burroughs so often presents himself as a victim in his story: he wants us to see that his outward, external behavior is "caused" by others, while he strives at the same time to reveal the enigmatic "heart" that is his true self.

Hence, for example, Burroughs says near the beginning of the episode dealing with his involvement with a counterfeiting ring that "all the plausible experiments which were performed by Philips [the counterfeiter] . . . were a series of the most consummate duplicities, which was ever performed." Where others, including many modern critics of his *Memoirs*, see him as a hardened counterfeiter, Burroughs actually asks his readers to see a dupe who is drawn into counterfeiting through the machinations of an evil man, Philips. Burroughs is simply a victim. Philips, Burroughs reports, "had the entire command of his feelings, so that his countenance or actions never betrayed his inward sensations . . . [and he was] lost to all feelings of fidelity, either towards the public . . . or towards individuals" (62). Philips, not Burroughs, is the modern nightmare, the Confidence Man or Flem Snopes who, without the (possibly) redeeming humor of a Simon Suggs, exploits and abuses his fellow man. However, we should note, Philips's exploitation of Burroughs is merely an extension of the sort of objectification that Burroughs sees society performing at all levels: society always forces us to wear a disguise. "[The] world view typical of the anti-masquerade authors [like many of Burroughs's contemporary critics], characterized everywhere by a fear of ontological promiscuity and a desire for firm conceptual boundaries, was itself distinctly modern, and becoming increasingly pervasive in the eighteenth century," Terry Castle has written (102). Philips presents an extreme case of the sort of objectification we all perform, and have performed upon us, as social beings in the modern world.

Philips is a literal counterfeiter of money, Burroughs only a metaphorical counterfeiter of social roles. After being run out of Pelham, Burroughs takes up with a friend in Pelham—he refers to him as Lysander—who has also been enchanted by Philips's deception. Lysander becomes, under Philips's tutelage, an actual counterfeiter, and he urges Burroughs to pass counterfeit coins for him. Burroughs refuses. Lysander responds with a specious defense of counterfeiting, insisting that since he "intends" to work no harm on others, he will break no law in passing false coins. Money, Lysander tells Burroughs, "'is of no consequence, only as we, by mutual agreement, annex to it a nominal value, as the representation of money'" (83). People who do not know any better will accord the false representation a real value. The analogy here to Burroughs's own recent "representation" in Pelham is signficant, of course, as is the fact that he is not forced to "pay" (through punishment) for the counterfeit behavior, while he will be forced to "pay" (three years in prison) for the act of passing counterfeit coins not of his own making.[17]

Burroughs tells us that Lysander's "arguments convinced [him], unfounded as they were" (84). The arguments apparently do not seem so convincing to Lysander either, since, as Larzer Ziff has pointed out, Lysander seems "doubtful that the coins will pass and sufficiently certain that Burroughs, if apprehended, will nevertheless not betray him" (65). We find, Lysander says about money, that "the only thing necessary to make a matter valuable, is to induce the world to deem it so" (83). Burroughs esteems his friend, reporting that "the sentiment of friendship [is] the uppermost object in [his] understanding" (87). Friendship causes him to accept the specious arguments. He is a victim of Lysander's plotting. Burroughs passes the false coins, is apprehended within minutes, tried, and convicted.

When it is discovered that he duped the Pelhamites and tried to pass counterfeit money, Burroughs is brought within the near-constant scrutiny of the penal system,[18] and his behavior is subjected to constant suspicion. Just as Franklin learns that the appearance of virtue can accrue credit and reputation ("character"), so Burroughs learns that deception and the appearance of deception accrues scrutiny and suspicion. Like James Moody, Burroughs becomes distrusted, an object of fear, alarm, and interest. "Many people visited me daily, out of curiosity, to see a character entirely new," he reports (93). Like Allen in England, Burroughs is a "sight" or curious exhibit. No matter what he tells these visitors, they disbelieve his words:

I do believe, if I had set out with warmth to prove to the world that I was a man, and not a woman, that a great number, from the circumstance, would have been able at once to look through the deception which I was endeavoring to lay them under, and known for certainty that I was, in reality, a woman; so strong was the desire of mankind, at that day, to elude my deceptions, which they thought I was master of, to the utmost degree. (94)

Like Moody and Franklin and Deborah Sampson and many others in the period, Burroughs comes to see the power that individuals have in projecting an image of themselves, though in Burroughs's case the image that others see is the direct opposite of what he claims to be trying to project. Some observers, Burroughs notes, even tried to look beyond the "surface" of his face, "to see if they could distinguish where that depth of knowledge lay which had set the world in an uproar" (101), an idea that he later mocks by having a "Physician" tell a disguised Burroughs that "I never saw a more striking contrast, than between the designing, deceitful countenance of Burroughs, and your [i.e., Burroughs's] open, frank, and candid countenance" (224).[19] The "outside" does not reveal the "inside" and, hence, "it was hard to eradicate" unfavorable opinions from the minds of the people, "even by the most pointed evidence" (223).

Burroughs's deceptions, which, he claims, were in essence generated or authored by others, create a surplus value that not only prevents others from seeing (what the narrator claims is) the "real" Stephen Burroughs but also gives rise to incidents in which Burroughs's "character" is knowingly or unknowingly assumed by others (221–223, 260, 263–264). As happens with the Tory spy, Moody, Burroughs's character looses its moorings in temporal and geographic space, circulating haphazardly within society as a site of social and cultural fears, "the most singular" character that could be imagined (263). It is here, I would argue, that Burroughs's *Memoirs* resonates most powerfully with that other late-eighteenth-century rumination on deception and counterfeiting, Charles Brockden Brown's *Wieland; or, The Transformation*, also published in 1798. Like Burroughs, Brown dramatizes the anxiety produced by a character who "speaks where he is not," by actions divorced from clear motivations, and by the problem of determining virtue (or vice) from external behavior or appearances.

Gordon Wood has written persuasively about deceit and causality in the late eighteenth century. The paranoid style manifested in the thinking of Thomas Jefferson, John Adams, and others, Wood writes, was "a mode of causal attribution . . . [which] presume[d] a world of autonomous, freely acting individuals who are capable of directly and deliberately bringing about events through their decisions and actions, and who thereby can be held morally responsible for what happens" (1982, 409). The Declaration of Independence is a case study of just this sort of attribution: George III, in the figure of the "he" that begins each point in the list of "facts . . . submitted to a candid world," becomes the authorizing cause of all the colonies' ills. This mode of attribution, Wood suggests, was a late-Enlightenment attempt "to hold men personally and morally responsible for their actions" in an age in which the causative force of God's will became attenuated (1982, 411). And in light of the "convulsive and . . . sprawling" American and French Revolutions (1982, 431), it was soon forced to begin to give way to more modern notions—Hegel's, for example, and later Marx's and Freud's—of causality.

Burroughs's *Memoirs* intersects with such paranoia. His conviction on charges of counterfeiting, for example, takes place (he claims) amidst Shays's Rebellion, itself an instance of fixing agency and blame for a diffuse social-economic-political-military "event" on one person.[20] The insurgents, Massachusetts farmers unable to pay their taxes in an inflationary economy, demand that the state issue more paper money—a dilemma that Lysander proposes to fix by counterfeiting paper money. One can see why Burroughs's punishment is so severe: he appears to be a man who, for the sake of gain and at a time of social unrest, will counterfeit socially agreed-upon markers like money and dress and name: at his trial, he tells us, the attorney general stated "that I had been a counterfeiter not only of the coin of the country, but had likewise counterfeited a name, a character, a calling: all which seemed to communicate this idea to the world, that I had given a loose to the practice of every enormity" (96). The accusation that the insurgents in Massachusetts had "given a loose to . . . enormity" drives the Connecticut Wits' attack on them in *The Anarchiad* (1786–1787). In "Shays's and Shattuck's mob-compelling name"—note that those two men can supposedly impel the otherwise unruly mob, can control the "mobile"—

> the jails open, and the thieves arise.
> Thy constitution, Chaos, is restor'd;
> Law sinks before thy uncreating word.
> (Humphreys et al., 6)

Paper money, *The Anarchiad*'s authors lament in their next installment, will only "introduce the long expected scenes of misrule, dishonesty, and perdition" (13). The rebels have rejected both specie and law, "giv[ing] a loose" to paper money and to the social chaos that their rejection of the legal system must necessarily engender.

Burroughs, like Jefferson and Adams and the Wits, also hopes to pin the "agency" for his behavior on specific causes: his education, his natural temper, his sentimental friendships. Life itself, he remarks near the end of volume one, is a negotiation between our "wish to be happy" and our experience of learning how "to form right estimates of the various effects which will follow the measures we pursue" (225). He recognizes, however, that society is not usually very insistent in attributing effects to their true causes. "The world, in general, for the same reason it calculates that the sun will rise tomorrow, because it rose today, imputes to him, who has been once in the fault, the commission of an hundred others" (212). "I found," Burroughs laments much earlier, "a censorious world little desirous of inquiring into circumstances" (43). Events have discernible causes, Burroughs agrees, but the world is not always interested in discovering them. As a result, Burroughs's character is loaded with what I have called a surplus value, his motives are seldom inquired into, and his future behavior is expected to conform to his past behavior. He becomes a kind of "monster" to many people, a mechanism whose "little secret springs" cannot be discerned,[21] and thus whose life is "a scene of fluctuation . . . uniformly irregular" (359). Neither he nor his motives can, it seems, be known, which is why "It was [sometimes] reported that the devil has assisted [him], in [his] efforts to break jail" (127). "O! ruthless mortals! said I, why so infatuated! Am I not a member of the same family with yourselves?" (107) Some people with whom Burroughs came into contact said that he was not.

As regards the self, Burroughs is in some ways no more radical than Graydon or Allen. Like them, he understands that actions, even apparently monstrous or enormous ones, have discernible causes, and he tries to fix responsibility for his on specific causes, albeit ones that others cannot see. Like Rousseau in the *Confessions*, Burroughs "never [takes] the . . . step to [a] much more radical subjectivist position. He [runs] his inner voice in tandem with the traditional way of understanding and recognizing human good" (Taylor, 362). Like other eighteenth-century experimenters such as Franklin, Burroughs knows that the self is primarily a social construct, shaped and controlled by social expectations and demands. Though his roguery and self-conscious role playing suggest a kind of modernity, Burroughs is in some ways as firmly embedded in self-biographical discourse and assumptions as are Rush and Rousseau.

But there is a radical element to Burroughs's story, one that suggests, in tentative ways, the full transposition in values that occurs by the mid–nineteenth century, when the notion of a self formed in accordance with a model or an ideal ("imitation" or "emulation," as I argued earlier) has fully given way to "Herderian expressivism, [in which] each person has his or her own original way of being" (Taylor, 184). Throughout *Memoirs*, as Daniel Cohen perceptively observes, Burroughs expresses a "distaste for established social values and hierarchies" (161), and accordingly he usually portrays himself as "a figure with serious ideas about society and with serious grievances against those who [dominate] it" (162). In his remarks on education, in his treatment at Dartmouth, in his attempt to purchase a library for the "people," in his posturing as a minister, and in many other ways, Burroughs dramatizes himself participating in the broader "American revolution against patriarchal authority" (as Jay Fliegelman puts it) or the broader "radicalism of the American Revolution" (as Gordon Wood puts it). Burroughs distrusts traditional sources of authority. "I am so far a republican," he says on the first page of his narrative, "that I consider a man's merit to rest entirely within himself, without any regard to family, blood, or connection" (3). He rejects classical notions of deference, while at the same time insisting (as did Franklin, Graydon, Rush, and these other experimenters) that some forms of deference be maintained: "I know much is due to government. Personal inconvenience is to be borne, rather than government should suffer any injury . . . upon the uninterrupted administration of justice by government, depends the welfare of the whole community" (161).[22] His resistance to imprisonment, to "punishment by servitude" (177), is not a resistance to punishment itself, but to the unnatural and unfeeling way it is carried out in Massachusetts (98–99). Like Rush, Burroughs wants to reform the penal system, not deny its potential efficacy in reforming individual criminals.

Hence, while Burroughs challenges traditional sites of authority, he accepts the notion that authority must, finally, rest somewhere, perhaps in a democratic government, perhaps in rights "which we inherited from nature" (291), and perhaps—most insistently—in common sense or sentimentality itself. Here is his most obvious connection to another "eccentric" of the age, Tom Paine, who, after denying the authority of the state, institutional religion, and the Bible, finds a ground for true knowledge in the perception of the universe through the principles of "mathematical science" (1995, 693). Burroughs and Paine, like the Wits whom William Dowling discusses in *Poetry and Ideology in Revolutionary Connecticut*, have in their Revolutionary years the "experience of seeing through ideology, of gazing past its subterfuges to a real world of naked power and domination underneath" (30), even as they begin to struggle to reconfigure the meaning of those underlying bases of power and authority.

Burroughs speaks, then, in language that is intended to appeal to a new and democratic audience. "But, said I, what is law, but the voice of the people? And what is the voice of the people but the language of the heart? . . . Surely, this is the idea which the language of nature strongly inculcates upon our minds" (128). Liberty, for Burroughs, is not simply "freedom," as it is for us, nor is it the right of a people to share in the government, as it was for classical republicans;[23] it is a state of personal independence: "[Imprisoned, I was] shut from the enjoyment of society, from performing a part among the rest of my fellow mortals, to make some establishment for myself, in this state of dependence; and from testing the sweets of liberty, for which we had so lately fought and bled" (98). By appealing to the sensibilities of people who conflated the Revolution with their own personal liberty from traditional sources of authority, Burroughs is in essence both appealing to and calling into being the emergent middle class. Unlike Crèvecoeur, Graydon, Rush, Franklin, and Allen, all of whom aspired to rise to elite social levels and all of whom epitomize the self in generalized terms, Burroughs attempts to find the meanings of his actions in himself, in a private self that lies behind or beyond or within the particular representations of face, dress, speech, and social behavior, representations that do not actually "represent" that self. Burroughs theorizes that that self is not yet unique: we are "members of one and the same family" (128); "the *human* character becomes really known" when we take off our daily, social masks (130, emphasis added). While it has become private, that self is not yet unique. However, the weight of his characterization of himself and his actions suggests that the self *is* both private and unique. Burroughs's problem in *Memoirs* is finding a way to portray or represent that private space. "Pray excuse my incoherent method of writing" (362), he asks his parents in one letter. In the end, his method has necessarily been incoherent to many readers because the method he chooses to adopt—sentimentalism, the appeal to our shared, common sense—tends to be read as insincere, and perhaps rightly so given Burroughs's characterization of himself. "Why," Elihu Hubbard Smith asks in his diary in 1795, "is there no certain, no unequivocal language, by which the unsupported voice of truth might speak conviction, and outweigh the united clamours of the legions of Falsehood!" (20). Words spoken where the author is not (as Smith's friend, Charles Brockden Brown, knew) cannot carry with them their own "certain" proof. We have consistently read Burroughs's sentimentalism as part of a confidence game (Gross; Daniel Williams, 1990), a reading that the theme of the narrative enforces, rather than as a technical problem that Burroughs himself faced in separating the performative self that makes him appear to be an early exemplar of the confidence man from his own protestations that he is typically "human."

We might think of Burroughs's readers as being in a position analogous to Burroughs himself in his dealings with Lysander. Intellectually, Burroughs knows that Lysander's arguments for counterfeiting are "unfounded" (84), yet he agrees to pass counterfeit money for him anyway. He agrees because "the sentiment of friendship" he feels toward Lysander and, especially, Lysander's wife urges him to ignore reason. "What would you have done, had you been in my situation?" Burroughs asks his readers. "Words had now become entirely out of the question, and only one thing remained to be done [i.e., to try to pass the money]" (86). Words deal with reason; only actions can demonstrate feelings. Allen, himself a master of "stratagems," would have understood Burroughs. But Burroughs's modern readers have sensed that his explanations for his actions are "unfounded"; modern readers have not permitted "sentiment" to override their suspicions. Burroughs's bid in *Memoirs* is precisely, however, to urge his readers to overcome their suspicions both of his stereotypical self (circulating wildly in post-Revolutionary society) and of his own words (as he explains his past), and to find a "common" sense with him in his frustrations with traditional social forms as he encountered them in the 1770s and 1780s.

"You say my character to you, is an enigma," Burroughs writes to his correspondent, "that I possess an uncommon share of sensibility, and at the same time, maintain an equality of mind which is uncommon" (1). The enigma is not one whose depths Burroughs can plumb in language.[24] He is trying to imagine an interiority, a sense of inwardness, via a common sense that ties him to other feeling human beings, ties him, as I say, democratically to others within a society configured, potentially, by the equality of heart, not the hierarchies of birth, status, or wealth.

Burroughs, in this sense, is revolutionary; he takes the American Revolution to be a social reconfiguration in which deference and hierarchy give way to equality and democracy. His *Memoirs* verges on the revolutionary in generic and discursive terms. He is still writing about a public self (hence, appropriately, he writes his "memoirs") whose actions are driven by common, emulable principles. He, too, in this sense, is writing in Benjamin Franklin's wake. But Burroughs also comprehends some of the values that autobiographers will fully adopt in their autobiographical narratives at midcentury: the belief that nature or a natural inner-accessed moral sense dictates proper behavior, the sense that other people see only external behavior while true motives ("character" or "personality") remain sensible only to the self, a sense of alienation or eccentricity, and a self-reliant belief that the "credentials" in one's head take precedence over any socially prescribed credentials imposed by the Aaron Woolworths of this world. Burrough's self in *Memoirs* is, indeed, enigmatic, a curious puzzle that cannot ever be seen clearly but can only on occasion be glimpsed by sympathetic and like-hearted readers.

❧ 7 ❧

Printed for the Authoress:

K. White and Elizabeth Fisher

SINCE THE 1960S, SCHOLARSHIP ON ALL ASPECTS OF women's lives during the Revolutionary and early national eras has flourished. We simply know more now about the physical, material, social, and intellectual dimensions of women's lives at the turn of the eighteenth century than we did thirty years ago. Full-length studies by scholars like Nancy Cott, Mary Beth Norton, Joy Day Buel and Richard Buel, Linda Kerber, Cathy Davidson, Laurel Thatcher Ulrich, Edith Gelles, Nina Baym, and Joan Gunderson, along with influential articles by scholars like Betsy Erkkila, Sharon Harris, and Carroll Smith-Rosenberg,[1] have in a variety of ways shown us how "the American Revolution fostered certain measurable changes in white women's lives, including an increased emphasis on the affectionate rather than the authoritarian family and a rise in the moral authority and stature of the mother within both the household and the republic" (Erkkila, 215). For the most part, these changes were not legal and political; they were, instead, intellectual and attitudinal: women began to gain "the knowledge, the language, the desire, and the power to foment further rebellion" (Erkkila, 219). "Remember the Ladies," Abigail Adams wrote to her husband in 1776. "If perticuliar care and attention is not paid to the Ladies we are determined to foment a Rebelion, and will not hold ourselves bound by any Laws in which we have no voice, or Representation" (Adams and Adams, 121). That "Rebelion" did not occur until much later, of course, when questions of voice and representation were addressed by state and federal legislation. But the way was prepared by several generations of women, beginning with Adams's, each of which challenged in its own way the social construction of femaleness as an inferior or secondary being.

Part of our reconstruction of women's lives has been the incorporation of women writers of the Revolutionary period into the canon. Recent years have seen the reprinting and classroom use of works by writers like Judith Sargent Murray, Mercy Otis Warren, Abigail Adams, and Hannah Webster Foster. Nevertheless, it is true that not one self-biography or autobiography by a woman writer in this period in America has canonical or even near-canonical status. From Elizabeth Ashbridge's *Some Account of the Early Part of the Life of Elizabeth Ashbridge* (1774; wr. before 1755) to Hannah Adams's *Memoir of Miss Hannah Adams* (1832)—or, more probably, to Harriet Jacobs's *Incidents in the Life of a Slave Girl* (1861)—no female self-biographer is studied or taught within the traditions of autobiography, captivity narratives, American women's writing, or American literature more generally. More famous and prolific writers like Murray and Foster did not pen self-biographies, and the names of the lesser-known women who did have been almost entirely forgotten.

My own initial readings into Revolutionary and post-Revolutionary narratives of selfhood did not turn up many women writers. Standard bibliographies and literary histories referred me to texts like Sarah Wister's *Journal* (wr. 1777–1778) and Mary Lewis Kinnan's *True Narrative of the Sufferings of Mary Kinnan* (1795), neither of which seemed to me to offer sophisticated or complex imaginings of personal identity. Both represented what I expected to find. I did not see much chance to discover forgotten or ignored texts. Following Susan Stanford Friedman, I assumed that women had been elided from the autobiographical tradition because "the model of separate and unique selfhood that is highlighted in [the work of most critics, including my own] establishes a critical bias that leads to the (mis)reading and marginalization of autobiographical texts by women and minorities" (34). I assumed, simply, that no women dared in the period under consideration to write aggressively and ambitiously in the public sphere. I anticipated having to write about women's self-conception in the period through diaries and journals, rather than formal self-biographical acts, or—if I were to stay true to my subject matter of formal, retrospective self-biography[2]—not writing about women at all. And I anticipated that I would find in those diaries and journals traditional conceptions of women's roles, of the sort that, indeed, I found in narratives like Wister's.

But I found two things that surprised me. First, women wrote a substantial number of self-biographical accounts in these years. Within the tradition of spiritual conversion narratives, writers like Sarah Hamilton (in *A Narrative of the Life of Sarah Hamilton* [1803]) tell stories of youthful indiscretion and later religious perseverance in the face of familial and social disapproval. Within the tradition of captivity narratives, writers like Susannah Johnson (in *A Narrative of the Captivity of Mrs. Johnson* [1814]) recount the well-rehearsed tale of Indian attack, captivity, forced march, deprivation, and finally "redemption." Other women tell less traditional stories: Anne Grant, a Scotswoman who lived in Albany from 1757 to 1768, recounts her youthful memories of growing up in upstate New York, idealizing the landscape in ways that anticipate Fenimore Cooper's romances, and idealizing her mentor, Mrs. Philip Schuyler, in ways that typify the emergent discourse of the "bonds of womanhood" (*Memoirs of an American Lady* [1808]); Lucy Brewer recounts her experiences as a prostitute and as a disguised sailor in the War of 1812 (*The Life of Louisa Baker* [1814], also reprinted as *The Female Marine*); and Abigail Bailey recounts her horror story of being married to a violent, unfaithful, lecherous, conniving husband, contriving her story as a sort of captivity narrative in which she is spiritually "redeemed" by her piety and materially redeemed by her success in gaining a divorce (*Memoirs of Mrs. Abigail Bailey* [1815]). Though they are even less visible in American literary history than writers like Benjamin Rush and Ethan Allen, women self-biographers in this period were definitely finding their way onto the page and into print.

Second, I was surprised to find that at least two female self-biographers wrote narratives that challenged my assumption that women writers, unlike their male counterparts, did not in this period begin to struggle to tell the story of how they came to be independent, often original, agents. I assumed that the radicalism inherent in the American Revolution was more immediately available to white men of all social classes than it was to women and to African-Americans. And, although I still think that is generally true, I have found that it is not categorically true. Both K. White in *A Narrative of the Life, Occurrences, Vicissitudes, and Present Situation of K. White* (1809) and Elizabeth Fisher in *Memoirs of Mrs. Elizabeth Fisher* (1810) write of themselves as agents of their own destiny, an agency that is figured initially on the titles pages of their narrative ("Schenectady: Printed for the Authoress," says White's title page; "New York: Printed for the Author," says Fisher's) and then insistently in the narratives themselves. In his *History of My Life*, Benjamin Franklin consistently puts women (his mother, his wife, his daughter) to the side or at a distance, in order to focus upon the male world of work, print, public discourse, and politics. But two female self-biographers, at least, writing twenty years after his death, set themselves as equals beside him and the other men who try to control their lives, providing us with unusual glimpses into the discursive formation of female self-identity in the post-Revolutionary period.

૪◦

I must state here at the outset my fundamental agreement with the argument, made by Teresa de Lauretis, Sidonie Smith, Mary Poovey, and others, that "technologies of gender" (the phrase is de Lauretis's) "hypostatized an ideology of sexually marked 'selfhood' in the nineteenth century that rigidly construed and partitioned masculine and feminine spheres of desire, fate, and discourse" (Sidonie Smith, 80). The ideology of metaphysical selfhood and the discourse of autobiography that textually manifests that ideology revolve around an "I" that "appears unitary, bold, [and] indivisible," but that in reality is "gendered and . . . male" (Sidonie Smith, 79). "Gender," Marlene Kadar writes, "has determined genre in the past" (7). For the most part, autobiographies figured only masculinity until well into the nineteenth century. When Hannah Adams's *Memoir* was published in 1832, the editors emphasized the author's reluctance to speak in public: she "composed reluctantly," they wrote, sensing that "the community could hardly care to know anything about . . . an individual as humble as herself" ("Introductory Note," n.p.). Their protection of her privacy recalls the editorial "protection" offered by Mary Rowlandson's friend, "Per Amicum," 150 years earlier. No wonder that, having ventured forth into the public, Adams repeatedly reminds us of her "nervous complaints" (16) and "constitutional want of bodily and mental firmness" (2);[3] she hesitates to reveal her inner self, opting instead to provide a narrative that oscillates between the "bonds of womanhood" (what Friedman refers to as "a culturally imposed group identity for women and minorities" in self-biographies [35]) and the publishing history of her theological and historical writings.

At the same time, it is possible to agree with Shirley Neuman that a "poetics of women's autobiographies . . . [should] pay considerable attention to the ways in which [female] narrators negotiate cultural prescriptions for women, by appropriating or re-writing androcentric models for autobiography" (218). People, in other words, are not passive in the face of dominant ideologies and discourses; subjects are both socially constructed and constructing. Eighteenth-century self-biographies, Felicity Nussbaum writes in *The Autobiographical Subject*, "offer a private space for experimentation, revision, and resistance to prevailing notions of identity" (xvii). "Women autobiographers in the eighteenth century ... speak in the codes and language that are available to them in texts that imitate and reflect the autobiographical subjects of the male hegemonic social formation" (138).[4] Women writers, Leigh Gilmore has written in *Autobiographics: A Feminist Theory of Women's Self-representation*, often "use self-representation and its constitutive possibilities for agency and subjectivity to become no longer primarily subject to exchange but subjects who exchange the position of object for the subjectivity of self-representational agency" (12). This, I will argue, is exactly the move that K. White and Elizabeth Fisher make in their early nineteenth-century self-biographies. Within my definition of autobiography, White and Fisher are among the earliest American autobiographers, writing themselves as agents in ways that Graydon, Rush, and Allen would have deplored for women *and for men*.

The title page of K. White's *Narrative* actually insists upon her agency in two ways: it tells us that she had the text printed for her, and it tells us that she "compiled and collated [it] by herself. . . . Feb. 1809." The story that she compiles and collates is a complex one. Born in Edinburgh in 1772, she is brought to America by her father, a Tory merchant who because of his loyalty to the king, George III, is forced to return to Scotland in 1780. Having moved to Stockbridge after her father left, White is taken captive by Indians for several months, redeemed, and then reunited with her mother and father. At seventeen, she falls in love with an American army officer, who, it turns out, is married to a women whom he does not love. He commits suicide one week before his scheduled wedding date with the author. After several months in mourning, she is urged by her father to marry a distant relation, a Mr. S. White, who "possessed insinuating manners" (48). As readers of eighteenth-century novels would have immediately suspected from the author's brief comment, S. White is a lecher, hypocrite, and liar. Soon after the wedding, he seduces the chambermaid and then flees Boston, leaving the chambermaid and her child destitute and White herself pregnant.

White's child apparently dies at birth, and she at that point enters the public world of trade, travel, and the law. She becomes a merchant in order to "acquire an independency, or at least, a compentancy [*sic*]" (54). Her husband's creditors sue her, however, and she is forced to appear in court to defend herself. She is acquitted. She then tries to start over in business in Providence, only to fail; then moves, consecutively, to Schenectady, Herkimer County, Canada, Buffalo Creek, Onondaga, and finally Albany, where she is living when the narrative ends. Along her peripatetic route, she is accused of being both a French spy (chapter VII) and a British spy (chapter X), toys with the affections of a young woman who thinks that White is a man, and tracks down her husband in Canada and forces him to give her a piece of land—a "separate maintenance" (117)—in exchange for her agreement not to go public with the fact of his bigamy. At the end of her narrative, in good health but poor, legally independent but bound by "fate," White reflects upon the "novel and eccentric" course (126) her life as a woman has taken.

She notes that some events in her story are so novel and so eccentric that readers might not accept them as true. Such "novel and eccentric" (123) scenes might cause some readers to laugh, she notes, although her intent is merely to describe what happened, without "insinuat[ing]" herself to the "readers by the aid of flowery fancy" (123). Of course, the word "insinuating" suggests the behavior of her husband, whose manners indeed turned out to be snakelike.[5] She will not behave in such despicable ways. Her life was eccentric, she insists, and the reader must understand that eccentricity in order to make sense of her story.

The figures of novelty and eccentricity—departing or deviating from the regular or established norm—apply to White's behavior as a woman. Her eccentric course has led her to poverty and isolation, an inverted picture of the still-emergent middle-class ideal of wedded, domestic bliss. "The errors of our own country women will check the vicious career of their sisters," White writes in the preface, "and teach, from their misfortunes, how the pit of misery may be shunned" (vi). Her experiences and the moral lesson they exhibit are, in other words, gendered. Yet, interestingly, White also appeals at the end of her narrative to the figure Alexander Graydon will invoke two years later: "when I contrast my present precarious situation with my former part of life, it brings forcibly to my mind, a sentiment, 'It is pleasing to progress from a low, inconvenient situation to a lofty and affluent one'" (127). Like Graydon, White has not "risen" in the world. Her particular experiences, however, relate specifically to women, both in that her deviations from life's "normal" or "regular" course have to be measured against cultural norms for women and in that they are narrated in order to prevent other women from sinking into such misery. Still, and at the same time, her story resonates across gender and race and class lines. Like many others who did not benefit from the material and financial forces affecting life in the new United States, White expresses dissatisfaction at the limitations imposed upon her. Meeting the expectations of some of her readers, no doubt, White claims at times that the "sportive goddess," fortune, made "her [a] victim"; more astute readers could see that, in reality, laws, public opinion, and the machinations of flesh-and-blood men determined her "eccentric" course.

White recognizes her eccentricity as a "wandering situation" (84), both a literal traveling beyond acceptable boundaries and a metaphorical challenging of cultural and social norms. Her narrative is continually concerned with thresholds: a "timid female" like myself, she writes at the beginning, "approaches the threshold of her 'tale of woe'" with a trembling step; but she then goes over it (9–10). Her engagement to her first lover promises to mark her entrance into that "eventful epoch in the history of most females" (36), an epoch that is delayed narratively by her fiancé's suicide, but that is entered soon after by her marriage to Mr. White.

Figuratively speaking, White is willing and able to cross all sorts of thresholds and boundaries. She turns out not to be the "timid female" afraid of telling her story that she invokes in the preface. Hence, for example, when she is sued for the first time, she attends a packed courtroom whose visitors have been "attracted [by] the novelty of the scene." White is not silent and passive, as might be expected: she challenges potential jurors until finally a jury sympathetic to her plight is sworn in (57). The jury returns a not-guilty verdict. In Herkimer County a few years later, White is arrested on suspicion of being a French spy. She wittily characterizes the justices before whom she is examined as "justasses" (75), and parries their ineffectual questions with ease and humor:

Justice—How do you support yourself?
Answer—By good eating and drinking.
Justice—That is no answer—How do you gain your livelihood?
Answer—By hard industry.
Justice—What occupation do you follow?
Answer—Travelling.
Justice—To what purpose?
Answer—Pleasure. (79)

These are not the answers of a shy and retiring woman, and in fact they allude to two of her most persistent concerns in the narrative: her body and her eccentric wanderings. In that instance, she is not only released from confinement, she initiates charges of false imprisonment against the justices and wins from them a "most humble apology . . . for their conduct towards me" (82–83).

Figuratively, White's very body—her "figure"—crosses accepted boundaries:

> Although in my younger years I was of slender form yet as I advanced in age, I became large in stature[,] somewhat of a masculine form, of a robust strong complexion, so that upon the whole I would not make a bad appearance as a man, were I dressed in masculine attire. My female readers will perhaps smile at the fact, but Nature had so "ordered it" and I could not remedy it. (63)

Nature pushes her toward masculinity, and White, seldom shy, sometimes assists. It is her "masculine appearance" (74) that causes the justices of Herkimer County to suspect her of spying; something in her appearance or behavior as a woman makes them suspicious of her identity. In Schenectady that "something" leads a "young lady struck with [White's] appearance" (64) to arrange an "interview" with her. White, whimsically, plays along, disguising herself further with a false beard and using doublespeak to lead the young lady on. The affair, with its mixed message of homoeroticism and irony, leads eventually to an "engagement . . . of matrimony" (68), until another suitor for the young lady's hand charges White with "attempting to seduce a lady in disguise"—an accurate charge, of course, only not in the way the other suitor imagined—and forces her to leave town. My "form," White sighs later in her travels, often tended to "become a subject of suspicion" (101).

White, I must emphasize, accepts her masculine appearance, and even plays upon the figure it presents. "'Tis true," she jokes in a poem near the end of her *Narrative*,

> I'm strong and masculine,
> What then? My size is justly mine,
> If living well can make it;
> The fat I boast I've justly gained,
> Yet if another it has claimed,
> Why he is free to take it.
> (104)

Her masculine appearance accompanies her growing sense of her own power at law and within society. When a "gentleman" accuses her of being a British spy (107), White responds by challenging him to that quintessential male test, a duel. She writes to her accuser: "you have dared to traduce my reputation and to wound my feelings, trusting to the fallacious hope that a woman's weapons were but her innocence and good conduct. But, sir, you shall find I am not totally destitute of others" (108). The accuser's response to her challenge is ill-written, misspelled, and almost illegible, and White prints it with glee: the "gentleman" was obviously not what he seemed. When, the next morning at the appointed site, he discovers that White is a woman, he tries to turn the duel into a boxing match; she puts a gun to his ear and makes him offer "concessions" to her in writing, concessions that of course she has to write for him. "'I acknowledge'," she ventriloquizes, "'to have circulated a report implicating the reputation of K— W—, and representing her as [a spy]'" (111–112). K. White will control her own representations, however extravagant or eccentric they might be.

White's boundary crossing extends to her own writing style. That she can write, and write well, is emphasized in the incident with the so-called gentleman, whose style of writing—"I hav sid noting to hurt your karractter that I nose off" (110), he writes, for example—counterpoints her own. While correct and clear, however, White's style is headlong in its rush to relate incidents. She breathlessly plunges forward into a story that, while she claims to "tremble" to tell it, shows her to be reveling in her newfound freedom and power. She uses dashes, ellipses, and exclamation points to press the reader forward into the story:

> [My first fiancé] united most fascinating manners and persuasive eloquence. He was assiduous in cultivating and encreasing my regard for him, and soon proposed to me. . . . . . his heart and hand! Young and giddy, as I was, I little knew the too fatal consequences of this attachment. He vowed, and sighed—and I, alas, consented to become his wife. The day was appointed to consummate the hymeneal rites, and to unite me to him for—life! But fortune had not done persecuting me. . . . (37)

Sylistically, White is not shy and withdrawn. She plays upon the stylistic conventions of sentimental fiction, but she drives us forward not to discover the expected ending of sentimental fiction—marriage or death—but to discover her own self-reliance. It is a remarkable performance.

This pushing at boundaries is generic, as well.[6] White nods in the direction of the spiritual narrative at the end of *Narrative*: "on the 10 July [1804] the 'grace of God,' under 'seal,' was poured out upon me. My soul was ever 'free and independent,' and the littleness and persecutions of relentless creditors I despised the more they accumulated these persecutions" (119–120). But that is, quite literally, the only reference in the narrative to her conversion, and I take it to be simply less relevant than the force of her self-characterization elsewhere. In the narrative itself, as her allusion to not "rising" in the world suggests, White is grappling with the "self," not the "soul," and like her contemporaries she is struggling to comprehend how that self knows itself, how it relates to other selves, and what, finally, undergirds it. Generically, then, her narrative is not a spiritual narrative but is instead an emergent autobiography of the sort I will now be concerned with in this book. Indeed, White's narrative is so insistent about the protagonist's agency, and so willing to find purpose and meaning in isolation—what White calls "my solitary situation" (127) —that it could be considered one of the earliest autobiographies written in the West.[7] Rousseau declared at the beginning of his *Confessions* that his purpose was "to display to my kind a portrait in every way true to nature" (17), a purpose that I take White to be repeating in 1809, though from the perspective of a spurned, marginalized woman.

In her representation of herself as vocal, aggressive, and independent, White notes only once her dissatisfaction with her own behavior: in her deception of the young lady to whom she becomes "engaged." "I feel [the] full weight [of the readers' censure]," she sighs. "I would have wished to have omitted this incident had not a regard to truth compelled me to narrate it" (67–68). Here, and elsewhere in her *Narrative*, White is willing to expose herself as she really is. She is masculine in appearance, and tells us. She marries a lecher and a hypocrite, and tells us. She misleads a young, innocent woman, and tells us. "[My] better judgment wholly condemned" my deception, she admits. Throughout her *Narrative*, it is men who are characterized as secretive and deceptive (and unwilling to admit it). It is men who "insinuate." Unlike White, men try hard not to "expose" themselves or their mistakes.

Take, for instance, her fiancé. Before he commits suicide, he leaves White a letter detailing his youthful mistake in marrying a woman he did not love. She, it turns out, proved unfaithful (anticipating the behavior of White's own husband later). White's fiancé cannot obtain a divorce from his wife, however, and hence he cannot marry White. "On either side," he writes despairingly to White, "exposure and misery are certain" (46). The fiancé has the choice either of returning to his wife, and being exposed as a cuckold, or of marrying White, and being exposed as a bigamist. He chooses romantic suicide, as, for example, does Harrington in William Hill Brown's *The Power of Sympathy* (1789), but he chooses it precisely because he cannot live with the exposure of his true self. He is already a cuckold, and he would be a bigamist if he married White. There is, of course, an ironic reversal in this since, typically, it is the woman who must fear "exposure." In Eliza Haywood's early feminist fiction, *Fantomina* (1724), the narrator remarks that Fantomina, about to deliver a child whose conception she has kept hidden for nine months, "would easily have found Means to have screened even this from the Knowledge of the World had she been at liberty to have acted," but her contractions "expose" her true state and lead to her punishment (246). In Hannah Foster's *The Coquette* (1797), Julia Granby notices Eliza Wharton's symptoms long before Eliza's pregnancy is finally exposed (138)—the seducer, Sanford, rightly fears Julia's "inquisitorial eye" (140) —but in the end the pregnancy is exposed to the wider public by the signs of childbirth, particularly "the marks upon her linen" (162). Without those marks, Eliza would have died as a stranger, unexposed, in a Boston boardinghouse; with them, she is publicly exposed as a fallen woman.

In White's narrative, it is the men who fear exposure. As she recounts her emigration to America, White tells the story of the ship captain who tried to force himself on Mrs. Carmichael, a passenger. Very few people, other than White's father, notice that "the captain's manners were far from pleasing to a female"; he dissembles his "real character . . . of a professed libertine" (12). Despite being reprimanded by White's father, the captain rapes Mrs. Carmichael during what White describes as a "deceitful . . . calm" (13). The captain succeeds in his attack precisely because he concealed his true self, just as, much later, Mr. White succeeds in marrying the protagonist because "his depravity was concealed under a veil which [only] in time was removed to display the consummate powers of treachery and falsehood" (50). They successfully insinuate themselves. Later, when she tracks down Mr. White in Canada as he is about to marry another woman—her own story, ironically, repeated—she records him having said: "I entreat you . . . to hear me [i.e., to hear his explanation]. I shall conceal nothing. . . . But you must be conscious to expose me in this country can answer no other purpose than driving me to a state of desperation" (97).[8] Like her first fiancé, the husband fears the consequences of his "exposure," while White herself, as I have said, takes responsibility in the narrative for exposing herself.

There is "Some ignus fatuus that leads astray, / And ruins many a woman every day," White writes in a poem late in the narrative. The "foolish fire" is, of course, man. Throughout her life, men present themselves either as fools, like the judges in Herkimer County or the "gentleman" who accuses her of being a British spy, or as deceptive hypocrites trying to lead women astray, like the ship captain or her husband. Men are overly aggressive, as well, usually to the point of violence. The ship captain rapes Mrs. Carmichael, and White is caned by the jealous suitor of her female "fiancé" (70). White herself, interestingly, begins to display some of these qualities as she takes on her more masculine appearance. She conceals her true intentions with the young lady, though she apologizes for it and "exposes" herself later. Once, tracked down by a jealous husband who thinks White (disguised as a man) has been making love to his wife, White responds to his "abusive" language by drawing a "brace of pistols" and threatening violence herself. I take White to be saying in this that, while women would do well to adopt man's aggressiveness at law and in social relations, they must stop short of adopting man's deceitfulness and violence. Accused of being a man by the jealous husband, White plays the role to extricate herself from the situation, but she does not actually engage in violence.

I am suggesting, then, that K. White's *Narrative* works against both traditional eighteenth-century conceptions of the role of women and then-emergent conceptions of the "bonds of womanhood" and republican motherhood. On the one hand, she urges women to become more aggressive, to recognize that their lives are shaped and controlled by men who usually deceive them, and to consider an option other than the traditional choice of marriage. The option is a lonely one, she points out; she is unable to settle in one location, and she regrets her consequent inability to form "one sincere friend" (125). But remaining single is an option, nonetheless. "I hope I may and will profit," even yet, by my decision to live alone, White declares at the very end of her narrative. That she should say so in print in 1809 is itself a remarkable fact. At the same time, White urges women not to become "too" masculine, for by adopting the masculine traits of deception and violence they will merely replicate the behavior that has misled so many women in the past. This is why White's own attempted seduction, while in disguise, of a young lady—an episode that stands at the very center of the narrative—demands from her such an unequivocal denunciation. Such behavior is no longer merely eccentric, a crossing of norms; it is masculine and insinuative, and hence must be repudiated.

This sort of reading of White's *Narrative* returns us to the question of audience: who is White writing for in 1809? Why does she take the time to "compile" and "collate" her adventures? The preface claims that, "in giving the characters of the times," authors should "contrast vice with virtue" in order to make virtue "seen" (v). Doing so will teach women how to avoid the sort of mistakes White made. "I am aware of the critics," White growls; "they have no claim to this production" (vi). Of course not. Graydon is speaking to the "critics," the powers that be; she is not. This "production" is for women, many of whom are unaware of vice and hence need to be taught to "see" it in order to avoid marrying the wrong man—or marrying at all. In this sense, White simply makes the same claim as do many early American novels. She even plays with the conventions of those novels in her narrative, conventions like sentimentalized language, arranged marriages, and perfidious lovers. But, remarkably, White offers a much different vision of her own, "real" self than most contemporary novels do of their female heroines. White is aggressive where they are passive. White is eccentric where they are normal. White chooses isolation and a life on the road where they choose a husband and domesticity. And, finally, White speaks publicly where they remain or become silent. Printed by the authoress? Who else would print it in 1809?

꙳

Christopher Castiglia has remarked that White's *Narrative* was "Embellished if not entirely fabricated" (110): her "eccentricity," he says, was permitted only "by [a] fictional license" through which she transformed both genre (the captivity narrative) and gender (111). There is no proof that White fabricated her story, however. In fact, a number of facts in White's story are apparently true. She reports, for example, that her family emigrated to America in "the ship Charming Susan" (10); that they were headed for "a settlement in the western world" (11); that the ship was lost in a storm, only to be rescued by another ship that provided water and direction (16); and that they finally landed safely in Boston (16–17). In *Voyagers to the West*, Bernard Bailyn tells the story of a ship called *Charming Sally*, whose Scottish passengers were bound for a settlement in northern New York. *Charming Sally* sailed in May 1775, foundered in an Atlantic storm, and was towed into port (in Philadelphia) in late August (1986, 592–596). The "principle facts" of the story, White remarks in a footnote, were told to her by her father, which would account for the errors; but the outline of the story essentially agrees with Bailyn's account.

Anyway, given postmodern assumptions about autobiography, it would perhaps not matter much to us if she had fabricated her story: identity itself is a construction, a fabrication; and no recounting of the history of a self can do without the conventions and figures of fictional narration. White's cross-dressing, real or imagined, one could argue, derives from eighteenth-century fictions like *Fantomina* and *Female Quixotism* (1801), just as Franklin's youthful indiscretions in *History of My Life* are derived from fictions like *Tom Jones* (1749). How could "true" self-biography avoid contamination by "fictional" self-biography? And vice versa?

Elizabeth Fisher's *Memoirs of Mrs. Elizabeth Fisher* also plays upon the conventions of eighteenth-century fiction, though her story is also apparently "true." In her case, we can more easily verify the general contours of her story, since the family she was born into was well known at the time. Her father was Henry Munro, a Scottish loyalist who served as a chaplain in New York before and during the Revolution. Fisher accurately describes his return to Scotland, his negotiations to settle a tract of land awarded to him by the crown, and the legal transfer of that land to his son, Peter Jay Munro, in 1800. These and other facts are contained in a nineteenth-century account written by Edward F. De Lancey, a descendant, and published in *The New York Genealogical and Biographical Register* in 1873. De Lancey's account is notable in that it does not mention a daughter, Elizabeth, by name; he notes only that Munro's first marriage produced a daughter, and that the mother died soon after. An editor at the *Register* added a footnote to the biography in which he points out that Elizabeth's mother's name is not known, and that Elizabeth married a Donald Fisher, had three children, and died in Montreal, date unknown. It sounds like the relatively normal life of public obscurity for a woman of the time.

But as Fisher tells it, her life was anything but normal. It was, if anything, novelistic. Her mother dies three days after giving birth to her, and her often-absent father later remarries a cruel stepmother who abuses her. The stepmother is Eve Jay, sister of John Jay. Fisher lacks a mother and a father who can or will educate her in the ways of the world. And like many another fictional heroine—most obviously, Clarissa—Fisher rejects the man chosen by her father to be her husband, and instead runs off with a man whom she "chooses" in desperation. Indeed, Clarissa's story echoes throughout Fisher's, particularly in the characters' conception of the value of land and property over honor. Fisher pushes her story, as Richardson pushed his, toward the paradigmatic.

Fisher's title page, even more than White's, calls attention to her agency. She emphasizes her authorship in at least three different ways: the title of her narrative, which implicitly claims that her "memoirs" are hers (her name is printed in large, bold capitals); the subtitle, which insists that the memoirs were "written by herself" (printed in italicized capitals); and the copyright information, which declares that the narrative was "printed for the author" (printed in capitals). The variety of types employed on the title page also calls attention to the role her half brother plays in the narrative, as she tells us that her own "domestic misfortunes" culminated in her being imprisoned for six years "at the instance of her [half] brother, Peter Jay Munro," at that time a lawyer and later a judge and minor politician in the state of New York. The inverted V shape of the paragraph summarizing her story visually draws the prospective reader's eye toward her half brother's name in bold capitals. The narrative promises, then, to be a public reply to her half brother's public role in her "cruel condemnation" to prison, yet a fourth way in which Fisher calls attention to herself. And, finally, in a fifth gesture toward herself, Fisher's unattributed epigraph states that "the mind that is armed with conscious virtue" cannot be shaken by the betrayal of friends or family or by circumstances more generally. Readers could assume, from the narrative summary in midpage, that hers was the unshaken mind.

Fisher overdetermines her agency because she is acutely sensitive to the way her audience reads narratives by women.[9] Midway through her *Memoirs*, she begins to call attention to that audience: "I must . . . relate some circumstances which may not be uninteresting to the public" (26); "I know not whether my conduct, in accepting this wench [a black slave girl], will be received with approbation by the public" (30); and "I believe the public in general will say that I have stood my trials through life with great fortitude" (42–43). She tries in the narrative to re-present herself, to revise the public's perception of her as a criminal and make it see her instead as a virtuous, well-meaning person, both a victim (of her half brother's machinations and of her father's neglect) and an agent. Fisher's

Memoirs is a battle of representations: hers, as she would like us to see her, versus her half brother's (and, through him, the legal system's).

Fisher justifies her agency by recounting, first, her victimization. Left for long periods of time with her stepmother, Eve Jay Munro, who was evidently emotionally and psychologically unstable (Richard Morris, 33), Fisher was psychologically and physically abused. Eventually, the neighbors intervened, and Fisher was sent away at the age of sixteen to spend a blissful summer with "a companion, a girl about my age, who went with me every where I pleased to go" (7).[10] When she returns to her family, she finds that her father has permitted a much older man to make his addresses to her: "of course, I could not like him" (8), she writes. Her father, like Clarissa's, is unfeeling and determined to put property ahead of her opinions; her stepmother is a witch; and her half brother is taken in by the Jay family, "as they are his relations." For myself, Fisher writes, "I had no relations. —I had to seek my living among strangers" (12). Though her language echoes Ruth's, Fisher's rejection by and of her family is unusual at a time when women were primarily defined by domestic relations. And when she tries to find a new domestic situation by marrying Mr. Fisher, she finds not contentment but strangeness and disagreeableness. Soon after their marriage, and despite eventually having five children together, they spend long periods apart. At one point, she contemplates suicide. "My father and stepmother . . . had separate beds for each other, which is a bad sign" (10), she comments at one point, and the same could be said for her and Mr. Fisher. By 1788, they had separated for good: "After this I never lived with Mr. Fisher as a wife" (25).

The last straw for their marriage is recounted by Fisher in an interpolated story after the fact. She wants, apparently, to make it seem as if it is a story she does not want to tell: "Without observing the order of time, I must go back and relate some circumstances . . ." (26). Among other things, her husband accuses her of infidelity, and brings her and the accused man before a justice of the peace to swear their innocence (35–36). This public humiliation, which anticipates her half brother's later treatment of her in court, sunders her from her second family: "you and I must bid adieu to each other," she tells him. Now, since her "father and brother paid no attention to [her] wants" (25), she is alone in the world. Following her imprisonment, even her children turn against her: "they seem to act towards me with great coolness" (45), she observes. "From this day," she writes near the end of the narrative, "I will deny all family connexion" (45).

Denied "normal" female roles—daughter, sister, wife, even mother—Fisher is driven to adopt an extreme resolve for a woman in 1810: "I must set out with a resolution to gain a living for myself, and think no more of brother nor children" (42). Conventionally, like K. White, she finds solace and "family" with God—"I found a friend . . . which was the Lord" (46)—but she also finds "solace" in her own agency. This other "solace" takes the shape both of the narrative itself, which represents an attack on her half brother and a defense of her actions,[11] and of her representation of herself in that narrative as an agent of her own destiny.

What is at stake for Fisher in the narrative is agency. What is at stake for most of the other characters—men—is land or property, commodities that in the early United States presupposed agency. Fisher's *Memoirs* is remarkable for the way it demystifies a woman's role in 1810 as a commodity, an object, equivalent to land or, at best, as a carrier of land or property for a father or husband or son. Fisher's father, the Reverend Harry Munro, spends a good bit of the narrative pursuing land or property: he marries Eve Jay expecting "something handsome from her father . . . but . . . [is] much disappointed" (5); he has "a patent of land granted him for his services in the army" in the Seven Years' War (6–7); he offers to marry Elizabeth to an older man "providing [the man's] father . . . make over part of his estate" to support her and her children in case of the proposed husband's death (9); he purchases two lots in Albany (10); and, after the American Revolution, he puts in a claim for his loss of "landed property in America," a claim that is eventually honored by the British government. Munro is continually, as a later character in American literature puts it, minding the main chance.

Elizabeth is involved in many of those transactions. She provides affidavits for her father's claim against the government after the Revolution. Rejecting her father's plan to marry her to an older man, she agrees to marry Fisher, against her father's wishes, only after he offers to "make over all his property to [her]" (13), a fact that still does not please her father completely. Later, he tries to settle them on his patent, where Mr. Fisher proves to be a bad farmer. In the late 1770s, buffeted by the events of the Revolution, father and daughter meet up again in Montreal, where, down on his luck, he is forced to ask for money from the daughter he has never forgiven for marrying against his wishes. In return for her kindness, apparently, and fearing that Mr. Fisher, who is older that his daughter, will leave her an unprotected widow, he gives her a "deed of his patent, telling [her] to take care of it, but never to say anything concerning it till after his head was laid in the grave" (22). Munro then returns to England, promising to serve the Fishers as an importer; but they do not hear from him for eight years. He contacts his daughter again only when he needs the signed affidavits proving the value of the land he has lost in the Revolution. Throughout the narrative, then, Fisher is dangled as bait for land, Fisher marries for land, and Fisher is given land to hold for her children.

Her father's decision to grant her his patent of two thousand acres is strange, given that he then sunders communication with her for eight years and contacts her again only when he needs her help: "his conduct was not so pleasing as I wished" (23–24), she sighs. But when, in 1800, she tries "the virtue of the deed" her father gave her, she faces even worse conduct. Her half brother is leasing the land to tenants at the time, and he immediately challenges her deed. "I know," she insists, ". . . that my father had given him a quit-claim of the same property I held the deed of" (39), but he enters a complaint against her for forgery, she is immediately jailed for four months, and at trial she is quickly convicted and "sentenced to the state's prison for life" (39). For her part, Fisher claims never to have seen the man who testified that he had seen her deed executed by someone other than her father, though she recognizes that the evidence is so "pointed" that the court had no choice but to convict her (43).

The swiftness with which she is jailed and, later, convicted suggests women's relative helplessness before the law in 1810, while her half brother's claim that she forged the deed suggests that, for Fisher, what is at stake in her narrative is precisely a real, true, accurate, noncounterfeited portrait of herself. She is determined to prove that she is not a "forger." Brother and sister disagree about what kind of woman Fisher is: in public, at trial, legally, she is "convicted" of being a misrepresenter of her father's "will"; in public, in print, textually, she refutes that charge and presents herself as a woman wronged by her father, mother, brother, and children and thus driven, passively in a sense, to assert control of her own destiny (an action that, as I have suggested, she mitigates through a lukewarm conversion to Christianity).

Following her pardon by the governor and subsequent release from jail, Fisher asks:

What is property? It is only lent, and we must soon leave it; then we shall no more contend who shall have the most—no state's prison to be sent to if we cannot agree—no false witnesses to swear against us. . . . I have been told . . . that if I would behave myself, my brother would not see me want for anything. I wish I knew what kind of behaviour he wishes. (43)

No doubt, her half brother did not approve of her "behaviour" when she published her *Memoirs*. But she and he have different ideas, obviously, of what constitutes proper conduct for a woman. He wants her to be passive and silent. She, having "said little, but thought a great deal" (29) for many years, has become aggressive and vocal: rejecting family (45), going directly to the "public" for emotional support (44), castigating her father and half brother and son, rejecting an offer of marriage (46), and threatening further publication of the "unnatural" situation in which she has been placed (48). And, of course, she has "printed for the author" the very narrative in which she reconfigures herself as a vocal agent of her own destiny and him as just another man out to take advantage of a woman.

At the end of their narratives, both White and Fisher are quite literally alone in the world. They are oddities in post-Revolutionary society: women who have come to define themselves through their own endeavors, including the act of narrating their own stories. White calls to her aid "some of the sentiments contained in Zimmerman," that is, the German author Johann Georg Zimmermann, whose *Solitude Considered with Respect to Its Influence on the Mind and the Heart* (1793) went through several American editions in the sixteen years prior to White's publication of her narrative. "In solitude," Zimmermann wrote, "every man surrenders himself, without restraint or limitations, to the guidance of his own ideas, and implicitly, adopts the sentiments which his taste, temper, inclination, and genius inspire" (30). Or as John Dennie would write in the 1817 collection of his "Lay Preacher" essays: "I commune with my own heart in the crowd, and can be still, even in the street. . . . He who accustoms himself to closet meditations will not only purify his heart but correct his judgment, form his taste, exercise his memory, and regulate his imagination" (106). Zimmermann also, it should be noted, discussed Rousseau's *Confessions* in some detail (e.g., 301–304), perhaps leading both White and Fisher to conceive of their narratives, like Rousseau's, as confessions. Thus, Fisher adopts some of Rousseau's strategies, particularly in four interpolated pages (32–35) in which she confesses to youthful indiscretions committed in secret but now revealed to the (presumably) sympathetic reader. Thus, perhaps, both women "resolved on an enterprise which [had] no precedent" (Rousseau 1953, 17) in their world: imagining that they had an independent, even unique, self, and that that self had a story to tell, a story that could not yet be sold commercially to a publishing house, but that had, by necessity, to be printed by the author.

White's and Fisher's narratives are not fully emerged as autobiographies. Both authors are trying to express a sense of inwardness or interiority, but they lack the narrative means to do so. Rousseau is consistently interested in the *Confessions* in how his "heart" and "character" are formed (see, e.g., 23) and in what makes them unique. He tries to express that uniqueness through a description of his interior landscape, a private realm in which Rousseau (and, potentially, others) can, as Thoreau later says, "know [him]self as a human entity; the scene, so to speak, of thoughts and affections" (429). Both women, I would argue, are looking for ways to describe the "scene" of a distinctive, unique self; White's emphasis on the body is one such attempt. But by and large they do so only obliquely. Their narratives turn more insistently to the external world and the traditional roles for women against which they define themselves.

Both authors clearly push their narratives toward an affirmation of ordinary life, and both begin to rely on nature as an inner moral source. There is a residual gesture toward religious conversion in their narratives, but notably there is no gesture toward federal or republican notions of self-effacement. Unlike Graydon and Rush and Allen, White and Fisher do not have the luxury of imagining themselves as disinterested. Their narratives are called into being precisely in order to *affirm* their visibility in the public world. Finding no connections where they are supposed to (as daughters, wives, and mothers) and finding none where male self-biographers found them (in politics, society, books, etc.), White and Fisher look to themselves as natural sources of moral authority. In these ways, they begin in their narratives to emerge as agents of their destinies.

◦§ 8 §◦

John Fitch and the Invented Self

IT IS AN IRONY OF AMERICAN LITERARY HISTORY THAT Benjamin Franklin's *History of My Life*, which so consistently and insistently describes a self formed in reaction and relation to others, has been enshrined as the first classic American autobiography.[1] His narrative clearly exists outside the emergent ideologies of romanticism and capitalism, and it exists outside the accompanying and also emergent discourses of autobiography and romantic individualism.[2] Seen generically and historically, I have argued, emergent autobiography in the nineteenth century can best be defined as any work written or told by one person in which the author struggles to tell the story of how s/he comes over time to be an independent, often original, agent. Franklin resists seeing himself in those senses, as do most of his contemporaries. He and they see themselves as products of imitation and emulation, bound within a social sense of self that emphasizes conformity and compatibility. Thoreau's fear in *Walden* that his "expression may not be extravagant enough, may not wander far enough beyond the narrow limits of my daily experience, so as to be adequate to the truth of which I have been convinced," would have been inexplicable to Franklin and Allen and Rush. They did not desire "to speak somewhere without bounds," as Thoreau puts it (580); they desired to speak within the known bounds of commonly held experience. Alexander Graydon, remember, insisted that he possessed "diffidence . . . a kind of morbid sensibility [to] ever making self the principle figure in [a] scene" (1811, 73). Thomas Jefferson, midway through his "memoranda and . . . recollections" (which we now refer to as his *Autobiography*), wearily sighs: "I am already tired of talking about myself" (43). Jefferson's narrative, James M. Cox has written, is a "memoir, which means that it will relate itself to the external world of the author in history, not to the inner world of self-reflection" (52). The

157

"inner world of self-reflection" is simply not available to most writers in the period, of course, and Jefferson is typical in the way that he diminishes "his personality, his inner feelings, his private relations" (Cox, 40) in his narrative. Franklin, Graydon, and Jefferson insist that they are dependent selves, deriving their identity from imitable and emulable predecessors. As the patriot-painter John Trumbull could put it late in life in his own memoirs: "My taste for drawing began to dawn early. It is common to talk of natural genius; but I am disposed to doubt the existence of such a principle in the human mind; at least, in my own case, I can clearly trace it to mere imitation" (5).

I have already discussed several self-biographers in the early national period who began to reconceptualize the self in terms of inwardness and independent agency. Another of Franklin's contemporaries who began to reconceptualize the self was John Fitch. An early proponent of the use of steam to power boats, John Fitch was born in 1744 in Connecticut. His life, as he narrates it, echoes Franklin's in a number of ways. Like Franklin, he was from a large family headed by a hardworking, industrious father. Like Franklin, he had little formal education, but managed to read fairly widely, become accomplished in a number of fields, and moved easily in the circles of men who possessed more formal educations. Like Franklin, he was an improver and an inventor. They both "tinkered" with machines and with ideas. And like Franklin, he wrote his self-biography in order both to prevent others from telling his story wrongly and to provide "useful lessons to mankind" (19).[3] The parallels between the two men—one the most famous American of his age, the other soon (and still) forgotten—run deep. As indentured servants, both left their masters before their time expired; as sons, both ran away from home in a defiant gesture of self-dependence; as young men, both organized social clubs for personal and social improvement; as philosophers, both moved from their parents' Protestantism to a deeply held deism; and as scientists, both tinkered with gadgets and played with numbers. They were remarkably similar in their backgrounds and interests.

But in 1790, the year of Franklin's death, Fitch began to recount his life in a narrative that he refers to as "a detail of my life" (19), a narrative that moves toward different conclusions about the formation of selfhood than does Franklin's. In his narrative, Fitch struggles to understand himself not as a social being formed by imitation and emulation, but as a unique being capable of original thought and independent agency. This uniqueness is expressed not only in Fitch's insistent demand to Thomas

Jefferson and the federal Board of Patent Commissioners to recognize his claim to be the inventor of the steamboat, a demand that dominated Fitch's consciousness after 1790, but also and concomitantly in the conception of selfhood he formulates in this curious self-biography, not published in any form until 1976.

Indeed, it is entirely possible that Fitch's narrative is a direct response to Franklin's.[4] Fitch's idea for the steamboat came to him in 1785, coinciding with Franklin's return to Philadelphia from Paris in that year. Fitch approached Franklin on at least one occasion for advice and help (see Prager, 9). The two men apparently shared several conversations, although in the end Franklin sent him elsewhere to seek aid. Franklin's *History of My Life*, parts of which he wrote in 1784 and 1788–1789, began to appear in print in 1790, the year of his death and the year Fitch sat down to write his own memoirs. Dr. Henry Stuber printed most of part one of Franklin's manuscript in *Universal Asylum and Columbian Magazine* from May 1790 through May 1791; and Mathew Carey printed a condensation of all four parts of the manuscript in *American Museum* in July and November of 1790. Fitch, presumably, could have read the excerpts.

Like Franklin's *History of My Life* and Rush's *Travels through Life*, neither of which was published in the author's lifetime nor authorized in a final form by them, Fitch's self-biography has a curious and complicated history. On the "12 day of January 1790," Fitch began to write a history of his work on the steamboat, work that dated to 1785, when he first had the idea of using steam to propel carriages or boats. Eventually that manuscript became a diary and a depository for notes, drafts, letters, and petitions. Fitch's modern-day editor refers to it, quite usefully, I think, as "The Steamboat History" (not to be confused with Fitch's 1788 pamphlet, *The Original Steam-Boat Supported*). The unwieldy manuscript begins with quite a bit of material about Fitch himself, but eventually becomes an archive of his attempts to publicize his experiments on the steamboat. In 1791 the Reverend Nathaniel Irwin, a close friend of Fitch's, urged him to write his memoirs, which Fitch accordingly did, dedicating this second manuscript to Irwin. This second manuscript focuses on Fitch's life from his birth to his invention/discovery of steam power in 1785, at which point, remember, the autobiographical material of "The Steamboat History" picks up his story. The second manuscript is supplemented by seven "postscripts" that Fitch wrote on the back of the fourth and final fascicle of "The Steamboat History," which, his editor tells us, "was turned over and upside down for this purpose"

(Fitch, 94, n. 61). The second manuscript (with its postscripts), which his modern-day editor refers to as Fitch's "Autobiography," is the one I want to examine in detail, containing as it does an extended and focused treatment of Fitch's entire life up to the time he wrote the narrative.

After completing the second manuscript, "A Detail of My Life," in 1792, Fitch sealed it and deposited it in the Library Company of Philadelphia with the request that it not be opened for thirty years. Apparently, he wanted to spare several of his friends embarrassment due to his revelations about their sexual misadventures.[5] The manuscript was duly opened after the thirty years had passed, and its information was used by biographers and historians in the mid–nineteenth century and beyond, either to write Fitch's life or to write him into accounts of the development of the steamboat in the United States. But the manuscript remained unpublished until 1976. The modern edition, called *Autobiography*, reprints the "Detail" manuscript in full and excerpts most of the "autobiographical" sections of "The Steamboat History."

In contrast to Franklin's effort a few years earlier to write himself as a self within society, imitating and emulating others, Fitch writes himself as "singular." I am, he remarks near the beginning of the manuscript, "one of the most singular men perhaps that has been born this age" (22). His singularity manifests itself in any number of ways. For example, he is treated in "singular" ways by other people: "The usage I met with in the house [of my master] perhaps was as singular as is to be found in the United States" (40), he complains. And "what was the most singular of all . . . was" (41) that his master would not let him use the tools of the trade, in this case clock repairing. His relationship with his master is typical of his relationships with everyone with whom he comes into contact. "Sir," Fitch writes to Irwin, "when I take a view of my Past life[,] as singular as it is[,] . . . I am sure I shall have the softest Cushen in Heaven to [be] Lit upon" (133).

His love life, to take another example, is singular, and this not simply in the way that he conceives of it, but in the fact that he talks about it so directly. I have pointed out that the private realm of emotions and passions was elided by most self-biographers in the period, including Jefferson, Franklin, Graydon, Rush, and Adams. Fitch's marriage, like theirs, is treated laconically. However, Fitch does not simply leave his marriage in the background of his achievements, as Franklin does in his reference to Deborah Reed Franklin as "a good & faithful Helpmate" through the years (1371); instead, he turns his account of it into a statement about his own independence and freedom. In December 1767, he married Lucy Roberts, who gave birth to a son in November of the following year. Two months later, Fitch "sat off [on] a journey from home and . . . never since found my way back" (45). He was, he says, convinced that he and his wife "could not live happy together" (46). Like K. White, he travels through the colonies/states without the burden of a family, alone but independent. Like Elizabeth Fisher, he denies his family. Indeed, the ensuing narrative demonstrates that he could not live happily with anyone. Witness the strange, "secret" (125) ménage à trois involving him, his business partner, and a female tavern owner. His partner, Harry Voight, a married man, carries on a long-running affair with the tavern owner, who is single. Fitch does not learn about the affair until she becomes pregnant. He separates the two and helps the woman give birth to the child, even though this leads the neighbors to think that he is the father of the child. Later, when the woman becomes pregnant by Voight again, Fitch sends her away, only to discover that she has taken his (Fitch's) name in order to protect her virtue. He insists—his audience, remember, is first and foremost a minister—that he is innocent of any actual "Crime" in the affair: he claims to accept her ruse in order to provide her with an excuse for the second pregnancy, thus protecting both her and Voight from the social stigma and crime of adultery. Thankfully, he sighs in 1791, "being so far advanced in years not many [events] so singular can accrue" to him now (129).

But singularity lies even deeper on him, as it did on K. White, whose "masculine" body led her into various scrapes. His very body, Fitch reports, was formed into "disproportioned shapes." His father imposed hard labor on him in youth, stunting his growth. At eighteen, "as nature required growth," he "started up all at once without giving nature time to consult herself" (32). He is, as a result, disfigured in some way that he will not specify, though he alludes to it at several points. I am, he says at one point, for example, "slendermade and [have] the appearance of one being considerably advanced in the consumption" (50), even though he apparently is not actually tubercular. I am not "a very handsome man" (137), he says; I am "contemptable" (102, 121) and "despicable [in] appearance" (123), with an "uncouth way of speaking and holding up extravigant Ideas" (124). His singularity is physical as well as social, and he insists upon it with a relentless fervor. He wants to be perceived as different, as singular, as "extravigant." Here, again, is an instructive difference between Fitch and Franklin, for Franklin rarely mentions his body in a personal way. Generalized comments about health can be found in *History of My Life*, but Franklin never particularizes those comments. It never occurs to him to describe and analyze his physical self.

Singularity finally seems to be a part of Fitch's very character. "I ever had a singular curiosity in seeing mechanical opperations" (33), he remarks at one point. He has no training in mechanical operations, yet, unaccountably, is fascinated by them. Later in the narrative, this intellectual singularity will allow Fitch to justify and explain his originality, but early on it merely seems perverse. He harshly criticizes his father for his bigotry and hypocrisy, and even turns to criticizing "heaven" for letting him be conceived by such a man. Such criticisms are, he notes, "unnatural," "irreverand," perverse. But they do come from him. They are "the truth" (25). From "the singularity of my make shape disposition and [fortune] in this world," he says mournfully, "I am inclined to believe that it was the design of heaven that I should be born on [the] very line [between two towns, Hartford and Windsor] and not in any township whatever" (22). From his very beginning, as it were, he is set apart from the rest of society, a separateness that he figures as singularity, unnaturalness, perversity, and liminality.[6] These figures, of course, are more similar to Thoreau's self-conception in *Walden* or to De Quincey's in *Confessions of an English Opium-Eater* (1821) than they are to Franklin's in his *History of My Life*.

Singularity was a word that had been in use for several centuries by the time Fitch took hold of it as an organizing trope for his self-biography in 1790. Samuel Johnson had defined it in his 1755 *Dictionary* as "Some character or quality by which one is distinguished from others" and "Character or manners different from those of others." The *Oxford English Dictionary* offers nine definitions, including one that seems closest to Fitch's meaning and which was first used by Laurence Sterne in 1768: "The fact or condition of departing or deviating from what is customary, usual, or normal; peculiarity, eccentricity, oddity, strangeness." To deny an apparently reasonable request, Samuel Richardson's Clarissa reports, "can carry only an appearance of singularity" (543); that is, unreasonable behavior makes a person eccentric or peculiar. By the nineteenth century, autobiographers like Thoreau and Barnum were concerned to both foster and articulate their eccentricities, but Clarissa and her avid eighteenth-century readers like Adams and Jefferson tried to resist theirs. What is remarkable in Fitch's "Detail of My Life" is both the extent of his singularity and its origins. The origins are various and include every source for human behavior that the eighteenth century could imagine: society (as we have seen), God, heaven, fate, nature, family, and the self. Wherever he turns, Fitch sees himself marked by others as eccentric and odd.

Family and society take the brunt of the blame, although it is not always clear whether Fitch was noticed by others because of his singularity or became singular because he was noticed. Like Franklin, whose brother beat him and whose friends took advantage of him early in life, Fitch says he was subjected to "tyranical" (95) family members, governors, and acquaintances. His brother unjustly beat him (23), his father unaccountably took him out of school (25), his master refused in what Fitch calls "most singular" behavior to teach him the trade of watchmaking (41), his fellow captives among the British in 1782 treated him "in the most tyranical manner" (95), and the militia during the Revolution mortified him by stripping him of his commission (57). But heaven, too, took great "pleasure" in "design[ing him] for some cruel fate," happy "to sport and tyrinize with [him]" (30). The government's denial of a sole patent to him for the steamboat in 1791 was simply another occasion when "fate"—in this case in the form of Thomas Jefferson—"sported" with him (70). But while Franklin frees himself from tyranny by choosing friends and family and a God who are increasingly "reasonable," Fitch withdraws into his eccentricity, into a conception of himself as fundamentally different from other people.

The most significant place where Fitch imagines his singularity is his invention of the steamboat. Seeing a gentleman pass him in a "Chair" drawn by a horse one day, Fitch is "struck" by the "thought . . . that it would be a noble thing if I could have such a carriage without the expense of keeping a horse."[7] The idea, he says, "strongly impressed my mind," and he immediately set about drafting plans for, first, a steam-driven carriage and, then, a steam-driven boat. He claims that the idea, both in its whole and in its parts, was essentially his. Even when a friend, learning of his idea, shows him pictures of a steam engine in the 1759 edition of *Philosophia Britannia*, Fitch insists that "Till then I did not know that there was such a thing in nature as a Steam Engine." In other words, he did not simply invent or discover the idea that steam could power a boat; he also independently invented or discovered the concept of a condensing steam engine! Seeing that someone had beat him to that invention "chagreaned me considerably," he says, but on the other hand it reassured him that he could procure "the force" of steam and so realize his first idea of a steamboat (113).

The most famous American inventor of the century, Benjamin Franklin, tinkered with objects or ideas, imitating or emulating in order to improve the performance of something. The glass lamps introduced in Philadelphia by Franklin were "his" invention, he says, only inasmuch as he could "claim" "some Merit . . . respecting the Form of our Lamps as differing from the Globe Lamps we at first were supplied with from London" (1425). He "studied & practis'd all Thevenot's Motions & Positions [for swimming]"; only then did he add "some of my own" (1351). His "Philadelphia Experiments" with electricity are modeled upon the experiments he observed in Boston in 1746; Franklin merely improves them and adds some of his own. Fitch's ideas did not come from previous models, like Franklin's lamps or experiments, nor did they come from books, like his swimming techniques or his writing style. They came to him—"struck" him, he reports several times in "Detail" and repeats in his 1788 defense of his steamboat—from out of thin air, and hence are essentially and originally his: "the principle part of the original thoughts of any part of the Works [of the steamboat] proceeded from me" (116), he insists. Unlike apprentices who imitated their masters and unlike "inventors" such as Franklin who emulated and improved the work of others, Fitch in his self-biographical account is the creator or inventor of things new "in nature" (113), that is, of the steamboat and—I want to argue—of a distinct, original self that is an agent of its own destiny.

The invention of the steamboat most interests Fitch, as the manuscript of his "Steamboat History" becomes, by turning the quarto-size notebook over and repaginating it, the continuation and conclusion of the narrative begun in "Detail." Metaphorically and textually, his life "became," as it were, the history of the steamboat. "Sir as I am sure that the remainder of my life [after 1790] cannot be filled with interesting matters I mean to confine the whole to the 4th Book of the Steam Boat History to which I refer you for the remained" (94), he writes to his correspondent. Both manuscripts begin in self-biography, only to become eventually an archive of the public documents dealing with Fitch and his steamboat. Personal narrative is transformed into the public history of a technological innovation. In that sense, Fitch, too, is in the end writing a self-biography or memoirs, rather than autobiography. But, before he is consumed by the steamboat, Fitch writes of the self in an innovative way. It is his "invention" of a distinct, original self that most interests me in this chapter, for his self-defense of the originality of his technological invention comes to depend, in great part, on his portrait of himself as eccentric, peculiar, "singular." Driven by failure from a "reasonable" dependence on society in any form—family, the apprentice system, other inventors—Fitch remakes himself as singular, participating in his culture's fascination in 1790 with the emergent concept of independent, distinct, original selfhood and anticipating the rise of a genre of writing devoted solely to its expression.

Recall Franklin's injunction at the end of his list of virtues in part two of *History of My Life*: "Imitate Jesus and Socrates." Like much else in that narrative, this injunction is deceptively simple. On one level, of course, it is surely meant to make us smile, as the old man pokes gentle irony at the young man's naïveté. He added this thirteenth virtue, he tells us, perhaps smiling himself, because a Quaker friend told him that he was "generally thought proud." But it is only gentle irony, for the command to imitate is fully a part of the Christian and classical view of selfhood that Franklin, no less than Jefferson and Washington and Adams, continued to adhere to late in the eighteenth century. Let me describe my father, Franklin says early in his narrative: "He had a mechanical Genius . . . and on occasion was very handy in the Use of other Tradesmen's Tools. But his great Excellence lay in a sound Understanding, and solid Judgment in prudential Matters, both in private and publick Affairs" (1315). Does that describe his father, or himself? Well, both. Franklin, one might say, actually "became" in his self-biography the father he so lovingly described. Franklin's God, similarly, is to be imitated, not through biblical commandments, but through man's use of his reason. The irony is gentle not because Franklin disbelieves the injunction to imitate, in other words, but because he now sees the young man's inability to approach Jesus's or Socrates's virtue. He became, Franklin sighs, satisfied with so much less than perfection:

> something that pretended to be Reason was every now and then suggesting itself to me, that such extreme Nicety as I exacted of my self might be a kind of Foppery in Morals, which if it were known would make me ridiculous; that a perfect Character might be attended with the Inconvenience of being envied and hated; and that a benevolent Man should allow a few Faults in himself, to keep his Friends in Countenance. (1390)

Note that it is "something that pretended to be Reason" that suggests this to him. Franklin unreasonably—but sociably—accepts behavior that is less than perfect. There is an even deeper level of irony here.[8]

Fitch, on the other hand, is much less concerned with whether he helps make society function more smoothly than he is with whether his own life is self-satisfying. When he returns from the Northwest Territory, for example, having surveyed 250,000 acres of "Valuable Lands," Fitch says that he was "morrally sure [he] should one day or other become a man of forturne" (108). Or, later, when he discusses his formation of a club or society for deists in America, Fitch declares that he had two purposes: one (Franklinian) was to "benefit ... mankind and support ... Civil Government"; the other was

> to let the world know as contemptable as I was and despised by all ranks of People from the first Officers of Government down to the Blacburry garls that I would call in all the world into my doctrines[,] the Jews with the fullness of the Gentile Nations[,] and establish one Area throughout the World. (116)

Franklin wants to imitate Jesus Christ and Socrates; Fitch wants to become their antitype, perhaps even wants to rise above them. "Only my despicable appearance and uncouth way of speaking and holding up extravigant Ideas and so bad an address must ever make me unpopular[,] but was I a hansom man and a good writer I could now do more than ever Jesus Christ or George Fox did" (123–124). When Fitch makes this claim he is not simply accepting deist views that Christ was merely mortal; he is moving beyond imitation and emulation as the defining methods of self-formation. The world remaining hostile and unaccommodating to him, Fitch retreats into singularity and originality to defend his ideas and to explain himself.

Seen in this way, many of Fitch's apparently casual references and ideas take on significance. As a young man, he was "nearly crazey after learning" (25), but his education, much more so than Franklin's, was haphazard and self-directed. His literary allusions in the narrative are therefore infrequent and often vague, as when he suggests that as a very young child watching ants and flies "made as lively impressions on my mind and perhaps as great as the Trojan War on the minds of heroes" (22). But at several points, he alludes much more specifically and significantly to specific literary figures. In 1782, on a western trip to survey land in Kentucky for a land-jobbing company he directed, Fitch is taken captive by Indians, forced to march to Detroit, and delivered to the British army. Moved to a prison barracks on an island in the St. Lawrence River, Fitch spends the rest of 1782 in captivity. But unlike Allen, who finds a community of sympathetic patriots in captivity, Fitch finds solitude and wealth: "my industery enabled me to be of service to myself and of great good to others" (91), he writes, so much so that "in about four months I got to be as rich as Roberson Cruso" (94). Defoe's novel, in both the full-length English editions and the American abridgements that began to appear in 1774, "offered the American reading public a theologically and hence politically acceptable model for filial disobedience, a justifiable assertion of independence" (Fliegelman 1982, 76). Fitch, like Franklin, early on enacts the story of the prodigal son; but Fitch never returns, either to his father, his wife, his family, or (in a sense) to society. He, like Burroughs and White and Fisher, has become a "pilgrim," wandering post-Revolutionary America with an agenda—independence, freedom, solitude— quite different from that of many of his contemporaries. Theologically, of course, Fitch's sense of himself as independent and free is figured, as I have already pointed out, by his sense that his deist doctrine makes him the equal or superior of Fox and Christ.

When, then, after being released on parole by the British, Fitch stops at a "decent well looking House" in New Jersey to put up for the night, he is asked his name: "I told them my name was Legons but wanted them to alter it to John Fitch" (101). On one level, this allusion is amusing: Fitch apparently liked to make other people feel uncomfortable, as the suggestion that they were putting Satan (or an insane person) up for the night might have made many people feel at the time. As Mark records the story in the New Testament, "a man with an unclean spirit" who lived in isolation, "secured [by his neighbors] with fetters and chains" and cutting himself with stones, escaped his bonds and ran up to Christ. Christ said to the man/devil: "'What is your name?' . . . 'My name is legion,' he answered, 'for there are many of us.'" Christ cast the devils plaguing this man into a herd of pigs, who immediately drowned themselves (Mark 5.1–20). That Fitch should, even amusingly, allude to himself as Satan is significant: he calls attention to himself as an "adversary," an outsider who, like Milton's Satan, defines himself in opposition to the forces that have shaped his existence. Another marginal figure of the era, Tom Paine, figuring the American quest for independence in 1776, also appropriated Satan's voice for independence: "as Milton wisely expresses, 'never can true reconcilement grow where wounds of deadly hate have pierced so deep'" (86). As Alina Clej remarks concerning De Quincey: "In [his] economy of the self, in his offering of the self as prodigal, as perpetual transgressor . . . a new fundamentally modern form of subjectivity appears" (11). Fitch imagines a romantic self.

In another gesture toward liminality and opposition, Fitch repeatedly identifies with American slaves. The behavior of his "tyrant brother" as he was growing up leads him to think that "could I be set into a Virginia field amongst their slaves with the severest driver at my back I would sooner engage in it than to go thro' the same again" (30–31). "I enjoyed myselfe," he barks at one point about his indentures, about "as well as most of the Virginia slaves who [have] liberty to go to a dance once a week" (32). Later, in captivity when he is forced to eat stolen food to stay alive, he remarks: "This circumstance . . . pleads powerfully with me in behalf of slaves who are kept on short allowance for theft" (79).

Crusoe, Satan, American slaves: Fitch finds himself in figures of isolation and oppression. He is, it seems to me, looking for a way to figure the concept of the self as an independent, active, (self-)shaping entity. Such an attempt has to "involve twisting existing terms into new and unfamiliar shapes," as Peter Carafiol has written; and it will "necessarily appear awkward, even to the writer who produced [it]" (166). Throughout the narrative, Fitch's attempt to do just that is also articulated by reference to two principles that other self-biographers like Jefferson and Graydon and Rush downplay: self-trust and ambition. Fitch learns early on to depend on himself: he does not tell his family that he rebelled against his master, "but trusted to my own abilities" to get out of the scrape. The same gesture is repeated time and time again, as when Fitch takes a watch apart and puts it back together without any assistance, "Which gave me confidence to undertake watches in future" (51). He does not need anyone's help (see also 102, 108, and 121). Ambition was a conflicted principle for Fitch's contemporaries, but not for Fitch. Even at the age of seventeen, "I at that time looked upon myself to be a man altho a very little one and was filled with a good deal of ambition" (33). Years later, after making himself an inventor and land-jobber, after peripatetically surveying much of what the new United States had to offer, Fitch leads his deist group (he imagines) as a sort of founding father. In 1790, the group votes, at Fitch's insistence, "to alter the date of our writings," beginning the calendar "in the 1st year of the Universal Society" on February 25, which is the anniversary of the first meeting of the society. Fitch desperately wants the year to begin on February 1, however, "but they did not know my Ambition and that I strenuously urged it because it was my Birth Day" (123). He is an originator, working, as even his "disciples" in the deist society know, with "Ideas [that] were all as wild as Steam Boat building" (122–123).

It is not surprising that Franklin always moves in the direction of society, not only by imitating and emulating other people, but by tinkering with social institutions like the post office and fire companies and colleges, by exploring the problems of urban experience, and by imagining himself from the first as "a leader among the Boys" who, even as a child, had a "projecting public spirit." Franklin is most at home when he is elbowing thousands of auditors at a sermon by George Whitefield or when he is politicking among the powerful and wealthy (1408–1409, 1412–1416, 1314). Whatever he was in real life, Franklin in his self-biography is a social self: typical, dependent, selfless. Fitch, like many of the romantic autobiographers to follow, is a separate self, and hence he continually figures himself as moving away from society, by continually alienating the people who try to help him, by repeatedly plunging into the as yet unsurveyed Ohio Territory, by demanding the sole patent and market rights to "his" idea of the steamboat, and by abandoning imitation and emulation as methods of self-formation.

His map of the Northwest Territory is a figure for his goal in "Detail of my Life." He begins the mapping project in emulation: "I . . . made a Draft of that Country from Hutchin's and Murrows Maps with the additions of my own knoledge." He did this, he reports, "to keep the Ideas of the Country in my mind," and to provide a cheap and accurate map to the many settlers about to descend upon Ohio. But what, finally, he represents on the map—what is new—is the uncharted territory that only he has "tested." The space he tries to represent is not yet the United States, though it will soon be; it is "natural" space, marked only by rivers and lakes and mountains. Similarly, in his narrative, he attempts to mark out space that is also uncharted: that of the self as a free, independent, self-determining agent. That space, too, will soon be mapped and inhabited by others, but in 1790 Fitch is its only pilgrim.

"Genius," Edward Young wrote in the mid–eighteenth century in his treatise on originality, "is [the] God within" (31). "Always in literature, and sometimes in life, originality is the one thing needful," Joseph Dennie wrote at the beginning of the nineteenth (84). It is Fitch, not the more famous Franklin, who first creates an American narrative self that begins to epitomize Young's assertion, who begins to see originality as "needful." Analyzing Fitch in a different context, that of the simultaneous emergence of literary/visual culture and the creation/division of labor in late-eighteenth-century America, Laura Rigal notes that Fitch repeatedly expresses "a rage for personhood" (59). The "opening of new territories in the western interior," she writes about Fitch's "Detail," "is linked inseparably to the (violent and painful) forging of new territories of subjective interiority, or new 'mental properties'" (71). Fitch steps beyond the world of "memoirs" and self-biographies and personal "histories" and struggles to express himself in what we now recognize as the discourse of autobiography. He conceives a world, like that conceived by historians following the French Revolution, in which radical discontinuity between people and between time periods is possible. He begins the calendar anew, as did the French revolutionaries. Fitch's invention of himself as distinct, original, and singular—something "new in nature" —is not conservative or progressive; it is radical and revolutionary. History, in this view, moves by leaps and bounds, by discontinuous alterations, much as, by analogy, ideas come to Fitch "out of nowhere." It is, indeed, how romantic historians like Hegel and Prescott come to understand the historical process, and how individuals like Thoreau come to understand their private selves. Franklin may be a founding father of the American political system, but Fitch is a founder, an originator, an inventor, of American autobiographical discourse. In his insistence on originality, on his own independent agency as inventor and self, Fitch, not Franklin, voices the emergent democratic conception that individual genius is the inimitable and unemulable God within.

❧ 9 ❧

"Res Privata": Cultivating the Self

in America, 1820–1830

Now that the republic—the *res-publica*—has been settled,

it is time to look after the *res-privata*—the private state,

—to see . . . that the *private* state receive no detriment.

—Henry David Thoreau, "Life without Principle"

IN PART ONE, I DISCUSSED AT LENGTH THREE SELF-biographies, one published in 1811 (Graydon's), one written in 1800 (Rush's), and one written and published in 1779 (Allen's). In part two, I have discussed four emergent autobiographies, one published in 1798 and 1804 (Burroughs's), two published in 1809–1810 (White's and Fisher's), and one written in 1792. I have not traced, in other words, a clear chronological development from self-biography to autobiography. Self-biographies continued to be written even as the autobiographical impulse fitfully emerged after 1790. The emergence of autobiography was not sudden and dramatic. In their narratives, Burroughs, White, Fisher, and Fitch reveal tendencies and impulses of the genre, though perhaps not fully executed examples of it.

I have, as well, been reluctant to push my analysis of the emergence of autobiography into the antebellum period. The urge in early national literary studies, as I pointed out in chapter 2, has often been to get to the midcentury United States as quickly as possible. I have been reluctant in part because I have found so much material to interest me in the thirty years from 1780 to 1810, but also because the emergence of the genre cannot be traced in a simple connect-the-dots manner. In this conclud-

171

ing chapter, however, I do want to extend my argument forward into the decade of the 1820s, when the genre of autobiography more fully emerged in the United States.

By 1810, I have argued, it was possible for authors in the United States to write autobiographies, as I have defined them. By 1830, that mode of self-understanding and self-expression had become dominant. What Thoreau at midcentury would refer to as the "res-privata" had, by 1830, become a primary concern of many writers, particularly those still held to the margins of politics and of financial and social success. This chapter surveys that decade, and in it I try to suggest the remarkable proliferation of narratives in which an author attempts to understand her or his lived experience in "autobiographical" ways. My method here necessarily changes from an extended discussion of one or two narratives to briefer, more suggestive discussions of a handful of narratives. These narratives represent a few examples, among many possible ones, of what came "after Franklin" in mid-nineteenth-century America

I begin with a nonnarrative text. The 1838 Franklin lectures, an annual series of public lectures initiated in the early 1830s and designed to enlighten the workingman in Boston, were delivered by William Ellery Channing. In *Self-Culture*, the printed version of his Franklin lectures, Channing proclaims that "the ground of a man's culture lies in his nature, not in his calling" (29). From our point of view, Channing's attitude is condescending—he is distributing advice from on high to the working class—but, still, it is one place from which to view the changed attitude toward the self in antebellum America. In contrast to the namesake of the lecture series, Channing places much less emphasis on work (one's "calling") as a component of one's self-conception. Franklin's *History of My Life* emphasizes his "calling" as a printer: how his father helped him choose a trade, how he apprenticed under his brother and did journeyman's work in London, how he worked with and against Keimer and others, how he augmented his business by expanding his printing operations into neighboring colonies, how he printed an advertisement for the British government in the Seven Years' War. Part one, especially, revolves around the printing trade, but even parts two and three continue to emphasize Franklin's business. His *History of My Life*, I insisted earlier and continue to insist here, is not about his individual "nature" or self; it is about the way he forms himself in accordance with other known models of thinking and behavior, including the models available in his calling. Franklin discovers his identity; he does not invent it.

Channing urges his audience to shifts its attention to "nature," by which he means the "powers" that we have, first, "of turning the mind on itself" (13) and, second, of "determining and forming ourselves" (14). On the face of it, perhaps, this formulation is not so different from Franklin's in part two of *History of My Life*. There, in several complicated and amusing extended metaphors, Franklin imagines the mind as both a garden and an ax. Contemplating his own desire for moral perfection, for example, he tells the story of the man who bought an ax from his neighbor, a blacksmith:

> the Man . . . desired to have the whole of its Surface as bright as the Edge; the Smith consented to grind it bright for him if he would turn the Wheel. He turn'd while the Smith press'd the broad Face of the Ax hard & heavily on the Stone, which made the turning of it very fatiguing. The Man came every now & then from the Wheel to see how the Work went on; and at length would take his Ax as it was without further Grinding. No, says the Smith, Turn on, turn on; we shall have it bright by and by; as yet 'tis only speckled. Yes, says the Man; but—*I think I like a speckled Ax best.* (1392, italics in original)

In this metaphor, another entity—"self" or consciousness—sharpens the moral sense (and in Franklin's other metaphor the "self" weeds the "garden" of the mind). We "see" ourselves and "shape" ourselves through a kind of "cultivation," a sharpening of the ax in the first metaphor, a pulling of weeds and strengthening of crops in the second. But weeds and crops are relative; corn in a cornfield is a crop, but corn in a bean field is a weed. Franklin knows which are weeds and which are crops by looking outside himself to parental models, to books, to social expectations. He builds his list of moral virtues by enumerating "the moral Virtues I had met with in my Reading" (1384), he tells us. Similarly, the ax, as Franklin points out, has a purpose (chopping) that determines its use. That purpose is not invented by the ax; it is determined by people who use axes. It has been *designed by someone else* to be useful, which is why Franklin humorously makes the point that it does not have to be completely free of rust. It chops as well with a few rust blemishes as does a perfectly polished axe, with much less effort in "sharpening" required.

Channing uses a metaphor similar to Franklin's: "To cultivate any thing, be it a plant, an animal, a mind, is to make grow. Growth, expansion is the end. Nothing admits culture, but that which has a principle of life, capable of being expanded" (15). Franklin's garden, like Candide's, is marked by logical limits, which experience has constructed according to the dictates of reason; and Franklin is content to shift easily between organic and inorganic metaphors. Channing's metaphor is always organic, and it always insists on the self's ability to expand or unfold: "Let me only say, that the power of original thought is particularly manifested in those, who thirst for progress, who are bent on unfolding their whole nature" (45). Faced with the vertiginous unfolding of knowledge —"progress" at first, then "revolution"—Crèvecoeur's fictional narrator flees Western society. However, Channing tells his audience to turn inward, to cultivate the mind or soul that is there, and it will, then, "unfold" or "expand" into an originality that marks us all as unique: "As the human countenance . . . is diversified without end in the race, and is never the same in any two individuals, so the human soul . . . expands into an infinite variety of forms, and would be wofully stinted by modes of culture requiring all men to learn the same lesson or bend to the same rules" (41–42).[1] By cultivating our self, Channing asserts, we will unfold our "natural" powers and thereby "free ourselves from the power of human opinion and example, except as far as this is sanctioned by our own deliberate judgment" (43). Each of us will become our own source of moral authority! *That* is a long way from Franklin's socially defined sense of "personal" identity.

Channing's lecture bears upon the genre of autobiography because it articulates the shift in values that accompanied and complemented the widespread emergence and acceptance of the autobiographical impulse.[2] These values include personal judgment as the sanction for behavior, nature or the natural self as the highest source of moral authority, and a sense of inward depth or inwardness (Channing's "unfolding"), which causes or leads to one's own originality or uniqueness. They include, as well, two other values that Channing articulates: an affirmation of ordinary life and a reverence for childhood as a formative age. On the first of these, Channing continues to assert the importance of work, but he emphasizes as well the other places, now, where self-culture can be pursued: a "clean, comfortable dwelling" (35); "close, tender, responsible connections" to others (30); the "seventh day" of the week, traditionally assigned to rest but now opened to personal improvement (72–73); and the "more and more time [that] will be redeemed from manual labor, for intellectual and social occupations" (73)—that is, what we now call leisure time. Lived experience as it is most highly valued moves into the spaces of the domestic and private. "A trade is plainly not the great end of [our] being, for [the] mind cannot be shut up in it" (29). And if mind must be cultivated attentively and continuously, then childhood must be revered as the bud that can fully flower later in life: "They, whose childhood has been neglected, though they may make progress in future life, can hardly repair the loss of their first years" (63).

The young Ralph Waldo Emerson, writing in his journal in 1827, remarked on several "Peculiarities of the Present Age": "It is said to be the age of the first person singular" (1982, 61), he noted. Emerson elsewhere insists that individual, lived experience is and must be primary: "The new individual," he wrote in 1839, "must work out the whole problem of science, letters, & theology for himself, can owe his fathers nothing. There is no history; only biography" (1982, 219). This, of course, is precisely what precipitates James's crisis in Crèvecoeur's *Letters*, and it is precisely what impels Burroughs and Fisher and Fitch to think about themselves in new ways. They owe their fathers nothing, and thus have to work out everything for themselves. "Every thing a man knows & does enters into & modifies his expressions of himself & therefore every character is different & experiences itself differently when it speaks with freedom" (1982, 70–71), Emerson wrote. Following Channing's assertion that we are as different as our countenances, Emerson is convinced that individuals are distinct, different, unique.

The passive phrasing of Emerson's assertion in 1827—"It *is said* to be the age of the first person singular"—suggests, perhaps, that Emerson was not yet convinced that the self had begun to receive its due. (One of the other "peculiarities" he noticed was the "disposition among men of *associating* themselves to promote any purpose" [61]. Such associations necessarily require a diminution of differences between individuals.) Teaching literary scholars like myself to note that the "tendencies of literature in different ages [are] observable," Emerson in 1823 claimed that not autobiographies but "Newspapers are [now] the proper literature of America, which affects to be so practical & unromantic a land" (1982, 39). By 1842, however, it had become clearer to him that "Autobiography & allo-biography go abreast; with every new insight we discover a new man" (1982, 354). Yet, even then, Emerson remained skeptical about how the self—and autobiography—had tended to be misused. Writing in 1839, he remarked that "we are misled by an ambiguity in the term Subjective. It is made to cover two things, a good & a bad. The great always introduce us to facts; small men introduce us always to themselves. . . .

The autobiography of the good is the autobiography of God" (1969, 320). Thus, Emerson's own work in biography and autobiography points to the universal or cosmic. *Representative Men* (1850) turns individual lives into typed lives that stand for higher human aspirations or abilities: for example, "[Goethe] is the type of culture" (1983, 758). In his own journals, Emerson is ever on the lookout for glimpses or insights into higher laws or powers that might draw his "self" into ever widening circles, circles that, if pursued, finally transcend or fragment the illusion of individual selfhood. Philosophically speaking, Emerson accurately saw that subjectivity—"the first person singular"—was a central concern of the age after 1830, even though he himself tried to think and write "through" the problem of the self.[3] Emerson accepted subjectivity and individual selfhood only to attempt to transcend it. His philosophy was enabled by the widespread and popular emergence of the autobiographical impulse.

The focus on "the first person singular," on the "cultivation" of the powers or expression of the individual, as Channing and Emerson described it in the 1820s and 1830s, led eventually in antebellum America to the publication of narratives like Henry David Thoreau's *Walden* (1854), with its emphases on cultivation (of beans, as well as the self), experience, and a deep, unfolding (or bottomless) self; Frederick Douglass's *Narrative of the Life of Frederick Douglass* (1845), Walt Whitman's *Leaves of Grass* (1855), P. T. Barnum's *Life of P. T. Barnum* (1855), Margaret Fuller's *Summer on the Lakes* (1844), Francis Parkman's *Oregon Trail* (1849), and Harriet Jacobs's *Incidents in the Life of a Slave Girl* (1861), among other narratives. It led to this first readily recognizable cluster of autobiographical texts in American literary history, texts that other critics have analyzed by focusing on the "modalities of self-display or self-concealment—ways of figuring and disfiguring the self" that they manifest (Porte, xi). This concern for the first-person singular "has, of course, long been recognized as a dominant issue in American Romanticism" (Porte, 20), but it takes my argument a bit further forward in time than I want to go in this study. We do not have to go so far to see the full emergence of autobiography in antebellum America.

In 1829, fifty years after Ethan Allen published his sentimental self-biography, Mathew Carey published *Auto Biographical Sketches. In a Series of Letters Addressed to a Friend*. Both narratives were published in Philadelphia, but there the similarities end. Carey is probably the first author to use a form of the word "autobiography" in the title of an original work. Carey, who had published parts of Franklin's *History of My*

Life in 1790, frames what is an economic treatise by claiming that he is writing so "that my friends and well-wishers might be able accurately to appreciate my character and conduct" (iv). Ostensibly, the larger purpose of his narrative was to defend the American system of internal national improvements championed in Congress by Henry Clay and others. But Carey begins by suggesting that his "character and conduct" stand in need of elucidation, perhaps because—so autobiography tells us—his interior or inward sense of personality, the natural self at the core of his identity, is hidden at a deep, relatively inaccessible level. His motives are obscure. "I am well aware that I incur the risque, indeed the certainty of being charged with egotism in this narrative" (3), Carey writes, gesturing toward the residual sense that vanity and egotism are traits that must be denied. But he does not deny them: he harps on how much money he spent on printing pamphlets to promote the American system, he repeatedly quotes himself as an incontrovertible authority on political economy, and he denigrates the men who lost money by not listening to him. Carey appropriates the term "autobiographical" to enlist his treatise in defense of the protective tariff and internal improvements, an impulse that at first might seem "self-biographical." His own behavior might appear to typify human behavior. But in the end he is probing the significance of his own actions, alienated behavior that the audience is asked to see as singular, not typical. Though masked by pages of economic facts and figures, Carey's narrative persona is original, inventive, an agent of its own destiny.

In her recent study of the experiences of the immediate post-Revolutionary generation, *Inheriting the Revolution*, the historian Joyce Appleby remarks that "Almost four hundred men and women of this cohort wrote autobiographies. . . . A testament to the flowering of modern subjectivity, these autobiographies fail to adhere to a formula, even to suggest the cohesion of a genre" (23). Appleby is surely right about the "flowering" of modern subjectivity in post-Revolutionary America. But her comment about the genre of autobiography is too hesitant. Certainly, various sorts of self-biography, including religious self-biography[4] and memoirs of public figures, continued to be written well into the antebellum period. And Carey's *Auto Biographical Sketches* speculated not on inwardness or subjectivity, but on his original and unique insight into the economy. Still, the genre of autobiography as I have defined it does begin to emerge fully in the 1820s. It achieves a recognizable coherence as a set of assumptions, conventions, and expectations.

In 1825, for example, Robert Stevenson Coffin published *The Life of the Boston Bard, Written by Himself*. Coffin was born in 1787 in a log cabin in Maine, and he eked out a living as a peddler and poet in the Northeast before he died in 1827, probably from tuberculosis. Before his death, he also published several volumes of poetry and many poems in newspapers, as well as this narrative of his life's experiences. Coffin's fellow poet, Daniel Bryan, to whom the *Life* is dedicated, insists in a strange moment in his *Appeal for Suffering Genius: A Poetical Address for the Benefit of the Boston Bard* (1826) that Coffin was not suffering from "the vice of intemperance" (n.p.), though it seems clear from the narrative that Coffin's father, at least, was a drunk. Bryan's remark suggests that Coffin was viewed by some people as an immoral eccentric, if not literally a drunk; but Bryan thinks instead that Coffin should be seen as a "genius," not simply eccentric but original. The internalization of genius, and its development as a concept to be distinguished from mere talent, was a feature of the early nineteenth century, of course, and both Coffin and Bryan resort to it to explain Coffin's nature.[5]

In his *Life*, Coffin exhibits a restlessness similar to that of Franklin, White, Burroughs, and Fitch: he refuses his first apprenticeship, leaves a series of masters in the apprenticeship he does choose (which, not surprisingly, is printing), and wanders the Northeast moved by whim or chance or opportunity. One opportunity, for example, occurs when he is asked to peddle books, and he quickly agrees. The next day he sets out from Hanover, New Hampshire, to Albany with (he claims) two thousand copies of Lucy Brewer's *Life of Louisa Baker* in tow. It is an amusing and instructive picture. Lucy Brewer first published her narrative in 1814 under the title of *An Affecting Narrative of Louisa Baker, a Native of Massachusetts*. By 1818, at least eighteen different editions of her narrative had been published, some of them under the title of *The Female Marine*. In her narrative, Brewer tells how she was seduced, became a prostitute, disguised herself as a man, and served in the War of 1812 on the USS *Constitution*. Brewer admits that she "had thoroughly studied the memoirs of Miss Sampson" (43) in crafting her own story of serving in the navy. Unlike Sampson, however, who was portrayed by Herbert Mann as a model of virtue (she disguised herself as a man out of a love for liberty), Brewer first becomes "a *voluntary* victim of vice" (23, emphasis added), and is even employed for three years as a prostitute before joining the navy. Her seduction may have been an initial fall, but Brewer chose the life of a prostitute that followed. At the end, Brewer's narrative takes the high moral road and encourages young readers to avoid "the fatal effects of an immoral life" (81), but surely the appeal of her narrative was precisely the fact that she did not experience many "fatal effects." Brewer flouts convention by voluntarily "falling" (for three years!) and then by disguising her "true" self, not out of patriotism (as did Sampson, who, remember, also did not publish her own story), but out of less noble desires.

We can see here the sense of a generic tradition developing: Sampson to Brewer to Coffin. Coffin tries to move beyond his models. "I have undertaken to write my life," he tells us, "and it must be written, let who will approve or condemn" (24). What he claims for himself is, first, originality, figured in his own self-christening as the "Boston Bard" and inaugurated in a youthful incident when he captures a pigeon in a rat trap: "the thought [of doing this] was original. . . . [T]he *Muse* inhabited the body of the ensnared pigeon, and . . . I caught them twain at once and the same moment" (14–15). It is hard to know if Coffin is pulling our leg here; he is, after all, known among the other apprentices at that time as a practical joker. But if the uninspired but prolific poetry that takes over the second half of the narrative is any indication, I do not think he is joking. He is—as he has someone report about him midway through the narrative—an "eccentric child of genius and misfortune" (101).

In contrast to Franklin, Graydon, Allen, and Rush, whom I discussed in part one, Coffin sees himself in opposition to others. When an early poem is attacked by a reader, he exclaims, "My stanzas are *worth* cursing! . . . [When] an anathema greeted my ear, my heart leapt for joy" (18). Early on, he knows what he wants because it is not what others want. Later, after he learns to write poetry that can pay "three dollars per yard" (97), he strives to protect that eccentricity, as it is his meal ticket. "Many of my poems may be puerile, tame, and insipid," he hisses; "but puerile, tame, and insipid as they may be, if they are worth stealing, they are worth something to the author, who would not have others suffer for his muse's imbecility" (174). He wants the protection of copyright because his ideas are unusual, because they are *his*. As Raymond Williams points out in his discussion of the word "individual," there are by the early nineteenth century two senses of "individualism": the individualism of singleness, or what one might call abstract individualism, "is based . . . on the quantitative thought, centred in mathematics and physics, of [the eighteenth century]. 'Uniqueness,' by contrast, is a qualitative category, and is a concept of the Romantic movement" (1985, 164). Self-biographies could be written in light of that first definition, but the emergent genre of autobiography depended upon the second. Coffin sees himself in just such a light throughout his narrative. The very end of his narrative reinforces this sense of unique identity. Coffin, following K. White, describes his body in detail (200), and then lists the private attributes that mark him as singular: "I often wash myself, and change my clothing on Saturdays" (200), "I am subject to melancholy reflections" (201), "I hate mosquitoes and detest egotism" (202). Inquiring minds may not want to know such details, but Coffin insists on relating them. In contrast to Carey, who claims "autobiography" in his title but tells us little about himself except as an investor, Coffin claims to hate egotism but his narrative is about nothing other than himself. "[S]mall men always introduce us to themselves," Emerson wrote condescendingly, but such introductions drove the emergence of the genre. Unfortunately for Coffin, his narrative was simply not interesting enough for anyone to care. "Enough of my whims have been stated whereby to give a pretty good '*guess*' at what sort of biped animal I am" (202), he smirks. Narratively speaking, he is a third-rate poet fascinated with what he takes to be his own originality and convinced that he is free of most social constraints. It was not selling in 1825.

I do not want to make light of those social constraints, for they were real. Though his father was a minister, Coffin was (apparently) indentured as a servant, survived a troubling home life, and never received much formal education. As I have been suggesting in part two, autobiography emerged in great part through the efforts of writers who sensed, as did Rousseau, that they had been marginalized by society or that they were naturally or normally eccentric. Coffin's *Life* is, in that sense, typical of the emerging genre, even if in the end it seems uncompelling, both to Coffin's contemporaries, enthralled by Lucy Brewer's exploits, and to modern readers.

It is also easy to understand why contemporaneous readers ignored William Grimes, who published *The Life of William Grimes, the Runaway Slave, Written by Himself* in 1825. Grimes's narrative, like Venture Smith's as-told-to *Narrative of the Life and Adventures of Venture, a Native of Africa* (1798),[6] tells the story of an "embittered" ex-slave, one who wrote both to vent his outrage at the "constitutional" system that denied him peace and contentment even in the North and to "claim [the] charity" of sympathetic readers.[7] Unlike the more famous slave narratives that began to appear in the 1840s, which were supported or controlled in one way or another by the antislavery movement, Grimes's *Life* was self-authorized and self-published. The story Grimes tells revolves around agency: "no law, no consequences, not the lives of millions, can authorize [the government] to take my life or liberty from me" (66). Long before Douglass stands up to Covey, Grimes turns to one of his overseers and threatens him: "I took up a stick, and told him if he put his hand upon me I would strike him; and marched toward him bold as a lion" (19). "I had too much sense and feeling to be a slave" (20), Grimes insists.

Grimes is interested in how that felt agency can be threatened, first and foremost—relentlessly—by slavery, of course, but in other ways, as well. He ponders how one old fortune teller could have predicted so accurately an incident in his life. Does that mean his life was predestined, already known to others? If so, in what sense could he imagine himself to be "free"? In another scene, he tells the story of driving his mistress and her sisters to a party, only to fall asleep while they were in the house. When they woke him up to take them home, he "did not know where [he] was, where [he] had been, nor where [he] was going" (33). It is a disconcerting experience, in which the self or his personal identity seems to vanish temporarily. He reports, as well, how an old female slave named Frankee, whom he was convinced was a witch, would "exercise her enchantments" by riding him at night: "I [would] then [be] entirely speechless; making a noise like one apparently choking, or strangling" (24). This "night-mare" is typical of Grimes's fear that he is at the mercy of other forces, including God, who comes to his aid once to prevent a whipping: "God delivered me from the power of the adversary" (17). Later, commenting on his escape from the South, Grimes reports: "it was his [i.e., God's] hand, and not my own artfulness and cunning, which enabled me to escape" (29). Yet unlike, say, John Marrant (in *A Narration of the Lord's Wonderful Dealings with John Marrant, a Black*), Solomon Bayley (in *A Narrative of Some Remarkable Incidents in the Life of Solomon Bayley . . . Written by Himself* [1825]), and George White (in *A Brief Account of the Life, Experience, Travels, and Gospel Labours of George White, an African*), Grimes does not in the end fully or even partially submit his agency to God, much less to the system of slavery that tries to deny him voice, "choking, or strangling" him. Not coincidentally, Grimes is unable to end his story happily, as do Marrant, Bayley, and White.

Like so many other early autobiographers, Grimes sees himself oppositionally. The first day he is taken inside a plantation house to work he is, he says, mistreated by the head servant, who wanted one of her own boys to have Grimes's position. Such treatment is normal for Grimes; and as the narrative progresses, he more and more initiates the opposition himself: manipulating white buyers to purchase him, going on a hunger strike to force one master to sell him or lose him, striking an old black slave driver, walking boldly past the town limits after dark while counting on his white complexion to let him pass as white. Though Grimes twice praises God for controlling affairs to his benefit, he more often imagines himself to be an independent agent. His masters, ironically, *lack* such agency: "I ought perhaps, to blame slavery more than my masters [for my mistreatment]. . . . I was therefore perhaps, difficult *to govern in the way in which it was attempted*" (20, italics in original). Faced with a black man who refuses to be subordinated, they act in ways that "slavery" has taught them, while Grimes thinks and acts for himself. He is unpredictable precisely because he thinks "outside" the system of slavery.

Grimes's agency is figured most eloquently on the title page and in the final paragraph. The title page announces his name and the by then familiar insistence that the work was "written by himself." Within the narrative, Grimes has at least three different names, so the assumption of his white father's surname on the title page is an aggressive act of appropriation. His conclusion is more startling. I am destitute, he reports, and do not know what will come next. "If it were not for the stripes on my back which were made while I was a slave, I would in my will, leave my skin as a legacy to the gover[n]ment, desiring that it might be taken off and made into parchment, and then bind the constitution of glorious happy *and free* America. Let the skin of an American slave, bind the charter of American liberty" (68). As William Andrews reads the passage, Grimes's scarified skin has been inscribed by "slavery's perverse pen"; to suggest that it could bind or enclose the Constitution is thus to demonstrate "major contradictions in the myth of America" (81). More subtly, the passage suggests not that slavery has *written on* Grimes's skin but that it has torn and lacerated it, a point Grimes repeatedly makes when he describes the whippings that slavery depended upon: "This poor man's back was cut up with the lash, until I could compare it to nothing but a field lately ploughed" (36). Black skin, as long as slavery and its apparatus exists, could *never* be used to bind the Constitution because it could never be tanned into a whole piece of parchment. Only when black skin remains whole, unlacerated, can it serve as binding; then, perhaps, slavery itself will no longer even exist. Yet, while slave skin is lacerated, and the Constitution is disordered (i.e., in need of "binding"), and Grimes's own physical "constitution could not bear" (47–48) what a slave South and unfair North did to him, Grimes at the end has a "will." He means, of course, a legal will, but he means, as well, a psychological will. In the domestic space he carves out with his wife (but which he will not describe for us) and in his refusal to succumb to the forces of racial and class prejudice (though he warns other, less able slaves to endure their condition [67]), Grimes claims for himself a personal agency that was emerging at numerous sites in the 1820s. Contrary to everything society has told him, he cultivates a self that is independent of all models. Grimes's character is not the outward sign of blackness, which should have condemned him to silence, but an internalized possession displayed and interpreted for us in his narrative.

It might be useful, here, to contrast Grimes's self-biography with the first self-biographical narrative actually written and published by an African-American, George White's *Brief Account of the Life, Experience, Travels, and Gospel Labours of George White, an African*, published in 1810. White's narrative records his conversion to Methodism and his subsequent and repeated attempts to become licensed as a Methodist minister, a goal that he finally achieves in 1807. "White is the first organization man in Afro-American autobiography" (Andrews, 53), and his narrative records a self subsumed narratively within conventional spiritual autobiography and socially within the institutionalized church structure of Methodism. Grimes chafes against society as it is; White accepts it. Grimes tries, in his closing metaphor, to figure his particularized life as useful for society;[8] White figures his life as "instrumental" (76) in God's plan for his children. The difference between Grimes and White points to an argument I have been developing since chapter 5: autobiography as a genre tells the story of how a person struggles to become an independent, often original, agent, and that genre developed in the United States from within the space occupied by marginalized, oppressed groups, including lower-class white men (Fitch), criminals (Burroughs), white women (White and Fisher), and African-American men (Grimes). Like Crèvecoeur's fictional narrator in *Letters from an American Farmer*, these writers were forced outside the systems that originally created or defined them, and then they struggled to comprehend themselves as agents independent of those or other systems. Forced, for whatever reason, outside those systems, they wrote themselves, hesitantly though persistently, as agents of their own destiny, figuring themselves as singular, isolated, self-generating, self-invented, and self-determining. They internalized character and personality, which the eighteenth century marked (if anxiously, as in Rush's thinking) as exterior attributes of socially determined roles, and in the process came to possess a unique self.

Another author who did this was Hannah Adams, whose *Memoir of Miss Hannah Adams* was published posthumously in 1832. Adams was a successful author from her debut in print in 1791 until her death in 1831. She published histories of New England, works on religious controversies, and an outline of Western Christianity. Like Grimes's *Life*, her autobiography was ostensibly written to appeal to the audience's charity, in the hopes that Adams's sister might have a financial "legacy" after the author's death. In *Memoir*, Adams denies that she had ambition: "It was poverty, not ambition, that first induced me to become an author, or rather a compiler" (22), she says. Ostensibly, she is not even an "author"; she is merely a "compiler." The word recalls the title of K. White's *Narrative*, but without White's overt, aggressive sense of independent agency. Adams's agency is occluded in the narrative in this way, and by her repeated denials of "authorship" and her claims of a "constitutional want of bodily and mental firmness." It is occluded, too, by the male editors who vouch for her humility, "modesty and unobstrusiveness" in an "Introductory Note" (n. p.), recalling the editorial framing of Mary Rowlandson's narrative 150 years earlier.

Still, despite this frame, and despite Adams's disavowals of authorship, and despite the theme of the "bond of sisterhood" that runs through the narrative, Adams sees her life story as a *publishing* history: her story is the story of her texts, which she authored on her own and which she pushed, insistently, into print. Women writers have it bad for two reasons, Adams notes: they are women and they are writers. "Arraigned not merely as writers, but as women, their characters, their conduct, and even their personal endowments, become the object of severe inquisition." The "penalties and discouragement attending authors in general fall upon women with double weight" (34), she sighs wearily. Like White and Fisher, Adams reveals that she has come to see that a life "passed in seclusion . . . [is] preferable to society in general" (6). She figures herself in isolation, in a "solitude" (17) that her "nervous complaints" (16) and "weakness and irritability in [her] nervous system" (2) protect. Constrained by social limitations on her ambition, she retreats to her imagination, which, even as a child, manifests "an early singularity of taste" (2).

Adams's agency is described most vividly in her self-assertive aggressiveness in her publishing endeavors, including her attempt to lobby Congress (through Fisher Ames) for a general copyright law (19–20) and her battle with an unnamed gentleman over the publication of one of her manuscripts (30). When her contracts with publishers indicate that she has been taken advantage of, she cuts a better deal by having a minister negotiate for her. Throughout her narrative, though with repeated gestures toward passivity, Adams imagines herself to be independent.

James Guild is yet another example of the emergence of the oppositional, independent, unique, cultivated self. Guild wrote what his modern editor has called his *Travel Diary*, though it is more retrospective than a simple diary, sometime after 1818. In it, he picks up his life story at the moment when he turns twenty-one and comes of age. "I sough[t] for some happier situation" than that of a farmer, he writes. "My disposition would not allow me to work on a farm" (300). He tries peddling, tinkering, silhouetting, painting, writing instruction, and even doctoring, as he wanders the Northeast in search of some way to "obtain a fortune" (300). "Now my sole object was to make money," he admits at one point. Eventually, Guild becomes successful painting miniatures, and at the end of the narrative—which breaks off abruptly—he is in London commencing his "profession as an artist" (312). That Guild should so often stumble into problems of representation in his career is revealing. He cuts profiles, takes likenesses, paints miniature portraits, writes songs, and even invents "a new Stile of writing" (287). As Gordon Wood has suggested, Guild is a new sort of American in 1818: restless, independent, ambitious, free. But that, like Coffin, he should attach himself to the mimetic arts suggests that his narrative has another dimension: it is an attempt to paint his own likeness, as it were. "The mapping of new territories of the self demanded a new cartography . . . ," Mechal Sobel has written. "Self-narratives were records of the great changes occurring in the self and were also agents of change in and of themselves. Creating narratives of their lives gave individuals coherence and purpose and gave structure to the self itself" (163). And, indeed, Guild, who often writes about himself in the third person, is concerned to show us how his mind works, what he thought at some particularly trying moment, how he learned from his "experience [that] if a man thinks he is something and puts himself forward he will be something" (279). Guild becomes what he wants to become. "How often do I think," he remarks, "of the famous writer when he was asked what was the greatest thing for a man to learn when he replied one's self; he was asked the second time what was the next, he still replied one's self, and the third, one's self" (302).

❧

Charles Taylor has sketched a schematic map tracing changes in the sources of moral authority in the course of Western history: "The map distributes the moral sources into three large domains: the original theistic grounding . . . ; a second one that centres on a naturalism of disengaged reason . . . ; and a third family of views which finds its sources in Romantic expressivism or in one of the modernist successor versions. The original unity of the theistic horizon has been shattered, and the sources can now be found on diverse frontiers, including our own powers and nature" (496). In the fifty years from 1780 to 1830 in the United States, that third "family of views" emerged as the impulse behind and logic for the genre of autobiography, even as some forms of what I have called "self-biography"—Taylor's first two categories—continued to be written and read.[9] Throughout this book, I have used Taylor's categories, which gauge the emergence of modern selfhood, to help trace the emergence of the literary genre of autobiography: inwardness (of the sort that Guild adopts in his *Travel Diary*), an affirmation of ordinary life (as Channing urges workers to remake themselves in their "leisure" time or as Fitch recounts the details of his domestic arrangements), and the natural self (as White and Coffin and Grimes begin to take themselves as the best and truest authority for behavior and identity). Franklin's *History of My Life*, as I read it, fits best in Taylor's second category, and thus serves as the background against which we can see the full emergence by 1830 of modern, autobiographical self-expression.

I have, as well, tried to describe that emergence through other sets of terms. Eighteenth-century identity, particularly for the unlettered, was imagined in terms of imitation and, for those who were ambitious, emulation. In cultures based primarily on oral and visual education, imitation and emulation served as the primary means of acquiring skills. Even for the educated, roles and identity were fabricated by reason and by tradition, and in those cases, too, imitation and emulation were the known and accepted processes by which one understood one's place in the world. They gave way, I argue, to the model of invention. The aristocratic, hierarchical, sociable culture of eighteenth-century Anglo-America was shaken to its foundations at the end of the century by the

American and French Revolutions; in narratives by Fitch, Burroughs, White, and Fisher—and, then, in more dramatic numbers of narratives in the 1820s and beyond—imitative and emulative models of self-fashioning on which hierarchy and tradition depend are displaced by self-invention. The relentless restlessness of modern autobiographers figures, on one level, this self-inventedness. As travel opportunities expand for the less wealthy, writers like Fitch and Burroughs and Guild and Coffin simply cannot sit still. Their peripatetic wanderings in search of wealth or contentedness expose them to ideas they have not had before, customs they have not imagined, people who can teach them new tricks. Crèvecoeur's fictional narrator is afraid to leave his farm for a "world so wide" (52); and, when he does, he is unnerved by the fact that neither religion nor reason could comprehend that world. The modern self might be initially threatened by the wider world—"Once I could (when with my master) enjoy the sweetes of society," Guild remembers, "although I had to work hard and with a discontented mind, but now I must . . . work for a living. . . . O misery what shall I do?" (259–260)—but it learns early on to accept that world, even to revel in it.

Invention is figured in other ways, as well. Fitch learns that he can, quite literally, invent new ideas in his head. Burroughs, Guild, and Coffin are insistently concerned in their behavior and careers with the problem of representation, and each seems to learn that everyone, in some sense, is a "forger." Identity is always "forged," either by society or by an individual. Those with intelligence and courage can "make" themselves a new identity, and in the process make character a possession to be defended against all forms of domination. It is possible to become what we imagine ourselves to be, simply by asserting that we *are* that thing: "if a man thinks he is something and puts himself forward he will be something," Guild writes.

Another way to think about the emergence of the self in narrative is through the construct of "personality." The *Oxford English Dictionary* defines "personality" as "That quality or assemblage of qualities which makes a person what he is, as distinct from other persons" (def. 2). This definition emerged as early as 1795. (One of its next cited, early uses was by Emerson in *Representative Men*!) The psychological definition of "personality"—"The unique combination of psychological qualities or traits . . . that make up each person. . . ." (def. 3)—emerged even later; Henry Maudsley's *Pathology of Mind* (1879) is cited as its first use. We are accustomed to thinking about Franklin's "personality" in his *History of*

My Life; we are accustomed to projecting the modern notion of personality back into time.[10] But that is surely an illusion. Franklin gives up very little of what we call "personality" in his memoirs: we do not learn his likes and dislikes, the way he thinks in certain circumstances, the way he feels (about his wife and children, for example), the way he looks or dresses.

In contrast, Burroughs, White, Coffin, and others begin to probe those spaces. Several authors insist that the physical body should be described, as it accounts for or explains some of his or her behavior. Domestic life is opened up to inspection, particularly if it is unusual or has been damaging. Thought processes are recorded, likes and dislikes discussed, attitudes explained. By the 1820s, in these narratives, "personality" has emerged as an available concept, and many writers take advantage of the textual opportunity to explain how theirs is, indeed, unique or distinct. As Raymond Williams writes: "a personality or a character, once an outward sign, has been decisively internalized [by the mid–nineteenth century], yet internalized as a possession, and therefore as something which can either be displayed or interpreted" (1985, 235). As the sociologist Roy F. Baumeister puts it: "During the 19th century, personality (rather than social rank and roles) came to be increasingly regarded as a, even *the*, central aspect of the self" (166, emphasis in original).

"All autobiographies are necessarily egotistical," P. T. Barnum writes in the preface to the second version of his life, *Struggles and Triumphs: or, Forty Years' Recollections of P. T. Barnum* (1869). Barnum is right. But, as I have argued, all self-biographical writing is not necessarily egotistical. "There are indeed aspects of the so-called modern sensibility that seem to arise first, or to be given special weight, in the Romantic period: interest in the self, especially the divided self, as a psychological entity; self-consciousness; insistence on originality and creativity; interest in 'organic form,' and so on," Joel Porte writes at the beginning of his study of the "modalities" of self-display in American romantic writing (11). Narratives by writers like John Fitch, Stephen Burroughs, K. White, Elizabeth Fisher, William Grimes, and many others point to that emergent interest in the early national and antebellum periods; they anticipate what would become a major and abiding interest of midcentury writers like Emerson, Thoreau, Fuller, Barnum, Douglass, Stephen Pearl Andrews, Whitman, and others. Writing as "the age of the first person singular" took shape, just as it emerged into discursive possibility, the writers I discuss in *After Franklin* represent some of the ways that the self could be imagined in post-Revolutionary and early national America. Only in some of those narratives does a natural or organic or romantic or determining self, the self of modern autobiography, come to be figured consistently and insistently: to do so simply was not possible prior to the 1810s. The writers I have discussed in part two represent, both in themselves and in juxtaposition to Franklin and Graydon and others, "the new nation's polyglot and socially fragmented world,"[11] a revolutionary landscape in which new kinds of voices emerged to test the concept that individuals are or could be or should be "egotistical." In that experimentation, they inaugurated a new kind of writing, which we now recognize as autobiography.

NOTES

I. THE AGE OF EXPERIMENTS

1. For bibliographic overviews of published materials through 1980, see William Spengemann, *The Forms of Autobiography: Episodes in the History of a Literary Genre* (New Haven: Yale University Press, 1980), 170–246; and James Olney, "Autobiography and the Cultural Moment: A Thematic, Historical, and Bibliographic Introduction," in *Autobiography: Essays Theoretical and Critical*, ed. James Olney (Princeton: Princeton University Press, 1980), 3–27. For recent work on autobiography, see the annual bibliography published in *Biography*, as well as bibliographies published on specific topics or themes in *A/B: auto/biography studies*. It is no doubt true that the subject of subjectivity, of which the criticism on autobiography forms a part, has been the primary focus of critical and philosophic discussion in the West in the late twentieth century, a point made by numerous commentators. Academic criticism in the 1990s even evolved into the creative expression of self-life-writing, as an increasing number of critics turned inward, writing about their own experiences. Why not? If, as Rousseau claimed about himself, "I am made unlike anyone I have ever met" (*The Confessions*, trans. J. M. Cohen [New York: Penguin, 1953], 17), then perhaps even the private lives of academics must hold some originality, some original or unique aspect of human existence about which others will want to learn.

2. Cf. Olney, "Autobiography and the Cultural Moment," 17.

3. Julia Watson remarks that "it has become a critical topos to begin discussions of the theory of autobiography by rehearsing the changing positions assumed by critics throughout the last three decades" ("Toward an Anti-metaphysics of Autobiography," in *The Culture of Autobiography: Constructions of Self-representation*, ed. Robert Folkenflik [Stanford: Stanford University Press, 1993], 57). I will not review these positions here, as they have been summarized by many other critics, including Watson.

4. Richard Dawkins, the zoologist, muses in an aside in a recent book "that the subjective feeling of 'somebody in there' may be a cobbled, emergent, semi-illusion" (*Unweaving the Rainbow: Science, Delusion, and the Appetite for Wonder* [Boston: Houghton Mifflin, 1998], 309). Dawkins is surely right. See, for example, Roy F. Baumeister, "How the Self Became a Problem: A Psychological Review of Historical Research," *Journal of Personality and Social Psychology* 52

(1987): 163–176. Following Baumeister, Charles Taylor, and others, I will argue that the emergent subjectivity which Dawkins refers to both develops its own literary genre (autobiography) and is itself, as the same time, developed and furthered by autobiography as an art form.

5. Cf. Shirley Neuman, "Autobiography: From Different Poetics to a Poetics of Difference," in *Essays on Life Writing: From Genre to Critical Practice*, ed. Marlene Kadar (Toronto: University of Toronto Press, 1992), 214; Marlene Kadar, "Coming to Terms: Life Writing—from Genre to Critical Practice," in *Essays on Life Writing*, 7; and Leigh Gilmore, *Autobiographics: A Feminist Theory of Women's Self-representation* (Ithaca: Cornell University Press, 1994).

6. On the earlier emergence of the novel, see Michael McKeon, *The Origins of the English Novel, 1600–1740* (Baltimore: Johns Hopkins University Press, 1987); and J. Paul Hunter, *Before Novels: The Cultural Contexts of Eighteenth-Century Fiction* (New York: Norton, 1990).

7. I made this argument in an earlier article: Stephen Carl Arch, "American Hunger: Society and Autobiography in America," *The Grove: Working Papers in English* (Jaen, Spain) 1 (1996): 11–25.

8. The literature discussing these changes is immense. I have been influenced by these diverse studies, among many others: C. B. Macpherson, *The Political Theory of Possessive Individualism* (Oxford: Clarendon Press, 1962); Timothy Reiss, *The Discourse of Modernism* (Ithaca: Cornell University Press, 1982); Joyce Appleby, *Capitalism and a New Social Order: The Republican Vision of the 1790s* (New York: New York University Press, 1984); Robert H. Wiebe, *The Opening of American Society: From the Adoption of the Constitution to the Eve of Disunion* (New York: Knopf, 1984); and Gordon Wood, *The Radicalism of the American Revolution* (New York: Knopf, 1992).

9. Only the four "major" novels of Charles Brockden Brown have managed in recent years to hold their own in scholarly interest, and of course that interest is a fairly recent phenomenon.

10. For example, Herbert Leibowitz moves from a chapter on Franklin to chapters on Louis Sullivan and other modernists (*Fabricating Lives: Explorations in American Autobiography* [New York: Knopf, 1989]); Kenneth Dauber moves from a chapter on Franklin to chapters on Brackenridge, Cooper, Poe, Hawthorne, and Melville (*The Idea of Authorship in America: Democratic Poetics from Franklin to Melville* [Madison: University of Wisconsin Press, 1990]); Cynthia Jordan moves from a chapter on Franklin to chapters on Brackenridge, Brown, Cooper, Poe, Hawthorne, and Melville (*Second Stories: The Politics of Language, Form, and Gender in Early American Fictions* [Chapel Hill: University of North Carolina Press, 1989]); Henry F. Sayre moves from Franklin to Adams and James (*The Examined Self: Benjamin Franklin, Henry Adams, Henry James* [1964; reprint, Madison: University of Wisconsin Press, 1988]); and James Barbour and Tom Quirk's collection of essays moves from Franklin to Melville and

Thoreau (*Writing the American Classics* [Chapel Hill: University of North Carolina Press, 1990]). Note, as well, the move in several of these studies from Franklin, who never wrote a novel or short story (of the sort that emerges in the 1830s and beyond), to novelists like Hawthorne and Melville.

11. Benjamin Franklin, *History of My Life*, published as *The Autobiography*, in *Writings*, ed. J. A. Leo LeMay (New York: Library of America, 1987), 1379, 1394, and 1363. Throughout the book, I will cite Franklin's writings as they appear in this edition, unless where so noted.

12. I am aware of the textual difficulties in dealing with Franklin's *History of My Life*. While I will at times treat it as a single, unified text, I am well aware that it is best read as three distinct texts, written at three distinct times. See, for example, David Levin, "The Autobiography of Benjamin Franklin: The Puritan Experimenter in Life and Art," *Yale Review* 53 (1964): 258–275; and Alfred Owen Aldridge, "Form and Substance in Franklin's *Autobiography*," in *Essays on American Literature in Honor of Jay B. Hubbell*, ed. Clarence Gohdes (Durham: Duke University Press, 1967), 47–62.

13. Robert Folkenflik, "Introduction: The Institution of Autobiography," in *The Culture of Autobiography: Constructions of Self-representation* (Stanford: Stanford University Press, 1993), 1–2.

14. I am aware that "self-biography" was itself a neologism dating from the 1790s. "Autobiography," in the long run in English, won out as a term for self-narratives, and I am comfortable using it to refer to the modern narratives of selfhood that began to emerge in this period. I want to retain the term "self-biography" to refer to older types of narratives (like Bradstreet's) that reflect a traditional or classical or Christian understanding of personal identity, which downplays or denies the "self" as an independent or autonomous entity.

15. See Michael T. Gilmore, "The Literature of the Revolutionary and Early National Periods," in *The Cambridge History of American Literature, Vol. 1, 1590–1820*, ed. Sacvan Bercovitch (Cambridge: Cambridge University Press, 1994), 538–693. My brief discussion here of American literary history was influenced by David Perkins, *Is Literary History Possible?* (Baltimore: Johns Hopkins University Press, 1992), esp. 1–27.

16. Let me conduct a brief historical survey of criticism to outline my point here. Writing in 1829, Samuel Lorenzo Knapp was uneasy because he feared that Revolutionary literature would be unable to dispel the claim made by "foreigners" that "there was no such thing as American literature" (*Lectures on American Literature* [New York, 1829], 4). Surveying colonial and Revolutionary literature from Jamestown and Plymouth plantation to the United States in the 1820s, Knapp was forced to look for signs of American eloquence in the Revolutionary period "throughout the history of all the transactions of that eventful period" (106)—that is, in public papers, speeches, pamphlets, and other texts that by 1829 were increasingly coming to be considered "unliterary." In other

words, Knapp was forced to look for signs of American literary maturity in texts that his own romantic aesthetic ideals elsewhere decry, as when he defines poetry as "natural to man. It is a sympathy of the human mind with the invisible world, in which the spirit is active in expounding, exalting, and reforming the realities it witnesses to something which belongs to upper natures, or divine essences" (139). By *that* sort of standard, no Miltons or Shakespeares or Wordsworths wrote in North America during or after the Revolution; by that sort of standard, *The Federalist Papers* and the speeches of Fisher Ames, prized by Knapp and others as examples of the maturation of the United States' national literary identity, fell short of recuperating American literature in the eyes of sophisticated readers. Try as he might, Knapp could not locate the literariness of American Revolutionary literature.

Writing in 1846, Margaret Fuller complained that American literature in her day was too imitative of English models; "we are not anxious to prove," she wrote, "that there is as yet much American literature" ("American Literature: Its Position at the Present Time, and Prospects for the Future," in *Margaret Fuller, American Romantic: A Selection from her Writings and Correspondence*, ed. Perry Miller [Garden City, N.Y.: Anchor Books, 1963], 230). She criticized the writings of a dozen mid–nineteenth-century American writers on the grounds that they were too English. Ironically, however, the writers "that led the way in the first half century of this republic," Fuller wrote, "were far better situated than we [in the mid–nineteenth century], in this respect." They were not overwhelmed with printed matter from Europe, and their patriotic readers were eager to read an American book. Many books written in those years, she asserted, were worthy to be read, even though they were essentially English (234). But Fuller mentioned no authors and no titles of books from those first fifty years. American Revolutionary literature exists in her account as a moment in time when the questions asked and answers given by American writers were basically English, even though the reading public may have accepted them as proleptically American. American literature had yet to be born in the Revolution, much less to begin to mature. In Fuller's account, the Revolution would not see real literary fruit until sometime after 1846. Unlike Knapp, she did not even feel constrained to *examine* what came before the rise of romantic literature in Bryant, Cooper, and others. Fuller could not locate the Americanness of American Revolutionary writers.

Ten years later, in their *Cyclopedia of American Literature* (1855), Evert and George Duyckinck cast American literature into three periods—colonial, Revolutionary, and nineteenth century—which taken together traced a progressive movement in American society from sacred to secular, ignorance to intelligence, oral eloquence to printed literature (*Cyclopedia of American Literature* [reprint, Detroit: Gale, 1965], vi–vii). The Revolutionary period became in their study a transitional moment when a "new spirit" was "introduced" into American literature, but that moment was merely preparatory to the romantic fulfillment in the mid–nineteenth century. The Duyckinks' historical and rhetorical move anticipated much of the scholarship to follow. In a similar move, for example, Charles F. Richardson in *American Literature, 1607–1885* (1886) cast American literature into the same three periods, with the progressive unfolding in his account being that of "race, climate and environment." Richardson's story is one of Anglo-Saxon immigrants (a "race" in his account) slowly becoming "American" under the pressure of "new geographical and political conditions" (*American Literature, 1607–1885*, 2 vols. [New York: Putnam's, 1886] I: 1). In his reading, the early colonists were British writers at the margins of the empire, largely ignored at home; Revolutionary orators and writers were heard back home, but they were "heeded less [for] their manner than their matter" (I: 178). That is, Richardson asserts, their *words* were not really heard; Europe took note of the fact only that, like a mosquito buzzing around one's head, a noise emanated from North America. Not until Washington Irving's fiction began to appear in 1819 did "American literature [find] a place in the European mind" (I: 258). This "dawn of imagination" would then see the full light of day in the work of Emerson, Poe, Cooper, Hawthorne, and others in the nineteenth century. For the Duyckincks and for Richardson, American Revolutionary literature served as a sort of halfway house or way station on the road to nineteenth-century romantic aestheticism (the Duyckincks) or political/ethnic nationalism (Richardson). Their analysis allowed them to locate the origins of literary "Americanness" a long time after the Puritans of New England and the Cavaliers of Virginia had produced feeble settlements and even feebler literature, but also a fairly long time before nineteenth-century writers like Hawthorne took the stage, thus offering a pre- or proto-history for the very qualities that made Hawthorne and others "American." All three scholars failed to find anything revolutionary about the literature of the American Revolution.

Barrett Wendell and Moses Coit Tyler, writing at the turn of the nineteenth century, saw in American literature a resolution of the political distance that separated Great Britain and the United States in 1900. Wendell asserted that America and England had for centuries "cherished" the same "ideals of morality and government," but that following the reign of Elizabeth in the early seventeenth century the "native tempers" of the two people began to diverge. By 1776, "despite their common language, neither of the kindred peoples . . . could rightly understand the other" (*A Literary History of America*, 4th ed. [New York: Charles Scribner's Sons, 1907], 521–524). At that time, according to Wendell, Americans were producing enthusiasm, political democracy, a love for abstract rights, and spontaneity, but not literature; English writers were producing great literature. In the nineteenth century, this relationship was inverted: America produced the great literature, and England produced political democracy (and, actually, great literature as well). "After three centuries of separation," Wendell concludes, "England and America [in 1900] are once more side by side. With them, in unison, lies the hope of imperial democracy" (526). The future can become, he hopes, an "earthly semblance of peace" where political democracy and literary eloquence can dwell in a perfect balance, as supposedly they had come to in nineteenth-century England and America.

Moses Coit Tyler saw the separation between Great Britain and the United States as occurring in the Revolution itself: "Accordingly, reaching this fatal point [of April 19, 1775]," Tyler wrote, ". . . the student of [American Revolutionary] literature becomes then and there conscious of crossing a great spiritual chasm—of moving from one world of ideas and sentiments to a world of ideas and sentiments quite other and very different" (*The Literary History of the American Revolution*, 2 vols. [1897; reprint, New York: Ungar, 1957], I: 406). For Tyler, this assumption freed his investigation: he could assert, in the context of tracing "the intellectual and emotional development of the Revolution" (II: 159), that works by writers like Franklin, Trumbull, Freneau, John Adams, and Hopkinson were indeed original and worthy of study. Falling on the correct side of the "chasm," they were originally "American." This move alone sets Tyler's history apart from all previous and many subsequent literary histories: Tyler found *literary* value in many Revolutionary texts that, since Knapp, had been considered outside the realm of belles lettres. His work is also set apart from his predecessors' by his focusing at great length in the course of his two volumes on the prose and poetry of the American Tories. His hope, after all, was "To show that this race feud [begun between Americans and Brits in 1775] need not, after all, be an endless one . . . [and] to bring together once more into sincere friendship, into a rational and a sympathetic moral unity, these divided members of a family capable . . . of leading the whole human race upward to all the higher planes of culture and happiness" (I: ix). Appealing to Richardson's category of race, Tyler compressed his three hundred years of separation into one hundred and turned that separation not to the purpose of American literary (and political and ethnic) isolationism but to the purpose of consolidating Anglo-American political and cultural hegemony on the world stage. Wendell and Tyler both imagined that literary history could help to bring into being an Anglo-American, English-speaking, twentieth-century empire. In their accounts, American Revolutionary literature is both a component of the empire's (temporary) disjunction and, especially in Tyler, a tool with which to bring the empire back into alignment.

Critics in the 1920s and 1930s repeated and regularized earlier claims that the American Revolution and its literature were transitions from one known thing (Puritanism or the Enlightenment or ignorance) to another known thing (romanticism or democracy or knowledge). Fred Lewis Pattee, for example, following Knapp and the Duyckincks, argued that literature should be defined "in terms of beauty . . . [and thus that] before 1776 America produced nothing at all" (*The First Century of American Literature, 1770–1870* [1935; reprint, New York: Cooper Square, 1966], 14). From the years from 1776 to 1815, Pattee wrote, "A few volumes have survived . . . to be classified as literature," but those years "produced no literature of note," being "from the standpoint of literary creation, the feeblest generation in American history" (263). Finally, he asserted, the years from 1815 to 1870 brought a "new era" (446) of profusive invention, a "seed-bed for everything that we find today in our modern literary world" (598). By 1935, Pattee was no longer concerned with reconciling England and America; he was fully invested in the American literary nationalism invented by Knapp, the Duyckincks, and Richardson in the mid–nineteenth century, and because of this the American Revolution serves only as an initiating political factor in his account, not as an important literary moment in its own right. Pattee's attitude had seen earlier light, of course, especially in Norman Foerster's 1928 collection of essays, in which Foerster and others (including Pattee) argued that "while American literature cannot be termed a national literature in the usual sense, it is assuredly not a mere reflection of English literature" (*The Reinterpretation of American Literature* [1928; rerint, New York: Russell and Russell], xxiii). American literature as a national phenomenon was about to be institutionalized by critics like Foerster and Pattee, and when this did occur American Revolutionary literature would retain its position as something transitional and abstract, not quite worthy of study in its own right.

Hence, *The Literary History of the United States* published by Robert Spiller and his associates in 1946 argues that "if America had not come of age in literature [by 1820]—and the work of [our] early writers is the best evidence it had not—at least the first stirrings of a vigorous and promising adolescence were evident" ([1946; reprint, revised ed., New York: Macmillan, 1953], 121). American liberals in the years from 1776 to 1820 "put into execution European ideas" (219)—the epigraph to the section of literary history dealing with "The Republic" is "inquiry and imitation" (113)—which led only to the "false literary dawn of the [seventeen] nineties and the 'dark ages'" that followed (130). True literature "had to wait for more settled times" (131). The more recent *Columbia Literary History of the United States*, edited by Emory Elliott and his associates (New York: Columbia University Press, 1988), promises to revise Spiller's history (xi–xii), but it too treats American Revolutionary literature as an inferior species of art, lacking in imagination, aesthetically unpleasing, and technically imitative. Only 65 pages of the *Columbia Literary History* focus on the forty-five years from 1765 to 1810; but 257 pages are spent on the fifty-five years from 1810 to 1865, a relationship of pages-per-year in the two periods of 1:3. And in those 65 pages American Revolutionary literature tends to be treated in condescending ways: Thomas Philbrick remarks, for example, that "no high art was to emerge from the [American] Revolution, but the very circumstances that worked against such a possibility . . . encouraged [later] American writers to go beyond the safely derivative and conventional limits that previously had circumscribed most of their efforts and to achieve a new intensity and range" (148). The literature of the American Revolution, Philbrick asserts, "looks forward" to the literature of the American Renaissance, even if it could not aspire to its success (143). Revolutionary American literature is "not art, [but] furnish[ed] the materials of art, as James Fenimore Cooper [and Herman Melville] knew" (145). Philbrick, who elsewhere has written eloquently on many of our early national writers, accepts the same assumptions as did Samuel Lorenzo Knapp in 1829, reaching, predictably, similar conclusions.

Recently, Philip Gura surveyed the scholarship of the 1990s on early American literature ("Early American Literature at the New Century," *The William and Mary Quarterly* 57 [2000]: 599–620). While recognizing the point I make here, Gura is nonetheless optimistic that the field has moved "further from the whiggish narratives, ways of merely getting from there to here in our teaching and scholarship" (618). One respondent to his essay, Michael P. Clark ("The Persistence of Literature in Early American Studies," *The William and Mary Quarterly* 57 [2000]: 641–646), takes a view closer to mine when he comments that, in many of the studies Gura discusses, "literature is relegated . . . to the same subordinate status it held in Hippolyte Taine's introduction to his history of English literature published in 1863–1867" (643), that is, the idea that "literature" is valuable only for reconstructing history, not for any aesthetic value it may possess.

17. Cathy Davidson, *Revolution and the Word: The Rise of the Novel in America* (New York: Oxford University Press, 1986); David S. Shields, *Oracles of Empire: Poetry, Politics, and Commerce in British America, 1690–1750* (Chicago: University of Chicago Press, 1990) and *Civil Tongues and Polite Letters in British America* (Chapel Hill: University of North Carolina Press, 1997); and William Dowling, *Poetry and Ideology in Revolutionary Connecticut* (Athens: University of Georgia Press, 1990).

2. FORMING SELVES IN REVOLUTIONARY AMERICA

1. Garry Wills has recently argued that the Latin title of Augustine's best-known work, *Confessiones*, should be translated as "testimony," rather than "confessions." Testimony, he says, "best covers [the] range of meanings for *confessio*" (*Saint Augustine* [New York: Penguin, 1999], xv).

2. On Bradstreet's reluctance to publish, see "The Author to Her Book," in *The Complete Works of Anne Bradstreet*, ed. Joseph R. McElrath, Jr., and Allen P. Robb (Boston: Twayne), 177–178.

3. As late as 1822, Robert Bailey still refers to his *Life and Adventures of Robert Bailey . . . Written by Himself* as "a memorandum of my life" (preface, n.p.).

"Spiritual autobiography" coalesced into a recognizable genre in the early seventeenth century, although no single term was used to refer to it.

4. See Olney, "Autobiography and the Cultural Moment," 5–6. It should be noted, however, that many nineteenth-century American authors continued to shy away from the use of the new word: Thoreau subtitled *Walden* "Life in the Woods"; Douglass and Barnum wrote narratives whose subtitles insist that the work was simply "Written by Himself"; Grant wrote his *Personal Memoirs*; and Adams penned *The Education of Henry Adams*. According to the *Oxford English Dictionary* (OED), the word "autobiography" was first used in 1809 in a review by Robert Southey. Felicity Nussbaum notes that Isaac Disraeli and Johann Herder used the term "self-biography" in 1796, and that one reviewer of Disraeli's *Miscellanies* used the term "autobiography" in 1797 but used it, as the OED notes, only to disapprove of its use (*The Autobiographical Subject: Gender and Ideology in Eighteenth-Century England* [Baltimore: Johns Hopkins University Press, 1989]), 1–27. Folkenflik locates the first use of the word "autobiography" (as an adjective) in 1786, and reviews the efforts by scholars to track its earliest uses (introduction, 1–20).

5. Similarly, I disagree with Susan Clair Imbarrato's recent assertion that eighteenth-century American narratives like Franklin's *History of My Life* are autobiographies that "declare the self as a work in progress moving from self-examination to self-construction" (*Declarations of Independency in Eighteenth-Century American Autobiography* [Knoxville: University of Tennessee Press, 1998], 2). My reading of the narratives of Franklin and his contemporaries sees them as embedded in eighteenth-century conventions, not looking forward to nineteenth-century ones. Earlier in her study, Imbarrato claims more tentatively that eighteenth-century self-biographies record "an emerging sense of the individual voice within an eighteenth-century context that moves away from a monarchical subordination of the individual and that anticipates a democratic celebration of the self" (*Declarations of Independency*, xvii). I find that assertion—with its qualifications of an "eighteenth-century context" and an "anticipation" of democratic selfhood—more plausible. In another recent study, Nancy Ruttenberg traces the emergence of what she calls "democratic personality" or the irruption of speech from the marginalized and dispossessed: "Far from speaking autonomously or unilaterally, as accountable individuals, democratic personality involved a transcendent legitimacy and supraindividual rationale for ignoring social restrictions upon public speech—indeed, it offered itself to the community as a passive instrument for the articulation of individual truths normally concealed from the natural minds of mortal men and women" (*Democratic Personality: Popular Voice and the Trial of American Authorship* [Stanford: Stanford University Press, 1998], 5). Ruttenberg is interested in many of the same narratives as I am, but she is interested in them less from a generic point of view than a cultural and political one.

6. For other references to "progress," see 76, 108, 130, and 196.

7. This explains, of course, why Letter III is so often excerpted and anthologized in the United States: the later letters undermine the myth so ably expounded in it.

8. I think here of Huck Finn, Lambert Strether, Nick Carraway, Professor St. Peter, and Tyrone Slothrop, all of whom experience a "defictionalizing" of their world. They are left, at the end, in symbolically liminal spaces that might represent either pure potentiality or death.

9. My argument here dovetails with Gerald N. Isenberg's when he argues that British romantic writers "fashioned a concept of the freedom of the unique self that made it not only the sole legitimate source of meaning and judgment but entailed its infinite expansion.... [But] they recoiled from their most advanced claims for the absolute authority and infinity of the self" (*Impossible Individuality: Romanticism, Revolution, and the Origins of Modern Selfhood, 1787–1802* [Princeton: Princeton University Press, 1992], 310–311).

10. Many American veterans would eventually be forced to lobby the United States government for compensation. See, for example, Israel Potter, *The Life and Remarkable Adventures of Israel Potter* (Providence, Rhode Island: 1824), 3–4, 51, and 105. The pension laws of 1818 and 1832 required veterans and/or their spouses to submit, in lieu of written records (which most veterans did not have), a full account of their military service (and proof of marriage for the spouse). The pension records of more than 80,000 applicants are on file in the Veterans Administration. Most of these pension-inspired narratives appear to have been written too late for me to analyze in this particular study. For an analysis of one of them see Alfred Young, "George Robert Twelves Hewes (1742–1840): A Boston Shoemaker and the Memory of the American Revolution," *The William and Mary Quarterly* 38 (1981): 535–572. Young has since expanded that article into a book, *The Shoemaker and the Tea Party: Memory and the American Revolution* (Boston: Beacon Press, 1999).

11. The point here is not that people did not deceive in earlier centuries, but that the deceivers themselves are by the late eighteenth century doing the speaking (an effect of increased literacy and accessibility to print culture) and that the audience is apparently fascinated by tales of successful deceptions. See also, for example, Lucy Brewer, *The Female Marine* (Boston, 1815). See, as well, my discussion below in chapter 9.

12. James Fenimore Cooper would make this a theme of his second novel, *The Spy* (1821). He answers the question by suggesting that they cannot be adequately reimbursed financially and socially but that they are emotionally, in their knowledge that they furthered the nation's goals. Moody would not have understood Cooper's romantic nationalism. Cooper's spy was possibly modeled upon Enoch Crosby. See H. L. Barnum, *The Spy Unmasked; or, The Memoirs of Enoch Crosby, alias Harvey Birch* (1828; reprint, Harrison, N.Y.: Harbor Hill Books, 1975). Cooper denied knowing about Crosby's story.

13. William J. Gilmore puts "the rise to dominance in public culture of secular interests," measured by sales of secular books like geographies, travel narratives, histories, and so on, "in the 1790s" (*Reading Becomes a Necessity of Life: Material and Cultural Life in Rural New England, 1780–1835* [Knoxville: University of Tennessee Press, 1989], 208). J. Todd White and Charles H. Lesser list 538 extant Revolutionary "Diaries, Journals, and Autobiographies," including some of the narratives I discuss here, many of them in manuscript (*Fighters for Independence: A Guide to Sources of Biographical Information on Soldiers and Sailors of the American Revolution* [Chicago: University of Chicago Press, 1977]). This number does not include all known self-biographical narratives written in America, 1770–1820.

14. Cf. Edward Gibbon's anecdote about acquiring "idioms" of classical authors and learning "the command . . . of a correct style" by translating Cicero into French and then back into Latin (*Memoirs of my Life*, ed. Betty Radice [New York: Penguin, 1990], 97).

15. Thus, in *Idler* 80 Samuel Johnson argues for the usefulness of biographies "in which the writer tells his own story" (what I am calling "self-biographies") because "The high and low, as they have the same faculties and the same senses, have no less similitude in their pains and pleasures. The sensations are the same in all, tho' produced by very different occasions" (1968, 347).

16. Well into and beyond this period, some evangelical Protestants, harking back to the Augustinian sense of self described by Bradstreet or the Quaker sense of self described by Woolman, continued to insist that God (or Satan) forms the "self," not man. See, for example, Freeborn Garrettson, *The Experience and Travels of Freeborn Garrettson* (Philadelphia, 1791). Rodger Payne has studied nineteenth-century American evangelical conversion narratives. He notes that many nineteenth-century "evangelical autobiographers were able to 'baptize' the modern concept of the independent and autonomous self into the larger discourse of Christian orthodoxy," though that assimilation was not complete until the mid–nineteenth century (*The Self and the Sacred: Conversion and Autobiography in Early American Protestantism* [Knoxville: University of Tennessee Press, 1998], 2). See, more generally, Payne, *The Self and the Sacred*, 33–49; and Richard Rabinowitz, *The Spiritual Self in Everyday Life: The Transformation of Religious Identity in Nineteenth-Century New England* (Boston: Northeastern University Press, 1989).

17. See, for example, the annotated bibliography in J. A. Leo LeMay and P. M. Zall, eds., *The Autobiography of Benjamin Franklin: A Genetic Text* (Knoxville: University of Tennessee Press, 1981), 365–374.

18. There is also an irony in that Franklin's world is one of tools and labor; he rises from the middle class to a preeminent place in the world, and thus seems to prefigure the struggles of men like Fitch and Burroughs to "rise" above their place. I would argue that Franklin's life, with some encouragement from his

manuscript self-biography but even more from contemporary redactions and reconstructions of his life, indeed was read that way from the very beginning (see Carla Mulford, "Benjamin Franklin and the Myths of Nationhood," in *Making America/Making American Literature*, ed. A. Robert Lee and W. M. Verhoeven [Amsterdam: Rodopi, 1996], 15–58); but that the actual text as Franklin imagined and wrote it tells a different, more conservative story.

19. This term "calling" suggests a predetermined place in the world; it was used in a culture where one's place *was* predetermined (by either God or society, or both). Robinson Crusoe's restlessness, which may or may not be "ambition," derives in part from his lack of a "calling," and in any case runs counter to his larger, predetermined "station" in life, in the middle class, a station that Crusoe finally accepts at the end of Defoe's novel. J. E. Crowley has studied the eighteenth-century conception of economic life and argues that, by retaining a notion of work as a "calling," the colonists fought "to maintain [a] sense of the social wholeness of the individual" (*This Sheba, Self: The Conceptualization of Economic Life in Eighteenth-Century America* [Baltimore: Johns Hopkins University Press, 1974], 12), despite actual evidence that ambition, selfishness, and acquisitiveness were on the rise.

20. Cf. Rousseau's contemporaneous assessment of himself: "I am made unlike any one I have ever met" (*Confessions*, 17). Rousseau's insistence on his own singularity means that he cannot assert that his narrative is "useful" in a traditional sense; we cannot imitate Rousseau the way that (theoretically) we can imitate Franklin. Rousseau, instead, continually asks his readers to "judge" him (169, 261, 335). Cf. Thoreau's insistence in *Walden* that readers not follow him to the actual Walden, but that each reader "explore your own higher latitudes . . . be a Columbus to whole new continents and worlds within you" (Henry David Thoreau, *Walden; or, Life in the Woods*, in *Henry David Thoreau*, ed. Robert F. Sayre [New York: Library of America, 1985], 578).

3. ALEXANDER GRAYDON AND THE FEDERALIST SELF

1. Alexander Graydon's *Memoirs of a Life, Chiefly Passed in Pennsylvania . . .* (Harrisburg, Pa.: John Wyeth, 1811) was republished by Blackwood's in Edinburgh in 1822. John Stockton Littell edited *Memoirs* and republished it in Philadelphia in 1846 under the title *Graydon's Memoirs of His Own Time*; and Littell's edition was reprinted twice, once in 1900 and once in 1969. Page references will be to the 1811 edition.

2. This thumbnail sketch is derived primarily from Graydon's own *Memoirs*, but I have also consulted the standard reference sources, as well as Graydon's obituary in *The Port Folio* 6, 4th series (1818): 56–58. Though *Memoirs* was published anonymously, Graydon was known to have been the author; see the review of

the 1811 edition in *The Port Folio* 7, 3d series (1812): 315–323, where the reviewer notes that *Memoirs* was "generally known to have been written by Alexander Graydon, Esq. of Harrisburg, and to be his own biography" (315). Not surprisingly, the reviewer does not refer to the narrative as an "autobiography." On the stance of anonymity in eighteenth-century America, see Michael Warner, *The Letters of the Republic: Publication and the Public Sphere in Eighteenth-Century America* (Cambridge: Harvard University Press, 1990). Graydon did sign his private letters, some of which survive.

3. See Richard P. McCormick, *The Second American Party System: Party Formation in the Jacksonian Era* (Chapel Hill: University of North Carolina Press, 1966), 3–5, 19–31; and Jared Charles Ingersoll, *Inchiquin, the Jesuit's Letters* (New York, 1810), 70.

4. See *The Port Folio* 6, 4th series (1818): 57. "Ideological" is not quite an anachronism, though Graydon would no doubt have (mis)understood it along the same lines as John Adams in his facetious comment to Jefferson: "Does it mean Idiotism? The Science of Non Compos Menticism. The Science of Lunacy? The Theory of Delerium? Or does it mean the Science of Self Love? Or Amour Propre? of the Elements of Vanity?" (Adams and Jefferson 1988, 501).

5. Few reviews of the 1811 edition appeared, and later British reviews of the 1822 Edinburgh edition were very harsh. See, for example, the anonymous review in *The Quarterly Review* 26 (January 1822): 364–374.

6. *The Columbia Literary History of the United States* merely refers to Graydon as an "arrogant" and "insufferable" person whose autobiography "is engagingly unorthodox" (153). William Gilmore, in *The Cambridge History of American Literature*, makes no mention of Graydon or his *Memoirs*, although he does note that until the 1980s "academic criticism accepted and elaborated [a] pejorative assessment of postrevolutionary culture" (541), including works like Graydon's *Memoirs*. Gilmore's optimism that the 1980s witnessed a change for the better has been challenged by William Spengemann in his review of *Cambridge History* ("E Pluribus Minimum," *Early American Literature* 29 [1994]: 276–294). Larzer Ziff briefly discusses Graydon's *Memoirs* (*Writing in the New Nation: Prose, Print, and Politics in the Early United States* [New Haven: Yale University Press, 1991], 185–186). I know of no other article-length studies of Graydon, but see the unpublished Ph.D. dissertation by Robert Reed Sanderlin "Alexander Graydon: The Life and Literary Career of an American Patriot" (University of North Carolina, 1968).

7. On Jefferson's relationship to the rise of modern liberalism, see Joyce Appleby, *Capitalism and a New Social Order*; and Michael Lienesch, "Thomas Jefferson and the American Democratic Experience," in *Jeffersonian Legacies*, ed. Peter S. Onuf (Charlottesville: University of Virginia Press, 1993), 316–339.

8. My use of the terms "dominant," "residual," and "emergent" has been influenced by Raymond Williams, *Marxism and Literature* (Oxford: Oxford Uni-

versity Press, 1977) and also by McKeon, *The Origins of the English Novel 1600–1740*.

9. On the cultural matrix that produced modern notions of authorship in America, see the recent studies by Grantland Rice, *The Transformation of Authorship in America* (Chicago: University of Chicago Press, 1997); and Christopher Grasso, *A Speaking Aristocracy: Transforming Public Discourse in Eighteenth-Century Connecticut* (Chapel Hill: University of North Carolina Press, 1999).

10. It is not clear how much of Franklin's *History of My Life* Graydon knew. Portions and paraphrases of Franklin's self-biography appeared in print as early as 1790; a French translation of part one appeared in 1791; and a retranslation into English of the 1791 edition appeared in 1793. Graydon could certainly have known part one well in 1811, and known parts two and three through the 1790 paraphrases. See Lemay and Zall, *The Autobiography of Benjamin Franklin*, xlviii–lviii.

11. Cf. Franklin, 1340–1342, 1361–1362.

12. Cf. Franklin, 1308–1312. Franklin's family was "obscure" (1311), Graydon's un-illustrious.

13. On the eighteenth-century public sphere, see Jürgen Habermas, *The Structural Transformation of the Public Sphere*, trans. Thomas Burger (Cambridge: Harvard University Press, 1991), esp. 27–43 and 51–67; Warner, *The Letters of the Republic*, 34–72; and the essays collected in Craig Calhoun, ed., *Habermas and the Public Sphere* (Cambridge: Massachusetts Institute of Technology Press, 1992). On Franklin and eighteenth-century print discourse, see Warner, *The Letters of the Republic*, 73–96; Lewis P. Simpson, "The Printer as a Man of Letters: Franklin and the Symbolism of the Third Realm," in *The Oldest Revolutionary: Essays on Benjamin Franklin*, ed. J. A. Leo LeMay (Philadelphia: University of Pennsylvania Press, 1976), 3–20; and Bruce Ingham Granger, *Benjamin Franklin: An American Man of Letters* (Ithaca: Cornell University Press, 1964), 5–18.

14. Graydon mentions Poor Richard's almanac (3), but for other published statements by Franklin on behavior, see *Writings*, 242–244, 320–322, 345–346, and 1294–1303. On the emergence in nineteenth-century America of an autonomous sense of self, accompanied by encouragements to self-construct personal identity, see Daniel Walker Howe, *Making the American Self: Jonathan Edwards to Abraham Lincoln* (Cambridge: Harvard University Press, 1997).

15. In a letter to Joseph Reed, president of the Supreme Executive Council, written thirty years before his recollections in *Memoirs*, Graydon stated his complaint more baldly: "that being exchanged, and having been disappointed in obtaining the Rank he [i.e., Graydon] conceived himself entitled to, he quitted the army, and is now enrolled in the Militia of Berks County. . . . [But] after having held the Rank of Captain in the Continental Army, he confesses that his feelings would have been wounded by being obliged to perform the Duty of a private Centinel in common with a set of men (the Peasantry of the Country,) with whom from their Education and manner of life he cou'd not associ-

ate. For notwithstanding the Principles of Equality upon which this and all free Government are founded, he presumes it will be admitted that in every society there are some Distinctions and Gradations of Rank arising from Education and other accidental circumstances" (letter dated 5 October 1780; *Pennsylvania Archives*, 2d series, 3: 380–381).

16. See 169, 172, and 288, respectively, for Graydon's allusions to each of these histories.

17. Frederick the Great of Prussia was a benevolent despot and a great patron of the arts—but he was still a despot.

18. By 1829, in the first literary history of the United States, Samuel Lorenzo Knapp could simply and without controversy declare: "The [American] publick [in 1776] had so long been in training for the evil times which came upon them, that every one was thoroughly prepared for all the difficulties which he had to encounter. . . . There were no discordant notes in the concert; all were in tune to any master hand that struck the chords" (94–95). Cf. John Adams's comment in an 1818 letter to Hezekiah Niles that "thirteen clocks were made to strike together" in 1776 (1851, 10: 283).

19. From a twentieth-century perspective, Charles Royster notes that Graydon was essentially correct: the "popular rage militaire vanished by the end of 1776 and never returned. Even in 1776 it was a weak echo of its loudest moments in 1775" (*A Revolutionary People at War: The Continental Army and American Character, 1775–1783* [Chapel Hill: University of North Carolina Press, 1979], 25).

20. Many journals and diaries written during the Revolution, like Jeremiah Greenman's, for example, record the monotony and tedium of the war; the anonymous *Adventures of Jonathan Corncob, Loyal American Refugee* (1787; reprint, Boston: David R. Godine, 1976) records a bawdy, satiric view of the Revolution; and other Federalists, like John Adams in retirement, wrote bitterly and irreverently about the developing myths surrounding the Revolution. On Adams, see Joseph Ellis, *Passionate Sage: The Character and Legacy of John Adams* (New York: Norton, 1993), 84–112.

21. Contrast this to Franklin's inclusion of the highly laudatory letters by Abel James and Benjamin Vaughan at the beginning of part two of *History of My Life*.

22. Of course, the formative influence of childhood on adult values is a central doctrine of literary romanticism, as witnessed by such works as Wordsworth's *Prelude* and Weems's *Life of Washington*. Graydon resists that emergent romantic formulation. He invokes the self of his childhood only to deny its relevance as a singular, specific phenomenon. The marble episode, which I mentioned earlier, points to general human nature, not to Graydon's particular, individual nature or self.

23. See also his comment after his exchange: "having now little before me, but the vapid occurrences of retired life, I shall here hold myself absolved from further attention to any matters merely of a personal or private nature" (287).

24. On the "modern" forces unleashed by the American Revolution, see Wood, *The*

Radicalism of the American Revolution, 227–369. On the emergence of the unrestrained economic man in the eighteenth century, see Crowley, *This Sheba, Self.*

25. Graydon might well have made a similar excuse for his own "highly wrought" attacks on Jefferson and other Republicans in the third section of *Memoirs*, as, for example, when he refers to the "malignant, Catilinarian spirit" of Jefferson's sect (325).

26. Allen, 29, 33–34, 42, 58–60, 65, 70, 74, and 77–79. Like Graydon, Allen expects his merit as a gentleman to be self-evidently obvious to others. See, for example, 42 and 70; and see my discussion in chapter 5 below.

27. See Lewis P. Simpson, "Federalism and the Crisis of Literary Order," *American Literature* 37 (1960): 253–266; and Stanley Elkins and Eric McKitrick, *The Age of Federalism* (New York: Oxford University Press, 1993), 21–25.

28. See also Habermas, *Structural Transformation*, 1–26; Simpson, "Federalism"; and Joseph Stevens Buckminster, "The Dangers and Duties of Men of Letters," in *The Federalist Literary Mind*, ed. Lewis P. Simpson (Baton Rouge: Louisiana State University Press, 1962), 95–102.

29. Concerning the classical ideal of literary value held by many in the Revolutionary generation, Robert Ferguson remarks: "Common assumptions such as the harmony of nature, the efficacy of reason, the importance of hierarchy and decorum, and the inherent structure of all knowledge were especially useful in an American aesthetics of order and control. By comparison, the subjective imagination, the originality, the fluid emotionalism and spontaneity of romanticism were inappropriate, even dangerous, to the goal of a collective sense of purpose" (*Law and Letters in American Culture* [Cambridge: Harvard University Press, 1984], 76). The "collective sense of purpose" is precisely what Graydon feared was being undermined by the ruthless scrambling of scheming individuals.

30. John P. Hewitt has in fact defined "the essence of modernity [as] its transformation of the boundaries of social order and individual existence. . . . [The] field of the modern imagination has widened to a societal [as opposed to a communal] scope" (*Dilemmas of the American Self* [Philadelphia: Temple University Press, 1989], 111, 115).

31. Graydon's *Memoirs* fits Spengemann's definition of historical autobiography (which I have insisted should be called self-biography, not autobiography): it "demonstrates the consonance of an individual life with an absolute, eternal law already in force and known through some immediate source outside the life that illustrates it" (1980, 60).

4. THE REVOLUTIONS OF THE MIND: BENJAMIN RUSH'S TRAVELS THROUGH LIFE

1. *Medical Inquiries and Observations*, vol. 1 (Philadelphia, 1789), 186–196. I refer here to the essay as reprinted under the title "Influence of the American Revo-

lution" in Benjamin Rush, *The Selected Writings of Benjamin Rush*, ed. Dagobert Runes (New York: Philosophical Library, 1947), 325–333. Throughout this chapter, simple page references to Rush's works will refer to *Selected Writings*; references to his other works will be noted parenthetically as *Travels* (Benjamin Rush, *The Autobiography of Benjamin Rush: His "Travels through Life" Together with his Commonplace Books for 1789–1813*, ed. George W. Corner [Princeton: Princeton University Press, 1948]); or as *Letters* (Benjamin Rush, *Letters of Benjamin Rush*, ed. L. H. Butterfield, 2 vols. [Philadelphia: American Philosophical Society, 1951]).

2. Cf. Rush's comment in a letter to Richard Price in 1786: "Most of the distresses of our country, and of the mistakes which Europeans have formed of us, have arisen from a belief that the American Revolution is over. This is so far from being the case that we have only finished the first act of the great drama. We have changed our forms of government, but it remains yet to effect a revolution in our principles, opinions, and manners so as to accommodate them to the forms of government we have adopted" (*Letters*, 388). John Adams also saw the Revolution and the war as two separate phenomena, but he maintained that the Revolution began long before the first shot was fired at Lexington and Concord: "What do we mean by the Revolution? The War? That was no part of the Revolution. It was only an Effect and Consequence of it. The Revolution was in the Minds of the People, and this was effected, from 1760 to 1775, in the course of fifteen Years before a drop of blood was drawn at Lexington" (Adams and Jefferson, 455).

3. See the standard biographical accounts by Nathan G. Goodman, *Benjamin Rush, Physician and Citizen, 1746–1813* (Philadelphia: University of Pennsylvania Press, 1934); Carl Binger, *Revolutionary Doctor: Benjamin Rush, 1746–1813* (New York: Norton, 1966); David Freeman Hawke, *Benjamin Rush: Revolutionary Gadfly* (Indianapolis: Bobbs-Merrill, 1971); and Donald J. D'Elia, *Benjamin Rush: Philosopher of the American Revolution* (Philadelphia: American Philosophical Society, 1974). On the yellow fever episode, see J. H. Powell, *Bring out Your Dead: The Great Plague of Yellow Fever in Philadelphia in 1793* (Philadelphia: University of Pennsylvania Press, 1949).

4. Rush also made use of John Redman Coxe's "gyrator," which, by centrifugal motion, forced a patient's blood away from the brain. See *Letters*, 961; and Rush, *Medical Inquiries and Observations upon the Diseases of the Mind* (Philadelphia, 1812), 224–226.

5. On the origins of reformative incarceration in Philadelphia, including solitary confinement, see Michael Meranze, *Laboratories of Virtue: Punishment, Revolution, and Authority in Philadelphia, 1760–1835* (Chapel Hill: University of North Carolina Press, 1996). On the rise of the penitentiary in colonial and Revolutionary America, see David J. Rothman, *The Discovery of the Asylum* (Boston: Little, Brown, 1971); and Adam Jay Hirsch, *The Rise of the Penitentiary: Prisons and Punishment in Early America* (New Haven: Yale University Press, 1992). On

the rise of the Western penitentiary and its modes of discipline, see Michel Foucault, *Discipline and Punish: The Birth of the Prison*, trans. Alan Sheridan (New York: Vintage, 1987).

6. Jay Fliegelman adduces Rush's tranquillizing chair as evidence of the "paradoxical ideal of the period ... the complementarity and mutuality of freedom and coercion" (*Declaring Independence: Jefferson, Natural Language, and the Culture of Performance* [Stanford: Stanford University Press, 1993], 139), but his method does not allow for sustained analysis of what the chair might mean in the "narrower" contexts of Rush's writings or the penal system or early national medicine.

7. See the account by Butterfield in *Letters*, 1213–1218 (the reference to "silly sansculottish stuff" is cited on 1214).

8. Rush notes at one point in the account that he is writing on June 2, 1800, and at another that he is writing in July 1800; but see also his comment at the very end of the narrative that "August 2cd 1798. This day [I] heard of the death of my dear and only sister Rachel Montgomery" (*Travels*, 43, 34, and 169).

9. The correspondence halted for fifteen years in part, of course, because Adams spent a portion of each year in Philadelphia (first as vice president, then as president). But it is also clear that there was a falling out between Adams and Rush in those years. See Adams's February 6, 1805, letter to Rush (Adams and Rush, 20–21).

10. The title Rush gave the narrative makes the same comment, though more obliquely: "Travels through life or an account of sundry Incidents and Events in the life of Benjamin Rush born December 24 1745 Old Style—written for the use of his children" (21). Many self-biographies continued to be written for the use of the author's children, as Bradstreet and Shepard had done in the mid–seventeenth century. See, for example, John Adams, *Autobiography of John Adams*, in *Diary and Autobiography of John Adams*, ed. L. H. Butterfield, 4 vols. (Cambridge: Harvard University Press, 1962), III: 254; and David Perry, *Recollections of an Old Soldier: The Life of David Perry* (Windsor, Vt.: 1822), 51.

11. Recently, a number of scholars have argued that the transition from Christian and classical notions of citizenship and authorship to liberal notions of citizenship and authorship was not sudden or sharp. See, for example, Rice, *The Transformation of Authorship*; and Grasso, *A Speaking Aristocracy*. On Rush's allegiance to both Christian and classical ideals, see D'Elia, *Benjamin Rush*; Joseph Alkana, "Spiritual and Rational Authority in Benjamin Rush's *Travels through Life*," *Texas Studies in Language and Literature* 34 (1992): 284–301; and John Kloos, *A Sense of Deity: The Republican Spirituality of Dr. Benjamin Rush* (Brooklyn, N.Y.: Carlson, 1991).

12. But see Rush's letters in 1765 to Ebenezer Hazard, in which he is already a vociferous opponent of the Stamp Act.

13. See also Henry May, *The Enlightenment in America* (Oxford: Oxford University Press, 1976), 208–211. On the influence of Davies, president of the College

of New Jersey when Rush was enrolled as a student, see Rush, *Letters*, 3–4; and Binger, *Revolutionary Doctor*, 22–25.

14. See also Fliegelman, *Declaring Independence*, 138–142. Rush and others in the late eighteenth century, Fliegelman proposes, enlarged the claims for the free agency of the human will, shifting more and more responsibility for behavior onto individuals; these enlarged claims "both masked and responded to a fear of constraining and determinate contingencies" (141). Simply expressed, the paradox, which I shall discuss below as Rush's self-biography touches upon it, is that behavior is determined by environment, but that individuals are still responsible for their behavior.

15. Clearly, however, Rush's relationship to Cullen is fraught with Freudian anxiety about the "father."

16. See, for example, Rush, *Medical Inquiries and Observations upon the Diseases of the Mind* (1812).

17. On self-effacement, see, for example, Fliegelman, *Declaring Independence*, 72–73; and Warner, *Letters of the Republic*, 42. However, their motives for believing in the concept of self-effacement differed, which is one of my points about seeing the shift from "classic to romantic" as a complex, convoluted, haphazard transition. On this latter point, see Marilyn Butler, *Romantics, Rebels, and Reactionaries: English Literature and Its Background, 1760–1830* (Oxford: Oxford University Press, 1981); as well as previously cited studies by Rice, Grasso, Fliegelman, Hedges, Ferguson, and others.

18. This is the fear that Charles Brockden Brown probes in his 1799 novel *Ormond; or, The Secret Witness*: "Ormond aspired to nothing more ardently than to hold the reins of opinion. To exercise absolute power over the conduct of others, not by constraining their limbs, or by exacting obedience to his authority, but in a way of which his subjects should be scarcely conscious. He desired that his guidance should controul their steps, but that his agency, when most effectual, should be least suspected" (1982, 177).

19. In "The Man at Home," written in 1798, Charles Brockden Brown commented: "According to this new mode of considering the subject, the world may, at present, be regarded as one vast hospital. . . . [There] is no one who is wholly uninfected" (in *The Rhapsodist and Other Writings*, ed. Harry R. Warfel [New York: Scholar's Facsimiles and Reprints, 1943], 86–87). Bill Christophersen has noted, rightly, I think, that "Brown's Gothic romances, on the whole . . . are *post*revolutionary fictions about the dangers of freedom, individualism, rationalism, and self-assertion" (*The Apparition in the Glass: Charles Brockden Brown's American Gothic* [Athens: University of Georgia Press, 1993], 25). Brown sees much of what Rush sees, but he is much less sanguine about our ability to remedy our condition.

20. The seal of the American Psychiatric Association has borne Rush's portrait since 1964. See Binger, *Revolutionary Doctor*, 196.

5. ETHAN ALLEN AND THE REPUBLICAN SELF

1. It has been available in its eighteenth- and nineteenth-century reprints and, as well, in two accessible twentieth-century reprints, one by Corinth Books (1961) and one by Applewood Books (1989). The Applewood edition is, apparently, a reprint of the edition issued in 1989 by the Vermont Historical Society, itself a reprint (with a new introduction) of the 1930 edition published by the Fort Ticonderoga Musuem. Throughout this chapter, I will be citing my own edition of Allen's *Narrative of the Captivity of Ethan Allen* (Acton, Mass: Copley Publishing, 2000), based on the first edition of 1779.

2. Any standard history of the American Revolution takes note, as Edward Countryman writes, of the "people's loss of initial enthusiasm" by 1778–1779 (*The American Revolution* [New York: Hill and Wang, 1985], 143).

3. On the concept of sensibility in eighteenth-century English culture, see G. J. Barker-Benfield, *The Culture of Sensibility: Sex and Society in Eighteenth-Century Britain* (Chicago: University of Chicago Press, 1992). On the sentimental in the literature of the period, see Janet Todd, *Sensibility: An Introduction* (London: Methuen, 1986); John Mullan, *Sentiment and Sociability: The Language of Feeling in the Eighteenth Century* (Oxford: Clarendon Press, 1988); and R. F. Brissenden, *Virtue in Distress: Studies in the Novel of Sentiment from Richardson to Sade* (New York: Harper and Row, 1976).

4. On the difference between sentiment and sensibility, see Todd, *Sensibility*, 6–9. Both terms apply in Allen's *Narrative*.

5. Another contemporaneous text that Allen's *Narrative* echoes is, of course, Tom Paine's *Common Sense*, which is hypersensitive to issues of youth and age, innocence and experience, liberty and slavery, purity and corruption.

6. See, for example, no. 69, in which Addison argues that "Nature seems to have taken a particular Care to disseminate her Blessings among the different Regions of the World, with an Eye to this mutual Intercourse and Traffick among Mankind, that the Natives of the several parts of the Globe might have a kind of Dependance upon one another, and be united together by their common Interest" (I: 213).

7. Cf. Paine's *Letter to the Abbé Raynal*. Paine argues that the American Revolution and the alliance with France "expel[led] prejudice"; they converted America in a way that would not have occurred had the United States "dropped quietly from Britain." "We see with other eyes; we hear with other ears; and think with other thoughts, than those we formerly used" (in *The Thomas Paine Reader*, ed. Michael Foot and Isaac Kramnick [New York: Penguin, 1987], 163).

8. On nerve theory and sensational psychology, see Barker-Benfield, *Culture of Sensibility*, 15–23.

9. See also 89; and cf. 2 Kings 19.3; Isaiah 22.5; etc.

10. It was part of the republican tradition that the heroic leader—Cincinnatus, or Cato, or Washington—should stand revealed to the people in his essential integrity. Cf. Henry Laurens's behavior when held by the British: he has a chance to escape from the guard on the way to London but does not do so, because the young man with him "reposed" his confidence in Laurens (Henry Laurens, *A Narrative of the Capture of Henry Laurens*, in *Collections of the South Carolina Historical Society* 1 [1857]: 23). Virtue must be demonstrated publicly.

6. THE ENIGMATIC CHARACTER OF STEPHEN BURROUGHS

1. See, for example, Rhys Isaac, *The Transformation of Virginia, 1740–1790* (1982; reprint, New York: Norton, 1988).
2. See, for example, Fliegelman, *Declaring Independence*.
3. The epistolary form also recalls Brown's *Edgar Huntly*, published the year after part one of Burroughs's *Memoirs*, which purports to be a letter from Edgar to his fiancée, Mary Waldegrave.
4. This is subtly different from the minister's suggestion—it is not the author's own opinion—in *Letters from an American Farmer* that "what we speak out among ourselves we call conversation, and a letter is only conversation put down in black and white" (44). There, writing is claimed to be a direct transcription of speaking; here, writing, though it seems to transcribe speech, alters the story in doing so: a "dull tale of egotisms" in verbal relation is "perused" in a different way in a written text.
5. Daniel Cohen claims that Burroughs did lead a band of counterfeiters in Canada, that he served more time in prison, that he resumed his career as a schoolteacher, and that he died in 1840, a converted Catholic and respected teacher (*Pillars of Salt, Monuments of Grace: New England Crime Literature and the Origins of American Popular Culture, 1674–1860* [New York: Oxford University Press, 1993], 158).
6. See also Lawrence Buell, *New England Literary Culture from Revolution through Renaissance* (Cambridge: Cambridge University Press, 1986), 339–340; Gary Lindberg, *The Confidence Man in American Literature* (New York: Oxford University Press, 1982), 303n and 304n; and Ziff, *Writing in the New Nation*, 59–67.
7. One's handwriting in the eighteenth century was referred to as a "character." Modern dictionaries retain some sense of "a style of printing or writing" as a "character" (*American Heritage Dictionary*). See Franklin, *Writings*, 1313, for example.
8. The novel, of course, is predicated upon just this assumption. "In reality," Fielding wrote in *Tom Jones* (1749), "there are many little circumstances too often omitted by injudicious historians, from which events of the utmost importance arise. The world may indeed be considered as a vast machine, in which the great

wheels are originally set in motion by those which are very minute, and almost imperceptible to any but the strongest eyes" (*The History of Tom Jones, a Found-ling*, ed. John Bender and Simon Stern [Oxford: Oxford University Press, 1996], 194).

Contrast Burroughs's notion in the quoted passage with Graydon's conser-vative resistance to understanding the "puerile" events of his youth as indicative of his personality. Burroughs's discussion of the importance of his "childish years" is tinged with the romantic belief that the child is closer to nature and closer to a natural self than is the grown adult. I will take up this idea further in chapter 9.

9. This complaint is registered in many American novels written in the early re-public. See, for example, Judith Sargent Murray, *The Story of Margaretta* (1798; in Sharon Harris, ed., *Selected Writings of Judith Sargent Murray* [New York: Oxford University Press, 1995], 153–272; and Tabitha Gilman Tenney, *Female Quixotism* (Boston, 1801).

10. Novel reading leads, in Burroughs's *Memoirs*, to his easy acceptance of Lysan-der's arguments that counterfeit money actually benefits the community (83–84). He cannot see the full implications of Lysander's selfishness. On a broad course of reading for a liberal education, see, for example, Jefferson's 1771 letter to Robert Skipwith (Thomas Jefferson, *Writings* [New York: Library of Amer-ica, 1985], 740–745).

11. "I have said enough to make it understood that punishment as punishment must never be inflicted on children. . . . Children's lies are all the work of mas-ters, and that to want to teach them to tell the truth is nothing other than to teach them to lie. . . . For us who give our pupils only lessons in practice and who prefer that they be good rather than learned—we do not exact the truth from them lest they disguise it, and we make them give no promises that they would be tempted not to keep. . . . If [his] difficult natural disposition compels me to come to some agreement with him, I will arrange things so carefully that the suggestion always comes from him, never from me. . . (Jean-Jacques Rous-seau, *Emile: or, On education*, trans. Allan Bloom [New York: Basic Books, 1979], 101–102.

12. See, specifically, *The Federalist Papers*, nos. 10, 35, 54–57, and 63; and, more gen-erally, *The Debate on the Constitution*, ed. Bernard Bailyn, 2 vols. (New York: Library of America, 1993). Saul Cornell, *The Other Founders: Anti-Federalism and the Dissenting Tradition in America, 1788–1828* (Chapel Hill: University of North Carolina Press, 1999), has recently analyzed the debate on the Constitu-tion from the point of view of anti-Federalism in the thirty years following ratification.

13. This is not an exhaustive list, but see Lawrence Buell, *New England Literary Culture*; Jay Fliegelman, *Prodigals and Pilgrims: The American Revolution Against Patriarchal Authority 1750–1800* (Cambridge: Cambridge University Press,

1982); Fliegelman, *Declaring Independence*; Thomas Gustafson, *Representative Words: Politics, Literature, and the American Language, 1776–1865* (Cambridge: Cambridge University Press, 1992); Michael Kramer, *Imagining Language in America: From the Revolution to the Civil War* (Princeton: Princeton University Prss, 1992); Christopher Looby, *Voicing America: Language, Literary Form, and the Origins of the United States* (Chicago: University of Chicago Press, 1996); David Simpson, *The Politics of American English, 1776–1850* (New York: Oxford University Press, 1986); and Ziff, *Writing in the New Nation*.

14. On the religious controversy that predated Burroughs's arrival in Pelham, see Stephen Marini, "The Religious World of Daniel Shays," in *In Debt to Shays: The Cultural Politics of an Agrarian Rebellion*, ed. Robert A. Gross (Charlottesville: University of Virginia Press, 1993), 239–277.

15. On the trope of theater in Revolutionary America (though usually as it was used in a national or epic sense), see Jeffrey Richards, *Theater Enough: American Culture and the Metaphor of the World Stage, 1607–1789* (Durham: Duke University Press, 1991), 245–297.

16. Cf. Burroughs's comment: "So true it is, that mankind will wear the veil of deception, generally, in all countries" (230).

17. One might argue that Burroughs's mistake was to pass someone else's "representation." He does much better when he tries to pass his own.

18. Given his insistence that the supervisory eye of our fellow man gives rise to our social disguises, one can anticipate how Burroughs might be affected by the scrutiny of the penal system. I will return to this point shortly.

19. Fliegelman remarks about this scene:

> In his criminal *Memoirs*, the notorious eighteenth-century forger Stephen Burroughs describes a conversation he had with a physician who knew him in his youth. Not recognizing Burroughs, who had disguised himself to avoid capture, the physician insists that, because physiognomy is an excellent index to "natural disposition," he can confidently assert: "I never saw a more striking contrast, than between the designing, deceitful countenance of Burroughs, and your open, frank, and candid countenance." The irony of the passage, an irony perversely confirming Lavater [who argued that facial expressions are infallible registers of personal character], is that the honest, open countenance is the countenance of deceit. (*Declaring Independence*, 37)

Fliegelman is a brilliant critic. But this passage is fraught with the sort of mistakes that critics using a New Historicist method are perhaps bound to commit, as the method deemphasizes the close reading of particular texts in favor of a "reading" of a concept or idea or institution pervading the larger culture. First, Burroughs was not, literally at least, a "forger"; he himself, remember, did not produce counterfeit money, he only passed it. Second, Burroughs does not tell us in the scene that he was disguised to "avoid capture"; he merely says that he was living among a people who at that time did not know his real name and character. Third, the physician claims only that he was once "'acquainted'" with a character named Burroughs; Burroughs himself remarks that the physician was merely from a part of the country "contiguous" to the one in which Burroughs grew up. Finally, Fliegelman's reading misses some of the irony that it purports to reveal: Burroughs himself offers the incident as a verification of what he claims is an "open, frank, and candid" heart, which his "countenance" actually affirms (even though his behavior might not, at times). Lavater, in other words, *is* confimed in the passage, not through Burroughs's manipulation of his facial expression but through his unselfconscious facial expression.

20. See David Szatmary, *Shays' Rebellion: The Making of an Agrarian Insurrection* (Amherst: University of Massachusetts Prss, 1980); and the essays in Gross, ed., *In Debt to Shays*. For a reflection on the "invention of responsibility" in the late eighteenth century, see Fliegelman, *Declaring Independence*, 140–150.

21. This metaphor provides another connection to Brown, who in *Edgar Huntly* investigates the "secret springs" of human behavior, an investigation that is figured by Edgar's and Sarsefield's construction of boxes:

> [The box's] structure was remarkable. It consisted of six sides, square and of similar dimensions. These were joined, not by mortice and tennon; not by nails, not by hinges, but the junction was accurate. The means by which they were made to cohere was invisible. . . . Mere strength could not be applied to raise [the lid], because there was no projecture which might be firmly held by the hand, and by which force could be exerted. Some spring, therefore, secretly existed which might forever elude the senses, but on which the hand, by being moved over it, in all directions, might accidently light. (1998, 739–742)

Brown's novel suggests that, in the end, that "secret spring" might well be the unconscious, and that not all actions can be traced to a rational, known cause or "spring."

22. As Burroughs writes to his parents in 1795: "that our times and changes are fixed and unalterable by the everlasting laws of nature, is what I most firmly believe; and therefore to remain quiet under whatever situation we may find ourselves, is a duty no less apparent" (362). This quietism depends on another, quite different kind of deference.

23. See J. G. A. Pocock, *The Machiavellian Moment: Florentine Political Thought and the Atlantic Republican Tradition* (Princeton: Princeton University Press, 1975), 526–552; and Gordon Wood, *The Creation of the American Republic, 1776–1789* (1969; reprint, New York: Norton, 1972), 61–65, 608–610.

24. I do not mean here an objective, true "plumbing"; as post-structuralists, we think we know quite well that language simply cannot provide us with such a

measure of reality. But the nineteenth-century nonfictional prose tradition, including autobiography and history, does come to believe that reality can be expressed through language, for example, in the symbolism with which Thoreau can suggest that his soul is like Walden Pond (depthless, clear, unchartable) or in the historical penetration to "essences" that Ranke uses to show the past "wie es eigentlich gewesen."

7. PRINTED FOR THE AUTHORESS: K. WHITE AND ELIZABETH FISHER

1. I refer to these book-length studies: Nancy F. Cott, *The Bonds of Womanhood: "Woman's Sphere" in New England, 1780–1835* (New Haven: Yale University Press, 1977); Mary Beth Norton, *Liberty's Daughters: The Revolutionary Experience of America, 1750–1800* (Boston: Little Brown, 1980); Joy Day Buel and Richard Buel, *The Way of Duty: A Woman and Her Family in Revolutionary America* (New York: Norton, 1984); Linda Kerber, *Women of the Republic: Intellect and Ideology in Revolutionary America* (New York: Norton, 1986); Cathy Davidson, *Revolution and the Word: The Rise of the Novel in America* (New York: Oxford University Press, 1986); Laurel Thatcher Ulrich, *A Midwife's Tale: The Life of Martha Ballard, Based on Her Diary, 1785–1812* (New York: Knopf, 1990); Edith Belle Gelles, *Portia: The World of Abigail Adams* (Bloomington: Indiana University Press, 1992); Nina Baym, *American Women Writers and the Work of History, 1790–1860* (New Brunswick: Rutgers University Press, 1995); and Joan Gunderson, *To Be Useful to the World: Women in Revolutionary America* (New York: Twayne, 1996). And, I refer to these articles: Betsy Erkkila, "Revolutionary Women," *Tulsa Studies in Women's Literature* 6 (1987): 189–223; Sharon Harris, introduction to *American Women Writers to 1800*, ed. Sharon Harris (New York: Oxford University Press, 1995), 3–30; and Carroll Smith-Rosenberg, "Subject Female: Authorizing American Identity," *American Literary History* 5 (1993): 481–511.

   This list is not exhaustive, of course, although it includes several of the most important studies of women in the Revolutionary and post-Revolutionary periods. It also does not mention the voluminous body of feminist criticism produced since the 1960s, which would be crucial for any full-length study of Revolutionary women writers. Instead, I confine myself below to comments on and references to some of the insightful feminist studies of women's autobiography.

2. I did decide, as I note in the preface, to analyze only formal, retrospective, written self-biographies.

3. The word "constitutional" ironically echoes Abigail Adams's comment to her husband in 1776 and suggests the political level at which Hannah Adams (no

relation to Abigail) was denied "bodily and mental firmness." But see my remarks on Hannah Adams's *Memoir* in chapter 9.

4. Much as, I will argue, White and Fisher imitate and reflect Franklin's (and others') model of American selfhood.

5. Perhaps White is aware that his first initial—"S."—calls attention as well to his snakelike qualities.

6. White's inclusion of her own poetry might be considered a subversion of generic expectations, as well, although I am not going to pursue the significance of her poetry here.

7. Cf. my readings of Burroughs (chapter 6) and Fitch (chapter 8).

8. It could, of course, answer other purposes, like revenge, but White is content to exchange her silence for property. She evinces here no sense of female solidarity, of the "bonds of womanhood": she does not tell her husband's Canadian fiancée about his "true" self. She simply does not see the other woman as a "sister." She takes the property and runs.

9. Presumably, she would not have been surprised by Castiglia's assertion that White was "fabricating" her story. She is sensitive to men's suspicions that, as Pope put it, a "powerful fancy works" in women's minds (*The Rape of the Lock* IV: 53).

10. This blissful summer anticipates the time, later, when Fisher and her "daughter Eliza . . . lived together very happy" just after Mr. Fisher's death (26).

11. Fisher also promises another edition of her *Memoirs* in which she "shall endeavour to show by letters and affidavits . . . how far I am guilty or innocent in this unnatural and unhappy circumstance . . . between my brother and myself" (47–48). That later edition was apparently never published, but the sheer threat of a such a public retaliation is itself significant.

8. JOHN FITCH AND THE INVENTED SELF

1. See, for example, Thomas Cooley, *Educated Lives: The Rise of Modern Autobiography in America* (Columbus: Ohio State University Press, 1976); Cynthia S. Jordan, *Second Stories*; and Warner, *Letters of the Republic*, among many other studies, as well as the many anthologies of American literature in which Franklin's narrative is extensively excerpted or entirely reprinted.

2. Cf. Christopher Looby's reading of Franklin in *Voicing America*: "A chief motive guiding Franklin's composition of the *Autobiography* . . . was a desire to contain the disruptive power of the Revolution" (101). Looby reads Franklin, accurately for the most part, I think, as a counterrevolutionary, a reading that squares in some ways with my own (though Looby, wrongly, I think, reads the narrative as "an autobiography . . . meant to represent Franklin's self" [123]).

3. Cf. Franklin, *Writings*, 1374 and 1377. All references to Fitch's writings in this chapter are to his *Autobiography* (his "Detail of My Life"), unless otherwise noted.

4. Rigal notes how Fitch constructed himself, more generally, in opposition authority figures (Laura Rigal, *The American Manufactory: Art, Labor, and the World of Things in the Early Republic* [Princeton: Princeton University Press, 1998], 56–60).

5. Rigal argues that Fitch also "identified with his writings so completely [that] he was unable to detach himself from his words or constitute them as an object (or book), and himself as their disembodied author" (81).

6. Rigal interprets these images of liminality and singularity "as an articulation of historical time-in-the-making; they mark the uneven creation, rationalization, and reorganization of labor (as works) by proliferating technologies of production and representation. . . . Instead of the author as representative producer, then, Fitch's 'Life' figures the uneven emergence of a culture of production" (64–65).

7. Cf. John Fitch, *The Original Steam-Boat Supported* (Philadelphia, 1788), where he claims that "the thought of a Steam-boat . . . first struck me by mere accident" (3).

8. Earlier, I discussed yet another level of irony in Franklin's choice of exemplars: Jesus and Socrates. Neither man, as far as we know, wrote anything in life, and hence both provide a startling contrast with Franklin, who—post-structuralists might say—inscribed himself and was inscribed in literally hundreds of newspapers, broadsides, journals, magazines, books, articles, and encyclopedias in the course of the century. Not to mention, Simon Schama reminds us, on all sorts of material objects after 1770, including a chamber pot that Louis XVI gave to one of his mistresses in order to cure her of her infatuation with Franklin (*Citizens: A Chronicle of the French Revolution* [New York: Knopf, 1989], 42–44).

9. "RES PRIVATA": CULTIVATING THE SELF IN AMERICA, 1820–1830

1. Augustine in *On Free Choice of the Will* makes a related move that points up the difference between the self-biographical and autobiographical impulses: "For when I contemplate within myself the unchangeable truth of numbers and their lair (so to speak) and inner sanctuary or realm—or whatever else we might call their dwelling-place and home—I am far removed from material objects. I may, perhaps, find something that I can think about, but nothing that I can express in words. So in order to be able to say anything at all, I return in fatigue to familiar things and talk in the customary way about what is right in front of me" (1993, 49). Augustine goes "inside himself" to discover the ineffable and

transcendent truth of numbers and wisdom, "an unchangeable truth that contains everything that is unchangeably true" (51). Channing urges his audience to delve within in order to unfold "their whole nature," a nature that is as unique as the human countenance.

2. More broadly, as Daniel Walker Howe argues in his study of the ideal of the "balanced" self-made man in nineteenth-century America, "American social thought in the nineteenth century showed a tendency to expand the number of people who were entitled to an autonomous sense of self, and the climate of opinion encouraged them to construct an identity of their own" (*Making the American Self*, 109). Howe's study complements mine, although he is less interested in narrative than I am and is more interested in the synthesis, via faculty pyschology, of evangelicalism and secular self-improvement in the antebellum period. Cf. also the fine article by Louis P. Masur ("'Age of the First Person Singular': The Vocabulary of Self in New England, 1780–1850" [*Journal of American Studies* 25 (1991): 189–211) in which he argues that nineteenth-century Americans recognized the emergent "self" and had three options open for dealing with it: deny it, improve it, or rely on it.

3. Jeffrey Steele, in *The Representation of the Self in the American Renaissance* (Chapel Hill: University of North Carolina Press, 1987), argues that Emerson detects individual personality only to see through it to a transcendent source beneath. Steele then shows how Fuller, Thoreau, and Whitman pursue Emerson's insight to see the self as a renewed being who accesses divine power within himself or herself, while Poe, Melville, and Hawthorne are skeptical of it, seeing the self as an opaque mask that reflects social demands and refracts unconscious impulses. Brian Harding argues that "since the self is problematized in [Emerson's, Whitman's, and Thoreau's] writings at the [very] moment it is most vigorously affirmed, it is hardly surprising that their subjectivity did not lead to the creation of autobiography. On the contrary, their use of the first person singular became a means of dissolving the solidity (or continuity) of the self" ("Transcendentalism and Autobiography: Emerson, Whitman, and Thoreau," in *First Person Singular: Studies in American Autobiography*, ed. A. Robert Lee [New York: St. Martin's, 1988], 59).

4. See Payne, *The Self and the Sacred*; and Rabinowitz, *The Spiritual Self in Everyday Life*. Both Payne and Rabinowitz detect an increasing interest in subjectivity even in Protestant self-biographies in the nineteenth century.

5. Samuel Taylor Coleridge and others developed the distinction between genius and talent in the early nineteenth century. See M. H. Abrams's discussion in *The Mirror and the Lamp: Romantic Theory and the Critical Tradition* (Oxford: Oxford University Press, 1953), 156–225; Raymond Williams, *Keywords: A Vocabulary of Culture and Society*, revised ed. (New York: Oxford University Press, 1985), 143–144; and Donald E. Pease, "Author," in *Critical Terms for Literary*

Study, ed. Frank Lentricchia and Thomas McLaughlin (Chicago: University of Chicago Press, 1995), 108–112.

6. Venture Smith's *Narrative* is "RELATED BY HIMSELF" (title page), but the editor's insistence in the preface that "nothing is added in substance to what he related himself" (369) calls attention to the problem of as-told-to narratives: we have no way of knowing what the editor/amanuensis added to the narrative, either substantively or stylistically. Two other as-told-to narratives that I do not discuss in *After Franklin* are Mary Jemison, *A Narrative of the Life of Mrs. Mary Jemison* (1824), which was dictated to and published by Dr. James Seaver; and John Tanner, *Narrative of the Captivity and Adventures of John Tanner*... (1830), which was "prepared for the press" by Edwin James. See Gordon M. Sayre, "Abridging between Two Worlds: John Tanner as American Indian Autobiographer," *American Literary History* 11 (1999): 480–499.

7. William Grimes, *The Life of William Grimes, the Runaway Slave, Written by Himself* (New York, 1825), iii, iv. The 1825 edition is extremely difficult to obtain. Many research libraries do not own a copy, even on microfilm. As far as I can tell, no later reprints of the 1825 edition ever appeared. Grimes himself reprinted the narrative in 1855, bringing his story up to date. That edition was reprinted in Arna Bontemps, ed., *Five Black Lives: The Autobiographies of Venture Smith, James Mars, William Grimes, the Rev. G. W. Offley, [and] James L. Smith* (Middletown, Conn.: Wesleyan University Press, 1971).

8. Grimes's metaphor anticipates the self-biographical writing of Thoreau and Whitman in the 1850s. In both *Walden* and *Song of Myself*, the unique self of the author is figured in ways that are designed to assist others in their journeys toward "themselves." See, for example, Whitman's remark, first, that "'Leaves of Grass' indeed (I cannot too often reiterate) has mainly been the outcropping of my own emotional and other personal nature—an attempt, from first to last, to put a Person, a human being (myself, in the latter half of the Nineteenth Century, in America) freely, fully and truly on record"; and, second, that "I have allow'd the stress of my poems from beginning to end to bear upon American individuality and assist it" ("A Backward Glance O'er Travel'd Roads," in *Walt Whitman: Complete Poetry and Selected Prose*, ed. Justin Kaplan [New York: Library of America, 1982], 671, 667).

9. As, for example, I read William Apes's *Son of the Forest: The Experience of William Apes, a Native of the Forest, Comprising a Notice of the Pequot Tribe of Indians* (New York, 1829). See Irene S. Vernon, "The Claiming of Christ: Native American Postcolonial Discourses," *MELUS* 24 (1999): 75–88.

10. Stephen Greenblatt, in *Renaissance Self-Fashioning: From More to Shakespeare* (Chicago: University of Chicago Press, 1984), studies the way that self-fashioning in the sixteenth century creates, in individual writers, "a distinctive personality, a characteristic address to the world, a consistent mode of perceiving and

behavior" (2). But, he also notes, this self-fashioning always "involves submission to an absolute power or authority situated at least partially outside the self" (9). The Protestant Reformation opens up the possibility of fashioning one's self or soul in accordance with new or different transcendent standards, but it does so not to set the individual "free" of all standards or restraints. Greenblatt's authors "fashion" the self only then to "cancel" the self, as he argues in the example of Thomas More (57).

11. Smith-Rosenberg, "Subject Female," 504.

LITERATURE CITED

Abrams, M. H. 1953. *The Mirror and the Lamp: Romantic Theory and the Critical Tradition*. Oxford: Oxford University Press.

Adams, Abigail, and John Adams. 1975. *The Book of Abigail and John: Selected Letters of the Adams Family, 1762–1784*. Ed. L. H. Butterfield, Marc Friedlander, and Mary-Jo Kline. Cambridge: Harvard University Press.

Adams, Hannah. 1832. *A Memoir of Miss Hannah Adams*. Boston.

Adams, John. 1850–1856. *The Works of John Adams*. Ed. Charles Francis Adams. 10 vols. Boston.

———. 1856. "A Dissertation on the Canon and Feudal Law." In *The Works of John Adams*. Ed. Charles Francis Adams. Boston: Little Brown and Co. Vol. I: 448–464.

———. 1962. *Autobiography of John Adams*. In *Diary and Autobiography of John Adams*. Ed. L. H. Butterfield. 4 vols. Cambridge: Harvard University Press. Vol. III: 251–Vol. IV: 254.

Adams, John, and Benjamin Rush. 1966. *The Spur of Fame: Dialogues of John Adams and Benjamin Rush, 1805–1813*. Ed. John A. Schutz and Douglass Adair. San Marino: The Huntington Library.

Adams, John, and Thomas Jefferson. 1988. *The Adams-Jefferson Letters*. Ed. Lester J. Cappon. Chapel Hill: University of North Carolina Press, 1959. Reprint, Chapel Hill: University of North Carolina Press.

Addison, Joseph, et al. 1961. *The Spectator*. Ed. Gregory Smith. 4 vols. 1711–1712. Reprint, London: Dent.

Adventures of Jonathan Corncob, Loyal American Refugee. 1976. Boston: David R. Godine.

Albanese, Catharine. 1976. *Sons of the Fathers: The Civil Religion of the American Revolution*. Philadelphia: Temple University Press.

Aldridge, Alfred Owen. 1967. "Form and Substance in Franklin's *Autobiography*." In *Essays on American Literature in Honor of Jay B. Hubbell*. Ed. Clarence Gohdes. Durham: Duke University Press. 47–62.

Alkana, Joseph. 1992. "Spiritual and Rational Authority in Benjamin Rush's *Travels through Life*." *Texas Studies in Literature and Language* 34: 284–301.

Allen, Ethan. 2000. *The Narrative of the Captivity of Colonel Ethan Allen*. Ed. Stephen Carl Arch. Acton, Mass.: Copley Publishing.

Ames, Fisher. 1983. *Works of Fisher Ames*. Ed. W. B. Allen. 2 vols. Indianapolis: Liberty Classics.

Andrews, William. 1988. *To Tell a Free Story: The First Century of Afro-American Autobiography, 1760–1865.* 1986. Reprint, Urbana: University of Illinois Press.

Apes, William. 1829. *A Son of the Forest: The Experience of William Apes, a Native of the Forest, Comprising a Notice of the Pequot Tribe of Indians.* New York: [Published] by the Author.

Appleby, Joyce. 1984. *Capitalism and a New Social Order: The Republican Vision of the 1790s.* New York: New York University Press.

———. 2000. *Inheriting the Revolution: The First Generation of Americans.* Cambridge: Harvard University Press.

Arch, Stephen Carl. 1996. "American Hunger: Society and Autobiography in America." *The Grove: Working Papers in English* (Jaen, Spain) 1: 11–25.

———. 1998. "John Fitch and the Origins of American Autobiography." In *Writing Lives: American Biography and Autobiography.* Ed. Hans Bak and Hans Krabbendam. Amsterdam: VU University Press. 9–15.

Ashbridge, Elizabeth. *Some Account of the Early Part of the Life of Elizabeth Ashbridge,* 1774. Reprint, Philadelphia, 1807.

Augustine, Saint. 1993. *On Free Choice of the Will.* Trans. Thomas Williams. Cambridge, Mass.: Hackett Publishing.

Bacon, Francis. 1999. *The New Organon.* In *Selected Philosophical Works.* Ed. and trans. Rose-Mary Sargent. Indianapolis: Hackett Publishing. 86–189.

Bailey, Abigail. 1989. *Memoirs of Mrs. Abigail Bailey.* 1815. In *Religion and Domestic Violence in Early New England: The Memoirs of Mrs. Abigail Bailey.* Ed. Ann Taves. Bloomington: Indiana University Press.

Bailey, Robert. 1822. *The Life and Adventures of Robert Bailey . . . Written by Himself.* Richmond: Printed for the Author.

Bailyn, Bernard. 1967. *The Ideological Origins of the American Revolution.* Cambridge: Harvard University Press.

———. 1986. *Voyagers to the West: A Passage in the Peopling of America on the Eve of Revolution.* New York: Knopf.

Banes, Ruth. 1982. "The Exemplary Self: Autobiography in Eighteenth-Century America." *Biography* 5: 226–239.

Barbour, James, and Tom Quirk. 1990. *Writing the American Classics.* Chapel Hill: University of North Carolina Press.

Barker-Benfield, G. J. 1992. *The Culture of Sensibility: Sex and Society in Eighteenth-Century Britain.* Chicago: University of Chicago Press.

Barnum, H. L. 1975. *The Spy Unmasked; or, The Memoirs of Enoch Crosby, alias Harvey Birch.* 1828. Reprint, Harrison, N.Y.: Harbor Hill Books.

Barnum, P. T. 1855. *The Life of P. T. Barnum, Written by Himself.* New York: Redfield.

———. 1981. *Struggles and Triumphs; or, Forty Years' Recollections of P. T. Barnum.* Ed. Carl Bode. New York: Penguin.

Baumeister, Roy F. 1987. "How the Self Became a Problem: A Psychological Review of Historical Research." *Journal of Personality and Social Psychology* 52: 163–176.

Bayley, Solomon. 1825. *A Narrative of Some Remarkable Incidents in the Life of Solomon Bayley . . . Written by Himself.* 2d ed. London: Harvey and Darton.

Baym, Nina. 1995. *American Women Writers and the Work of History, 1790–1860.* New Brunswick: Rutgers University Press.

Bercovitch, Sacvan, ed. 1994. *The Cambridge History of American Literature.* Cambridge: Cambridge University Press.

Binger, Carl. 1966. *Revolutionary Doctor: Benjamin Rush, 1746–1813.* New York: Norton.

Bogel, Fredric V. 1984. *Literature and Insubstantiality in Later Eighteenth-Century England.* Princeton: Princeton University Press.

Bontemps, Arna, ed. 1971. *Five Black Lives: The Autobiographies of Venture Smith, James Mars, William Grimes, the Rev. G. W. Offley, [and] James L. Smith.* Middletown, Conn.: Wesleyan University Press.

Bradstreet, Anne. 1981. *The Complete Works of Anne Bradstreet.* Ed. Joseph R. McElrath, Jr., and Allen P. Robb. Boston: Twayne.

Brewer, Lucy. 1817. *The Female Marine.* 5th ed. Boston.

Bridenbaugh, Carl. 1981. *Early Americans.* Oxford: Oxford University Press.

Brissenden, R. F. 1976. *Virtue in Distress: Studies in the Novel of Sentiment from Richardson to Sade.* New York: Harper and Row.

Brown, Charles Brockden. 1943. *The Rhapsodist and Other Writings.* Ed. Harry R. Warfel. New York: Scholar's Facsimiles and Reprints.

———. 1982. *Ormond; or, The Secret Witness.* Ed. Sydney J. Krause and S. W. Reid. Kent: Kent State University Press.

———. 1986. *Jane Talbot, a Novel.* In *Clara Howard in a Series of Letters, with Jane Talbot, a Novel.* Ed. Sydney Krause, et al. Kent: Kent State University Press. 149–439.

———. 1998. *Three Gothic Novels.* Ed. Sydney J. Krause. New York: Library of America.

Brown, Gillian. 1990. *Domestic Individualism: Imagining Self in Nineteenth-Century America.* Berkeley: University of California Press.

Bryan, Daniel. 1826. *The Appeal for Suffering Genius: A Poetical Address for the Benefit of the Boston Bard; and the Triumph of Truth, a Poem.* Washington City, N.Y.

Buckley, Jerome Hamilton. 1984. *The Turning Key: Autobiography and the Subjectivist Impulse since 1800.* Cambridge: Harvard University Press.

Buckminster, Joseph Stevens. 1962. "The Dangers and Duties of Men of Letters." In *The Federalist Literary Mind.* Ed. Lewis P. Simpson. Baton Rouge: Louisiana State University Press. 95–102.

Buel, Joy Day, and Richard Buel, Jr. 1984. *The Way of Duty: A Woman and Her Family in Revolutionary America.* New York: Norton.

Buel, Richard, Jr. 1972. *Securing the Revolution: Ideology in American Politics, 1790–1815.* Ithaca: Cornell University Press.

Buell, Lawrence. 1986. *New England Literary Culture from Revolution through Renaissance.* Cambridge: Cambridge University Press.

Burroughs, Stephen. 1988. *Memoirs of Stephen Burroughs.* 1798. 1804. New York: Dial, 1924. Reprint, Boston: Northeastern University Press.

Burstein, Andrew. 1996. *The Inner Jefferson: Portrait of a Grieving Optimist.* Charlottesville: University of Virginia Press.

————. 1999. *Sentimental Democracy: The Evolution of America's Romantic Self-image.* New York: Hill and Wang.

Butler, Marilyn. 1981. *Romantics, Rebels, and Reactionaries: English Literature and Its Background, 1760–1830.* Oxford: Oxford University Press.

Caldwell, Tanya. 1999. "'Talking Too Much English': Languages of Economy and Politics in Equiano's *Interesting Narrative.*" *Early American Literature* 34: 263–282.

Calhoun, Craig, ed. 1992. *Habermas and the Public Sphere.* Cambridge: Massachusetts Institute of Technology Press.

Carafiol, Peter. 1991. *The American Ideal: Literary History as a Worldly Activity.* New York: Oxford University Press.

Carey, Mathew. 1829. *Auto Biographical Sketches, in a Series of Letters Addressed to a Friend.* Philadelphia: John Clarke.

Casper, Scott. 1999. *Constructing American Lives: Biography and Culture in Nineteenth-Century America.* Chapel Hill: University of North Carolina Press.

Castiglia, Christopher. 1996. *Bound and Determined: Captivity, Culture-Crossing, and White Womanhood from Mary Rowlandson to Patty Hearst.* Chicago: University of Chicago Press.

Castle, Terry. 1986. *Masquerade and Civilization: The Carnivalesque in Eighteenth-Century English Culture and Fiction.* Stanford: Stanford University Press.

Channing, William Ellery. 1838. *Self-Culture: An Address Introductory to the Franklin Lectures, Delivered at Boston, September, 1838.* Boston: Dutton and Wentworth.

Christophersen, Bill. 1993. *The Apparition in the Glass: Charles Brockden Brown's American Gothic.* Athens: University of Georgia Press.

Clark, Michael P. 2000. "The Persistence of Literature in Early American Studies." *The William and Mary Quarterly* 57: 641–646.

Clej, Alina. 1995. *A Genealogy of the Modern Self: Thomas De Quincey and the Intoxication of Writing.* Stanford: Stanford University Press.

Coffin, Robert Stevenson. 1825. *The Life of the Boston Bard, Written by Himself.* Mount Pleasant, N.Y.

Cohen, Daniel A. 1993. *Pillars of Salt, Monuments of Grace: New England Crime Literature and the Origins of American Popular Culture, 1674–1860.* New York: Oxford University Press.

Colbourn, Hugh Trevor. 1965. *The Lamp of Experience: Whig History and the Intellectual Origins of the American Revolution.* Chapel Hill: University of North Carolina Press.

Cooley, Thomas. 1976. *Educated Lives: The Rise of Modern Autobiography in America.* Columbus: Ohio State University Press.

Cornell, Saul. 1999. *The Other Founders: Anti-Federalism and the Dissenting Tradition in America, 1788–1828*. Chapel Hill: University of North Carolina Press.

Corner, George. 1948. Introduction to *The Autobiography of Benjamin Rush: His "Travels through Life" Together with his Commonplace Book for 1789–1813*. Ed. George Corner. Princeton: Princeton University Press. 3–15.

Cott, Nancy F. 1977. *The Bonds of Womanhood: "Woman's Sphere" in New England, 1780–1835*. New Haven: Yale University Press.

Countryman, Edward. 1985. *The American Revolution*. New York: Hill and Wang.

Couser, G. Thomas. 1979. *American Autobiography: The Prophetic Mode*. Amherst: University of Massachusetts Press.

————. 1989. *Altered Egos: Authority in American Autobiography*. New York: Oxford University Press.

Cox, James M. 1989. *Recovering Literature's Lost Ground: Essays in American Autobiography*. Baton Rouge: Louisiana State University Press.

Crèvecoeur, J. Hector St. John de. 1981. *Letters from an American Farmer and Sketches of Eighteenth-Century America*. Ed. and intro. Albert Stone. New York: Penguin.

Crowley, J. E. 1974. *This Sheba, Self: The Conceptualization of Economic Life in Eighteenth-Century America*. Baltimore: Johns Hopkins University Press.

Damrosch, Leo. 1989. *Fictions of Reality in the Age of Hume and Johnson*. Madison: University of Wisconsin Press.

Dauber, Kenneth. 1990. *The Idea of Authorship in America: Democratic Poetics from Franklin to Melville*. Madison: University of Wisconsin Press.

Davidson, Cathy. 1986. *Revolution and the Word: The Rise of the Novel in America*. New York: Oxford University Press.

Dawkins, Richard. 1998. *Unweaving the Rainbow: Science, Delusion, and the Appetite for Wonder*. Boston : Houghton Mifflin.

De Lancey, Edward F. 1873. *The New York Genealogical and Biographical Register*, Vol. IV, no. 3 (July): 113–124.

de Lauretis, Theresa. 1987. *Technologies of Gender: Essays on Theory, Film, and Fiction*. Bloomington: Indiana University Press.

De Prospo, R. C. 1992. "Marginalizing Early American Literature." *New Literary History* 23: 233–265.

The Debate on the Constitution. 1993. Ed. Bernard Bailyn. 2 vols. New York: Library of America.

Defoe, Daniel. 1960. *Robinson Crusoe*. 1719. Reprint, New York: Signet.

D'Elia, Donald J. 1974. *Benjamin Rush: Philosopher of the American Revolution*. Philadelphia: American Philosophical Society.

Dennie, John. 1943. *The Lay Preacher*. Ed. and intro. Milton Ellis. New York: Scholar's Facsimiles and Reprints.

Doten, Ethan. 1936. "Ethan Allen's Original Something." *The New England Quarterly* 11: 361–366.

Dowling, William. 1990. *Poetry and Ideology in Revolutionary Connecticut.* Athens: University of Georgia Press.

———. 1999. *Literary Federalism in the Age of Jefferson: Joseph Dennie and "The Port Folio," 1801–1812.* Columbia: University of South Carolina Press.

Duyckinck, Evert A., and George L. Duyckinck. 1965. *Cyclopedia of American Literature.* 1855. Reprint, Detroit: Gale.

Elkins, Stanley, and Eric McKitrick. 1993. *The Age of Federalism.* New York: Oxford University Press.

Elliott, Emory. 1982. *Revolutionary Writers: Literature and Authority in the New Republic, 1725–1810.* New York: Oxford University Press.

———, gen. ed. 1988. *Columbia Literary History of the United States.* New York: Columbia University Press.

Ellis, Joseph. 1979. *After the Revolution: Profiles of Early American Culture.* New York: Norton.

———. 1993. *Passionate Sage: The Character and Legacy of John Adams.* New York.

Emerson, Ralph Waldo. 1969. *The Journals and Miscellaneous Notebooks of Ralph Waldo Emerson.* Vol. VIII. Ed. A. W. Plumstead and Harrison Hayford. Cambridge: Harvard University Press.

———. 1982. *Emerson in His Journals.* Ed. Joel Porte. Cambridge: Harvard University Press.

———. 1983. *Ralph Waldo Emerson: Essays and Lectures.* Ed. Joel Porte. New York: Library of America.

Equiano, Olaudah. 1789. *The Interesting Narrative of the Life of Olaudah Equiano, or Gustavas Vassa, Written by Himself.* London.

Erkkila, Betsy. 1987. "Revolutionary Women." *Tulsa Studies in Women's Literature* 6: 189–223.

The Federalist Papers. 1961. By Alexander Hamilton, James Madison, and John Jay. Ed. Clinton Rossiter. New York: New American Library.

Fennell, James. 1814. *An Apology for the Life of James Fennell, Written by Himself.* Philadelphia: Moses Thomas.

Felton, Silas. 1959. *The Life or Biography of Silas Felton Written by Himself.* Ed. Rena L. Vassar. *Proceedings of the American Antiquarian Society* 69: 119–154.

Ferguson, Robert. 1984. *Law and Letters in American Culture.* Cambridge: Harvard University Press.

———. 1986. "'We Hold These Truths': Strategies of Control in the Literature of the Founders." In *Reconstructing American Literary History.* Ed. Sacvan Bercovitch. Cambridge: Harvard University Press. 1–28.

Fessenden, Thomas Green. 1804. *Terrible Tractoration!! A Poetical Petition against Galvanizing Trumpery and the Perkinistic Institution.* New York.

———. 1805. *Democracy Unveiled; or, Tyranny Stripped of the Garb of Patriotism.* Boston.

Fielding, Henry. 1996. *The History of Tom Jones, a Foundling.* Ed. John Bender and Simon Stern. 1749. Reprint, Oxford: Oxford University Press.

Fisher, Elizabeth Munro. 1810. *Memoirs of Mrs. Elizabeth Fisher.* New York.

Fitch, John. 1788. *The Original Steam-Boat Supported.* Philadelphia.

———. 1976. *The Autobiography of John Fitch.* Ed. Frank D. Prager. Philadelphia: American Philosophical Society.

Fliegelman, Jay. 1982. *Prodigals and Pilgrims: The American Revolution against Patriarchal Authority 1750–1800.* Cambridge: Cambridge University Press.

———. 1993. *Declaring Independence: Jefferson, Natural Language, and the Culture of Performance.* Stanford: Stanford University Press.

Foerster, Norman. 1988. *The Reinterpretation of American Literature.* 1928. Reprint, New York: Russell and Russell.

Folkenflik, Robert. 1993. "Introduction: The Institution of Autobiography." In *The Culture of Autobiography: Constructions of Self-representation.* Ed. Robert Folkenflik. Stanford: Stanford University Press. 1–20.

Foster, Hannah Webster. 1986. *The Coquette.* Ed. Cathy N. Davidson. Oxford: Oxford University Press.

Foucault, Michel. 1987. *Discipline and Punish: The Birth of the Prison.* Trans. Alan Sheridan. New York: Vintage.

Franklin, Benjamin. 1908. *Works.* Ed. John Bigelow. 12 vols. New York.

———. 1987[a]. *History of My Life.* Published as *The Autobiography.* In *Writings.* Ed. J. A. Leo LeMay. New York: Library of America. 1305–1469.

———. 1987[b]. *Writings.* Ed. J. A. Leo LeMay. New York: Library of America.

Friedman, Susan Stanford. 1988. "Women's Autobiographical Selves: Theory and Practice." In *The Private Self: Theory and Practice of Women's Autobiographical Writings.* Ed. Shari Benstock. Chapel Hill: University of North Carolina Press. 34–62.

Fuller, Margaret. 1963. "American Literature: Its Position in the Present Time, and Prospects for the Future." In *Margaret Fuller, American Romantic: A Selection from her Writings and Correspondence.* Ed. Perry Miller. Garden City, N.Y.: Anchor Books. 227–250.

Garrettson, Freeborn. 1791. *The Experience and Travels of Freeborn Garrettson.* Philadelphia.

Gelles, Edith Belle. 1992. *Portia: The World of Abigail Adams.* Bloomington: Indiana University Press.

Gibbon, Edward. 1990. *Memoirs of My Life.* Ed. Betty Radice. New York: Penguin.

Gilmore, Leigh. 1994. *Autobiographics: A Feminist Theory of Women's Self-representation.* Ithaca: Cornell University Press.

Gilmore, Michael T. 1994. "The Literature of the Revolutionary and Early National Periods." In *The Cambridge History of American Literature,* Vol. 1, 1590–1820. Ed. Sacvan Bercovitch. Cambridge: Cambridge University Press. 538–693.

Gilmore, William J. 1989. *Reading Becomes a Necessity of Life: Material and Cultural Life in Rural New England, 1780–1835.* Knoxville: University of Tennessee Press.

Goodman, Dena. 1989. *Criticism in Action: Enlightenment Experiments in Political Writing.* Ithaca: Cornell University Press.

Goodman, Nathan G. 1934. *Benjamin Rush, Physician and Citizen, 1746–1813.* Philadelphia: University of Pennsylvania Press.

Granger, Bruce Ingham. 1964. *Benjamin Franklin: An American Man of Letters.* Ithaca: Cornell University Press.

Grant, Anne. 1903. *Memoirs of an American Lady.* 1808. Reprint, New York: Dodd, Mead.

Grasso, Christopher. 1999. *A Speaking Aristocracy: Transforming Public Discourse in Eighteenth-Century Connecticut.* Chapel Hill: University of North Carolina Press.

[Graydon, Alexander]. 1811. *Memoirs of a Life, Chiefly Passed in Pennsylvania, within the Last Sixty Years; with Occasional Remarks upon the General Occurrences, Character, and Spirit of That Eventful Period.* Harrisburg, Pa.: John Wyeth.

———. 1882. Letter to Jedidiah Morse. 5 March 1789. *Pennsylvania Magazine of History and Biography* 6: 114–117.

———. 1890. Letter to Joseph Reed. 5 October 1780. *Pennsylvania Archives*, 2d series, 3: 380–381.

Greenblatt, Stephen. *Renaissance Self-fashioning: From More to Shakespeare.* Chicago: University of Chicago Press, 1980.

Greene, John C. 1989. *American Science in the Age of Jefferson.* Ames: Iowa State University Press.

Greenman, Jeremiah. 1978. *Diary of a Common Soldier in the American Revolution, 1775–1783: An Annotated Edition of the Military Journal of Jeremiah Greenman.* Ed. Robert Bray and Paul Bushnell. Dekalb: Northern Illinois University Press.

Grimes, William. 1825. *The Life of William Grimes, the Runaway Slave, Written by Himself.* New York.

Gross, Robert A. 1993. "The Confidence Man and the Preacher: The Cultural Politics of Shays's Rebellion." In *In Debt to Shays: The Cultural Politics of an Agrarian Rebellion.* Ed. Robert A. Gross. Charlottesville: University of Virginia Press. 297–320.

Guild, James. 1937. *From Tunbridge, Vermont, to London, England—the Journal of James Guild, Peddler, Tinker, Schoolmaster, Portrait Painter, from 1818 to 1824.* Ed. Arthur Wallace Peach. Vermont Historical Society, *Proceedings* 5: 250–313.

Gundersen, Joan. 1996. *To Be Useful to the World: Women in Revolutionary America.* New York: Twayne.

Gura, Philip. 2000. "Early American Literature at the New Century." *The William and Mary Quarterly* 57: 599–620.

Gustafson, Thomas. 1992. *Representative Words: Politics, Literature, and the American Language, 1776–1865.* Cambridge: Cambridge University Press.

Habermas, Jürgen. 1991. *The Structural Transformation of the Public Sphere*. Trans. Thomas Burger. Cambridge: Harvard University Press.

Hamilton, Sarah. 1803. *A Narrative of the Life of Sarah Hamilton*. Boston.

Harding, Brian. 1988. "Transcendentalism and Autobiography: Emerson, Whitman, and Thoreau." In *First Person Singular: Studies in American Autobiography*. Ed. A. Robert Lee. New York: St. Martin's. 57–71.

Harris, Sharon, ed. 1995. *Selected Writings of Judith Sargent Murray*. New York: Oxford University Press.

———, ed. 1996. *American Women Writers to 1800*. New York: Oxford University Press.

Hartz, Louis. 1955. *The Liberal Tradition in America: An Interpretation of American Political Thought since the Revolution*. New York: Harcourt, Brace.

Hawke, David Freeman. 1971. *Benjamin Rush: Revolutionary Gadfly*. Indianapolis: Bobbs-Merrill.

Haywood, Eliza. 1996. *Fantomina; or, Love in a Maze*. In *Popular Fiction by Women, 1660–1730: An Anthology*. Ed. Paula R. Backscheider and John J. Richetti. New York: Oxford University Press. 227–248.

Hedges, William. 1973. "Benjamin Rush, Charles Brockden Brown, and the American Plague Year." *Early American Literature* 7: 295–311.

———. 1974. "Charles Brockden Brown and the Culture of Contradictions." *Early American Literature* 9: 107–142.

———. 1979. "The Myth of the Republic and the Theory of American Literature." *Prospects* 4: 101–120.

———. 1981. "The Old World Yet: Writers and Writing in Post-Revolutionary America." *Early American Literature* 16: 3–18.

Hewitt, John P. 1989. *Dilemmas of the American Self*. Philadelphia: Temple University Press.

Hindle, Brook. 1981. *Emulation and Invention*. New York: New York University Press.

Hirsch, Adam Jay. 1992. *The Rise of the Penitentiary: Prisons and Punishment in Early America*. New Haven: Yale University Press.

Howard, Leon. 1953. "The Late Eighteenth Century: An Age of Contradictions." In *Transitions in American Literary History*. Ed. Harry Hayden Clark. Durham: Duke University Press. 51–89.

Howe, Daniel Walker. 1997. *Making the American Self: Jonathan Edwards to Abraham Lincoln*. Cambridge: Harvard University Press.

Huang, Nian-Sheng. 1994. *Benjamin Franklin in American Thought and Culture, 1790–1900*. Philadelphia: American Philosophical Society.

Hume, David. 1996. "My Own Life" (1777). In *British Literature, 1640–1789: An Anthology*. Ed. Robert DeMaria, Jr. Oxford: Blackwell Publishers. 962–967.

Humphreys, David, et al. 1967. *The Anarchiad*. Ed. Luther C. Griggs. 1861. Reprint, Gainesville: Scholar's Facsimiles and Reprints.

———. 1968. *An Essay on the Life of... Israel Putnam*. In David Humphreys, *Miscellaneous Works*. Ed. William K. Bottorff. Gainseville: Scholar's Facsimiles and Reprints. 241–330.

Hunter, J. Paul. 1990. *Before Novels: The Cultural Contexts of Eighteenth-Century English Fiction*. New York: Norton.

Imbarrato, Susan Clair. 1998. *Declarations of Independency in Eighteenth-Century American Autobiography*. Knoxville: University of Tennessee Press.

Ingersoll, Charles Jared. 1810. *Inchiquin, the Jesuit's Letters*. New York.

Irving, Washington. 1978. *The Sketch Book of Geoffrey Crayon, Gent*. Ed. Haskell Springer. Boston: Twayne.

Isaac, Rhys. 1988. *The Transformation of Virginia, 1740–1790*. 1982. Reprint, New York: Norton.

Isenberg, Gerald N. 1992. *Impossible Individuality: Romanticism, Revolution, and the Origins of Modern Selfhood, 1787–1802*. Princeton: Princeton University Press.

Iser, Wolfgang. 1974. *The Implied Reader: Patterns of Communication in Prose Fiction from Bunyan to Beckett*. Baltimore: Johns Hopkins University Press.

Jacob, Margaret. 1988. *The Cultural Meaning of the Scientific Revolution*. New York: Knopf.

Jay, Paul. 1984. *Being in the Text: Self-representation from Wordsworth to Roland Barthes*. Ithaca: Cornell University Press.

Jefferson, Thomas. 1985. *Writings*. New York: Library of America.

Jellison, Charles A. 1969. *Ethan Allen: Frontier Rebel*. Syracuse: Syracuse University Press.

Jemison, Mary. 1824. *A Narrative of the Life of Mrs. Mary Jemison*. By James E. Seaver. Canandaigu, N.Y.

Johnson, Paul. 1991. *The Birth of the Modern: World Society, 1815–1830*. New York: Harper Collins.

Johnson, Samuel. 1967. *A Dictionary of the English Language*. London, 1755. Reprint, New York: AMS Press.

———. 1968. *Essays from the "Rambler," "Adventurer," and "Idler"*. Ed. W. J. Bate. New Haven: Yale University Press.

Johnson, Susannah. 1814. *A Narrative of the Captivity of Mrs. Johnson*. Windsor, Vt.

Jordan, Cynthia S. 1989. *Second Stories: The Politics of Language, Form, and Gender in Early American Fictions*. Chapel Hill: University of North Carolina Press.

Jordan, Winthrop D. 1973. "Familial Politics: Thomas Paine and the Killing of the King, 1776." *Journal of American History* 60: 294–308.

Kadar, Marlene. 1992. "Coming to Terms: Life Writing—from Genre to Critical Practice." In *Essays on Life Writing: From Genre to Critical Practice*. Ed. Marlene Kadar. Toronto: University of Toronto Press. 3–16.

Kant, Immanuel. 1988. "What is Enlightenment?" In *The Portable Enlightenment Reader*. Ed. Isaac Kramnick. New York: Penguin. 1–7.

Kenshur, Oscar. 1993. *Dilemmas of Enlightenment: Studies in the Rhetoric and Logic of Ideology*. Berkeley: University of California Press.

Kerber, Linda. 1986. *Women of the Republic: Intellect and Ideology in Revolutionary America*. New York: Norton.

Kloos, John. 1991. *A Sense of Deity: The Republican Spirituality of Dr. Benjamin Rush*. Brooklyn, N.Y.: Carlson.

Knapp, Samuel Lorenzo. 1829. *Lectures on American Literature*. New York.

Kramer, Michael. 1992. *Imagining Language in America: From the Revolution to the Civil War*. Princeton: Princeton University Press.

Lasch, Christopher. 1991. *The True and Only Heaven: Progress and Its Critics*. New York: Norton.

Laurens, Henry. 1857. *A Narrative of the Capture of Henry Laurens*. In *Collections of the South Carolina Historical Society* 1: 18–68.

Lawrence, D. H. 1977. *Studies in Classic American Literature*. 1923. Reprint, New York: Penguin.

Leibowitz, Herbert. 1989. *Fabricating Lives: Explorations in American Autobiography*. New York: Knopf.

Lejeune, Philippe. 1989. *On Autobiography*. Trans. Katherine Leary. Minneapolis: University of Minnesota Press.

Lemay, J. A. Leo. 1986. *Benjamin Franklin's Autobiography: An Authoritative Text, Backgrounds, Criticism*. New York: Norton.

Lemay, J. A. Leo, and P. M. Zall, eds. 1981. *The Autobiography of Benjamin Franklin: A Genetic Text*. Knoxville: University of Tennessee Press.

Levin, David. 1964. "The Autobiography of Benjamin Franklin: The Puritan Experimenter in Life and Art." *Yale Review* 53: 258–275

———. 1967. *In Defense of Historical Literature: Essays on American History, Autobiography, Drama, and Fiction*. New York: Hill and Wang.

Lienesch, Michael. 1993. "Thomas Jefferson and the American Democratic Experience." In *Jeffersonian Legacies*. Ed. Peter S. Onuf. Charlottesville: University of Virginia Press. 316–339.

Lindberg, Gary. 1982. *The Confidence Man in American Literature*. New York: Oxford University Press.

Locke, John. 1964. *An Essay Concerning Human Understanding*. Ed. A. D. Woozley. New York: Meridian.

Looby, Christopher. 1996. *Voicing America: Language, Literary Form, and the Origins of the United States*. Chicago: University of Chicago Press.

McCormick, Richard P. 1966. *The Second American Party System: Party Formation in the Jacksonian Era*. Chapel Hill: University of North Carolina Press.

McDonald, Forrest. 1979. *E Pluribus Unum: The Formation of the American Republic, 1776–1790*. 1965. Reprint, Indianapolis: Liberty Press.

MacIntyre, Alasdair C. 1981. *After Virtue: A Study in Moral Theory*. London: Duckworth.

McKeon, Michael. 1987. *The Origins of the English Novel, 1640–1740*. Baltimore: Johns Hopkins University Press.

Macpherson, C. B. 1962. *The Political Theory of Possessive Individualism.* Oxford: Clarendon Press.

McWilliams, John. 1976. "The Faces of Ethan Allen: 1760–1860." *The New England Quarterly* 49: 257–282.

Mann, Herbert. 1972. *The Female Review; or, Life of Deborah Sampson.* 1797. Reprint, New York: Arno Press.

Marini, Stephen. 1993. "The Religious World of Daniel Shays." In *In Debt to Shays: The Cultural Politics of an Agrarian Rebellion.* Ed. Robert A. Gross. Charlottesville: University of Virginia Press. 239–277.

Marrant, John. 1996. *A Narrative of the Lord's Wonderful Dealings with John Marrant, a Black.* In *Unchained Voices: An Anthology of Black Authors in the English-Speaking World of the 18th Century.* Ed. Vincent Carretta. Lexington: University Press of Kentucky. 110–133.

Marx, Leo. 1964. *The Machine in the Garden: Technology and the Pastoral Ideal in America.* New York: Oxford University Press.

Mason, Philip. 1982. *The English Gentleman: The Rise and Fall of an Ideal.* London: André Deutsch.

Masur, Louis P. 1991. "'Age of the First Person Singular': The Vocabulary of the Self in New England, 1780–1850." *Journal of American Studies* 25: 189–211.

Mather, Cotton. 1702. *Magnalia Christi Americana.* London.

Matthews, Jean V. 1991. *Towards a New Society: American Thought and Culture, 1800–1830.* Boston: Twayne.

May, Henry. 1976. *The Enlightenment in America.* Oxford: Oxford University Press.

Meranze, Michael. 1996. *Laboratories of Virtue: Punishment, Revolution, and Authority in Philadelphia, 1760–1835.* Chapel Hill: University of North Carolina Press.

Meyer, Donald H. 1976. *The Democratic Enlightenment.* New York: Putnam's.

Miller, Samuel. 1803. *A Brief Retrospect of the Eighteenth Century.* 2 vols. New York.

Mitchell, W. J. T. 1995. "Representation." In *Critical Terms for Literary Study.* Ed. Frank Lentricchia and Thomas McLaughlin. 2d ed. Chicago: University of Chicago Press. 11–22.

Moody, James. 1783. *Lieut. James Moody's Narrative of His Exertions and Sufferings in the Cause of Government.* 2d ed. London.

Morgan, Edmund. 1988. *Inventing the People: The Rise of Popular Sovereignty in England and America.* New York: Norton.

Morris, John N. 1966. *Versions of the Self: Studies in English Autobiography from John Bunyan to John Stuart Mill.* New York: Basic Books.

Morris, Richard B. 1975. *John Jay: The Making of a Revolutionary, 1745–1780: Unpublished Papers.* New York: Harper and Row.

Mott, Frank Luther. 1957. *A History of American Magazines.* Cambridge: Harvard University Press.

Mulford, Carla. 1996. "Benjamin Franklin and the Myths of Nationhood." In *Making America/Making American Literature.* Ed. A. Robert Lee and W. M. Verhoeven. Amsterdam: Rodopi. 15–58.

Mullan, John. 1988. *Sentiment and Sociability: The Language of Feeling in the Eighteenth Century*. Oxford: Clarendon Press.

Neuman, Shirley. 1992. "Autobiography: From Different Poetics to a Poetics of Difference." In *Essays on Life Writing: From Genre to Critical Practice*. Ed. Marlene Kadar. Toronto: University of Toronto Press. 213–230.

Norton, Mary Beth. 1980. *Liberty's Daughters: The Revolutionary Experience of America, 1750–1800*. Boston: Little, Brown.

Nussbaum, Felicity A. 1989. *The Autobiographical Subject: Gender and Ideology in Eighteenth-Century England*. Baltimore: John Hopkins University Press.

Nye, Russell. 1969. "Michel-Guillaume St. Jean de Crèvecoeur: *Letters from an American Farmer*." In *Landmarks of American Writing*. Ed. Hennig Cohen. New York: Basic Books. 32–45.

Olney, James. 1972. *Metaphors of Self: The Meaning of Autobiography*. Princeton: Princeton University Press.

———. 1980. "Autobiography and the Cultural Moment: A Thematic, Historical, and Bibliographic Introduction." In *Autobiography: Essays Theoretical and Critical*. Ed. James Olney. Princeton: Princeton University Press. 3–27.

Ong, Walter J. 1982. *Orality and Literacy: The Technologizing of the Word*. New York: Methuen.

Paine, Thomas. 1987. *The Thomas Paine Reader*. Ed. Michael Foot and Isaac Kramnick. New York: Penguin.

———. 1995. *Collected Writings*. New York: Library of America.

Pascal, Roy. 1960. *Design and Truth in Autobiography*. Cambridge: Harvard University Press.

Pattee, Fred Lewis. 1966. *The First Century of American Literature, 1770–1870*. 1935. Reprint, New York: Cooper Square.

Payne, Rodger M. 1998. *The Self and the Sacred: Conversion and Autobiography in Early American Protestantism*. Knoxville: University of Tennessee Press.

Pearce, Roy Harvey. 1947. "The Significance of the Captivity Narrative." *American Literature* 19: 1–20.

Pease, Donald E. 1995. "Author." In *Critical Terms for Literary Study*. Ed. Frank Lentricchia and Thomas McLaughlin. Chicago: University of Chicago Press. 105–117.

Pell, John. 1929. *Ethan Allen*. Boston: Houghton Mifflin, 1929.

Perkins, David. 1992. *Is Literary History Possible?* Baltimore: Johns Hopkins University Press.

Perry, David. 1822. *Recollections of an Old Soldier: The Life of David Perry*. Windsor, Vt.

Philbrick, Thomas. 1970. *St. John de Crèvecoeur*. New York: Twayne.

Plumstead, A. W. 1977. "Hector St. John de Crèvecoeur." In *American Literature, 1764–1789: The Revolutionary Years*. Ed. Everett Emerson. Madison: University of Wisconsin Press. 213–231.

Pocock, J. G. A. 1975. *The Machiavellian Moment: Florentine Political Thought and the Atlantic Republican Tradition*. Princeton: Princeton University Press.

Poovey, Mary. 1988. *Uneven Developments: The Ideological Work of Gender in Mid-Victorian England*. Chicago: University of Chicago Press.

Pope, Alexander. 1993. *Alexander Pope: A Critical Edition of the Major Works*. Ed. Pat Rogers. Oxford: Oxford University Press.

The Port Folio. 1812. Vol. 7, 3d series (April): 315–323.

The Port Folio. 1818. Vol. 5, 4th series (April): 317–318.

The Port Folio. 1818. Vol. 6, 4th series (July): 56–58.

Porte, Joel. 1991. *In Respect to Egotism: Studies in American Romantic Writing*. Cambridge: Cambridge University Press.

Potter, Israel. 1824. *The Life and Remarkable Adventures of Israel Potter*. Providence.

Powell, J. H. 1949. *Bring out Your Dead: The Great Plague of Yellow Fever in Philadelphia in 1793*. Philadelphia: University of Pennsylvania Press.

Prager, John. 1976. Introduction to *The Autobiography of John Fitch*. Philadelphia: American Philosophical Society. 1–15.

Rabinowitz, Richard. 1989. *The Spiritual Self in Everyday Life: The Transformation of Religious Identity in Nineteenth-Century New England*. Boston: Northeastern University Press.

Reiss, Timothy. 1982. *The Discourse of Modernism*. Ithaca: Cornell University Press.

[Review of Graydon's *Memoirs*]. 1822. *The Quarterly Review* 26 (January): 364–374.

Rice, Grantland. 1997. *The Transformation of Authorship in America*. Chicago: University of Chicago Press.

———. 1999. "Cognitive Patterns and Aesthetic Deformations in Post-Revolutionary American Writing: A Preliminary Inquiry." In *Reciprocal Influences: Literary Production, Distribution, and Consumption in America*. Eds. Steven Fink and Susan S. Williams. Columbus: Ohio State University Press. 13–23.

Richards, Jeffrey. 1991. *Theater Enough: American Culture and the Metaphor of the World Stage, 1607–1789*. Durham: Duke University Press.

Richardson, Charles F. 1886. *American Literature, 1607–1885*. 2 vols. New York: Putnam's.

Richardson, Samuel. 1985. *Clarissa*. Ed. Angus Ross. New York: Viking.

Rigal, Laura. 1998. *The American Manufactory: Art, Labor, and the World of Things in the Early Republic*. Princeton: Princeton University Press.

Rothman, David J. 1971. *The Discovery of the Asylum*. Boston: Little, Brown.

Rousseau, Jean-Jacques. 1953. *The Confessions*. Trans. J. M. Cohen. New York: Penguin.

———. 1979. *Emile; or, On Education*. Trans. Allan Bloom. New York: Basic Books.

Rowlandson, Mary. 1990. *A True History of the Captivity and Restoration of Mrs. Mary Rowlandson*. In *Journeys in New Worlds: Early American Women's Narratives*. Ed. William L. Andrews et al. Madison: University of Wisconsin Press. 27–65.

Royster, Charles. 1979. *A Revolutionary People at War: The Continental Army and American Character, 1775–1783*. Chapel Hill: University of North Carolina Press.

Rush, Benjamin. 1787. "Address to the People of the United States." *American Museum* I (January): 8–11.

———. 1812. *Medical Inquiries and Observations upon the Diseases of the Mind*. Philadelphia.

———. 1947. *The Selected Writings of Benjamin Rush*. Ed. Dagobert Runes. New York: Philosophical Library.

———. 1948. *The Autobiography of Benjamin Rush: His "Travels through Life" Together with his Commonplace Book for 1789–1813*. Ed. George W. Corner. Princeton: Princeton University Press.

———. 1951. *Letters of Benjamin Rush*. Ed. L. H. Butterfield. 2 vols. Philadelphia: American Philosophical Society.

Ruttenberg, Nancy. 1998. *Democratic Personality: Popular Voice and the Trial of American Authorship*. Stanford: Stanford University Press.

Sanderlin, Robert Reed. 1968. "Alexander Graydon: The Life and Literary Career of an American Patriot." Ph.D. diss. University of North Carolina.

Sayre, Gordon M. 1999. "Abridging between Two Worlds: John Tanner as American Indian Autobiographer." *American Literary History* 11: 480–499.

Sayre, Henry F. 1988. *The Examined Self: Benjamin Franklin, Henry Adams, Henry James*. 1964. Reprint, Madison: University of Wisconsin Press.

Schama, Simon. 1989. *Citizens: A Chronicle of the French Revolution*. New York: Knopf.

Seed, David. 1988. "Exemplary Selves: Jonathan Edwards and Benjamin Franklin." In *First Person Singular: Studies in American Autobiography*. Ed. A. Robert Lee. New York: St. Martin's. 37–56.

Shaffer, Arthur H. 1975. *The Politics of History: Writing the History of the American Revolution, 1783–1815*. Chicago: University of Chicago Press.

Shepard, Thomas. 1972. *God's Plot: The Paradoxes of Puritan Piety, Being the Autobiography and Journal of Thomas Shepard*. Ed. Michael McGiffert. Amherst: University of Massachusetts Press.

Shields, David S. 1990. *Oracles of Empire: Poetry, Politics, and Commerce in British America, 1690–1750*. Chicago: University of Chicago Press.

———. 1997. *Civil Tongues and Polite Letters in British America*. Chapel Hill: University of North Carolina Press.

Simpson, David. 1986. *The Politics of American English, 1776–1850*. New York: Oxford University Press.

Simpson, Lewis P. 1960. "Federalism and the Crisis of Literary Order." *American Literature* 37: 253–266.

———. 1976. "The Printer as a Man of Letters: Franklin and the Symbolism of the Third Realm." In *The Oldest Revolutionary: Essays on Benjamin Franklin*. Ed. J. A. Leo Lemay. Philadelphia: University of Pennsylvania Press. 3–20.

———, ed. 1962. *The Federalist Literary Mind*. Baton Rouge: Louisiana State University Press.

Smith, Elihu Hubbard. 1973. *The Diary of Elihu Hubbard Smith.* Ed. James E. Cronin. Philadelphia: American Philosophical Society.

Smith, Sidonie. 1992. "Resisting the Gaze of Embodiment: Women's Autobiography in the Nineteenth Century." In *American Women's Autobiography: Fea(s)ts of Memory.* Ed. Margo Culley. Madison: University of Wisconsin Press. 75–110.

Smith, Venture. 1996. *A Narrative of the Life and Adventures of Venture, a Native of Africa.* In *Unchained Voices: An Anthology of Black Authors in the English-Speaking World of the Eighteenth Century.* Ed. Vincent Carretta. Lexington: University Press of Kentucky. 367–398.

Smith-Rosenberg, Carroll. 1993. "Subject Female: Authorizing American Identity." *American Literary History* 5: 481–511.

Sobel, Mechal. 1997. "The Revolution in Selves: Black and White Inner Aliens." In *Through a Glass Darkly: Reflections on Personal Identity in Early America.* Ed. Ronald Hoffman, Mechal Sobel, and Frederika Teute. Chapel Hill: University of North Carolina Press. 163–205.

Spengemann, William. 1980. *The Forms of Autobiography: Episodes in the History of a Literary Genre.* New Haven: Yale University Press.

———. 1994[a]. "E Pluribus Mimimum." *Early American Literature* 29: 276–294.

———. 1994[b]. *A New World of Words: Redefining Early American Literature.* New Haven: Yale University Press.

Spiller, Robert, et al., eds. 1953. *The Literary History of the United States.* 1946. Reprint, revised ed., New York: Macmillan.

Steele, Jeffrey. 1987. *The Representation of the Self in the American Renaissance.* Chapel Hill: University of North Carolina Press.

Stoever, William K. B. 1978. *'A Faire and Easy Way to Heaven': Covenant Theology and Antinomianism in Early Massachusetts.* Middletown: Wesleyan University Press.

Strozier, Charles B. 1995. "Benjamin Rush, Revolutionary Doctor." *American Scholar* 64: 415–421.

Szatmary, David. 1980. *Shays' Rebellion: The Making of an Agrarian Insurrection.* Amherst: University of Massachusetts Press.

Tanner, John. 1956. *Narrative of the Captivity and Adventures of John Tanner (U. S. Interpreter at the Sault de Ste. Marie) during Thirty Years Residence among the Indians in the Interior of North America.* Ed. Edwin James. 1830. Reprint, Minneapolis: Ross and Haines.

Taylor, Charles. 1989. *Sources of the Self: The Making of Modern Identity.* Cambridge: Harvard University Press.

Thoreau, Henry David. 1985. *Walden; or, Life in the Woods.* In *Henry David Thoreau.* Ed. Robert F. Sayre. New York: Library of America. 320–587.

Tichi, Cecelia. 1977. "Worried Celebrants of the American Revolution." In *American Literature, 1764–1789: The Revolutionary Years.* Ed. Everett Emerson. Madison: University of Wisconsin Press. 275–291.

Todd, Janet. 1986. *Sensibility: An Introduction*. London: Methuen.

Trumbull, John. 1953. *The Autobiography of John Trumbull*. Ed. Theodore Sizer. 1841. Reprint, New Haven: Yale University Press.

Tyler, Moses Coit. 1957. *The Literary History of the American Revolution*. 2 vols. 1897. Reprint, New York: Ungar.

Ulrich, Laurel Thatcher. 1990. *A Midwife's Tale: The Life of Martha Ballard, Based on Her Diary, 1785–1812*. New York: Knopf.

Vernon, Irene S. 1999. "The Claiming of Christ: Native American Postcolonial Discourses." *MELUS* 24: 75–88.

Warner, Michael. 1990. *The Letters of the Republic: Publication and the Public Sphere in Eighteenth-Century America*. Cambridge: Harvard University Press.

Watson, Julia. 1993. "Toward an Anti-metaphysics of Autobiography." In *The Culture of Autobiography: Constructions of Self-representation*. Ed. Robert Folkenflik. Stanford: Stanford University Press. 57–79.

Weber, Donald. 1988. *Rhetoric and History in Revolutionary New England*. New York: Oxford University Press.

Weems, Mason Locke. 1962. *Life of Washington*. Ed. Marcus Cunliffe. 1809. Reprint, Cambridge: Harvard University Press.

Weintraub, Karl Joachim. 1978. *The Value of the Individual: Self and Circumstance in Autobiography*. Chicago: University of Chicago Press.

Wendell, Barrett. 1907. *A Literary History of America*. 4th ed. New York: Charles Scribner's Sons.

White, George. 1993. *A Brief Account of the Life, Experiences, Travels, and Gospel Labours of George White, an African*. In *Black Itinerants of the Gospel: The Narratives of George White and John Jea*. Ed. Graham Russell Hodges. Madison: Madison House. 51–85.

White, J. Todd, and Charles H. Lesser, eds. 1977. *Fighters for Independence: A Guide to Sources of Biographical Information on Soldiers and Sailors of the American Revolution*. Chicago: University of Chicago Press.

White, K. 1809. *A Narrative of the Life, Occurrences, Vicissitudes, and Present Situation of K. White. Compiled and Collated by Herself . . . Feb. 1809*. Schenectady: Printed for the Authoress.

Wiebe, Robert H. 1984. *The Opening of American Society: From the Adoption of the Constitution to the Eve of Disunion*. New York: Knopf.

Wilentz, Sean. 1984. *Chants Democratic: New York City and the Rise of the American Working Class, 1788–1850*. New York: Oxford University Press.

Wilkinson, James. 1816. *Memoirs of My Own Times*. Philadelphia.

Williams, Daniel. 1989. "Zealous in the Cause of Liberty: Self-creation and Redemption in the *Narrative of Ethan Allen*." *Studies in 18th-Century Culture* 19: 325–347.

———. 1990. "In Defense of Self: Author and Authority in the *Memoirs of Stephen Burroughs*." *Early American Literature* 25: 96–122.

Williams, Raymond. 1977. *Marxism and Literature*. Oxford: Oxford University Press.

———. 1985. *Keywords: A Vocabulary of Culture and Society*. Revised ed. New York: Oxford University Press.

Wills, Garry. 1978. *Inventing America: Jefferson's Declaration of Independence*. New York: Random House.

———. 1999. *Saint Augustine*. New York: Penguin.

Winans, Robert B. 1983. "Bibliography and the Cultural Historian: Notes on the Eighteenth-Century Novel." In *Printing and Society in Early America*. Ed. William L. Joyce. Worcester: American Antiquarian Society. 162–182.

Wood, Gordon. 1972. *The Creation of the American Republic, 1776–1787*. 1969. Reprint, New York: Norton.

———. 1982. "Conspiracy and the Paranoid Style: Causality and Deceit in the Eighteenth Century." *The William and Mary Quarterly* 39: 401–441.

———. 1992. *The Radicalism of the American Revolution*. New York: Knopf.

Woolman, John. 1961. *The Journal of John Woolman*. New York: Corinth.

Young, Alfred. 1981. "George Robert Twelves Hewes (1742–1840): A Boston Shoemaker and the Memory of the American Revolution." *The William and Mary Quarterly* 38: 535–572.

———. 1999. *The Shoemaker and the Tea Party: Memory and the American Revolution*. Boston: Beacon Press.

Young, Edward. 1966. *Conjectures on Original Composition*. 1759. Reprint, Leeds: Scholar's Press.

Ziff, Larzer. 1991. *Writing in the New Nation: Prose, Print, and Politics in the Early United States*. New Haven: Yale University Press.

Zimmermann, Johann Georg. 1804. *Solitude Considered with Respect to its Influence on the Mind and the Heart*. Trans. J. B. Mercier. 1793. Reprint, Boston.

INDEX